PENGUIN BOOKS
HOW TO STAY SMART IN A SMART WORLD

'Gigerenzer exposes the hunger for autocratic power, the political naivety and the commercial chicanery that lie behind the rise of AI – he does his best to educate and energise us against this future'
Simon Ings, *The Times*

'A fascinating invitation to keep thinking for ourselves . . . Vital reading for a world populated by algorithms'
Konstantinos Katsikopoulos, University of Southampton

'In clear, unencumbered, and unpretentious prose, Gigerenzer demystifies the logic of our 'smart' societies. And despite cataloguing many depressing examples of the ambitions of big tech, the overall message of the book – and indeed the author's view of human nature – is empowering'
John Zerilli, co-author of *A Citizen's Guide to Artificial Intelligence*

'This inspiring book dispels many myths about the predictive power of connectionist AI, describes its failures to tackle uncertain and unstable phenomena, and relaunches the simulationist psychological approach as the best way towards an ethical and Human AI'
Riccardo Viale, University of Milano Bicocca

'Anyone worried about the age of AI will sleep better after reading this intelligent account' *Publishers Weekly*

'A seriously compelling, eye opening, and well researched investigation' *Library Journal*

T0173718

ABOUT THE AUTHOR

Gerd Gigerenzer is Director of the Harding Centre for Risk Literacy at the University of Potsdam and partner of Simply Rational: The Institute for Decisions. He is former Director of the Centre for Adaptive Behaviour and Cognition at the Max Planck Institute for Human Development and a former Professor of Psychology at the University of Chicago. He is the author of several books on heuristics and decision-making, including *Risk Savvy* and *Reckoning with Risk*.

GERD GIGERENZER

How to Stay Smart in a Smart World

Why Human Intelligence Still Beats Algorithms

PENGUIN BOOKS

PENGUIN BOOKS

UK | USA | Canada | Ireland | Australia
India | New Zealand | South Africa

Penguin Books is part of the Penguin Random House group of companies
whose addresses can be found at global.penguinrandomhouse.com.

First published in Germany by C. Bertelsmann Verlag 2021
First published in Great Britain by Allen Lane 2022
Published in Penguin Books 2023

003

Printed and bound in Great Britain by Clays Ltd, Elcograf S.p.A.

A CIP catalogue record for this book is available from the British Library

The authorized representative in the EEA is Penguin Random House Ireland,
Morrison Chambers, 32 Nassau Street, Dublin DO2 YH68

ISBN: 978-0-141-99504-5

www.greenpenguin.co.uk

MIX
Paper from
responsible sources
FSC® C018179

Penguin Random House is committed to a
sustainable future for our business, our readers
and our planet. This book is made from Forest
Stewardship Council® certified paper.

For Athena

Contents

Introduction

'Daddy, when you were young, before computers, how did
you get into the Internet?'

A seven-year-old in Boston[1]

'If robots do everything, then what are we going to do?'

A five-year-old in a Beijing kindergarten[2]

Imagine a digital assistant who does everything better than you. Whatever you say, it knows better. Whatever you decide, it will correct. When you come up with a plan for next year, it will have a superior one. At some point you may give up making any personal decisions on your own. Now it's the AI that efficiently runs your finances, writes your messages, chooses your romantic partner and plans when it's best to have children. Packages will be delivered to your door with products you didn't even know you needed. A social worker may turn up because the digital assistant predicted that your child is at risk of severe depression. And, before you waste time agonizing over which political candidate you favour, your assistant will already know and cast your vote. It's just a matter of time until tech companies run your life, and the faithful assistant morphs into a supreme superintelligence. Like a flock of sheep, our grandchildren will cheer or tremble in awe of their new master.

In recent years, I have spoken at many popular artificial intelligence (AI) events and am repeatedly surprised at how widespread unconditional trust in complex algorithms appears to be. No matter what the topic was, representatives of tech companies assured listeners that a machine will do the job more accurately, quickly and cheaply. What's more, replacing people by software might well make the world a better place. In the same vein, we hear that Google knows us better than we know ourselves and that AI can predict our behaviour almost perfectly, or soon will be able to do so. Tech companies proclaim this ability when they offer their services to advertisers, insurers or retailers. We too tend to believe it. Even those popular authors who paint doomsday pictures of robots ripping the guts out of humans assume the near-omniscience of AI, as do some of the tech industry's most outspoken critics who brand the business as evil *surveillance capitalism* and fear for our freedom and dignity.[3] It is this belief that makes many worry about Facebook as a terrifying Orwellian surveillance machine. Data leaks and the Cambridge Analytica scandal have amplified this worry into fearful awe. Based on faith or fear, the storyline remains the same. It goes like this:

> AI has beaten the best humans in chess and Go.
>
> Computing power doubles every couple of years.
>
> Therefore, machines will soon do everything better than humans.

Let's call it the *AI-beats-humans* argument. Its two premises are correct, but the conclusion is wrong.

The reason is that computing power goes a long way for some kinds of problems, but not for others. To date, the stunning victories of AI have been in well-defined games with fixed rules such as chess and Go, with similar successes for face and voice recognition in relatively unchanging conditions. When the environment is stable, AI can surpass humans. If the future is like the past, large amounts of data are useful. However, if surprises happen, big data – which are always data from the past – may mislead us about the future. Big data algorithms missed the financial crisis of 2008 and in 2016 predicted Hillary Clinton's victory by a large margin.

In fact, many problems we face are not well-defined games but situations in which uncertainty abounds: finding true love, predicting who will commit a crime and reacting in unforeseen emergency situations are examples. Here, more computing power and bigger data are of limited help. Humans are the key source of uncertainty. Imagine how much more difficult chess would be if the king could violate the rules at a whim and the queen could stomp off the board in protest after setting the rooks on fire. With people involved, trust in complex algorithms can lead to illusions of certainty that become a recipe for disaster.

To appreciate that complex algorithms are likely to succeed when situations are stable but will struggle with uncertainty exemplifies the general theme of this book, staying smart in a smart world:

Staying smart means understanding the potentials and risks of digital technologies, and the determination to stay in charge in a world populated by algorithms.

I wrote this book to help you understand the potential of digital technologies, such as AI, but even more important, the limitations and risks of these technologies. As these technologies become more widespread and dominant, I want to provide you with strategies and methods to stay in charge of your life rather than let yourself get steamrollered.

Should we simply lean back and relax while software makes our personal decisions? Definitely not. Staying smart does not mean obliviously trusting technology; nor does it mean anxiously mistrusting it. Instead, it is about understanding what AI can do and what remains the fancy of marketing hype and techno-religious faiths. It is also about one's personal strength to control a device rather than being remote-controlled by it.

Staying smart is not the same as digital skills for using technology. Educational programmes worldwide seek to increase digital skills by buying tablets and smart whiteboards for classrooms and teaching children how to use them. But these programmes rarely teach children how to understand the risks delivered by digital technology. As a consequence, most digital natives shockingly cannot tell hidden ads from real news and are taken in by the appearance of a website. For instance, a study of 3,446 digital natives showed that 96 per cent of them do not know how to check the trustworthiness of sites and posts.[4]

A *smart world* is not just the addition of smart TVs, online dating, and gimmicks to our lives. It is a world *transformed* by digital technology. When the door to the smart world was first opened, many pictured

a paradise where everyone had access to the tree of truthful information, which would finally put an end to ignorance, lies and corruption.
Facts about climate change, terrorism, tax evasion, exploitation of the
poor and violations of human dignity would be laid open. Immoral
politicians and greedy executives would be exposed and forced to
resign. Government spying on the public and violations of privacy
would be prevented. To some degree, this dream has become reality,
although the paradise has also been polluted. What is really happening, however, is a transformation of society. The world does not simply
get better or worse. How we think about good and bad is changing.
For instance, not long ago, people were extremely concerned about
privacy and took to the streets to protest against governments and
corporations that tried to surveil them and get hold of their personal
data. A wide spectrum of activists, young liberals and mainstream
organizations held massive protests against the 1987 German census,
fearing that computers could de-anonymize their answers, and angry
people plastered the Berlin Wall with thousands of empty question-
naires. In the 2001 census in Australia, more than 70,000 people
declared their religion as 'Jedi' (after the movie *Star Wars*), and still in
2011, British citizens protested against questions infringing on their
privacy, such as ones concerning religion.[5] Today, when our smart
home records everything we do 24/7, including in our bedroom, and
our child's smart doll records every secret it is entrusted with, we shrug
our shoulders. Feelings of privacy and dignity adapt to technology,
or risk becoming concepts of the past. The dream of the internet was
once freedom; for many, freedom now means free internet.

Since time immemorial, humans have created impressive new technologies that they have not always used wisely. To reap the many
benefits of digital technology, we need the insight and courage to
remain smart in a smart world. This is not the time to sit back and
relax, but to keep our eyes open and stay in charge.

Staying in Charge

If you are not a devil-may-care person, you might occasionally worry
about your safety. Which disaster do you think is more likely to happen in the next ten years?

- You will be killed by a terrorist.
- You will be killed by a driver distracted by a smartphone.

If you opt for the terrorist attack, you are among the majority. Since the 9/11 attack, surveys in North America and Europe have indicated that many people believe terrorism to pose one of the greatest hazards to their lives. For some, it is the greatest fear. At the same time, most admit to texting while driving without much concern. In the ten years before 2020, 36 people on average were killed annually in the US by terrorists, Islamic, right-wing or other.[6] In that same period, more than 3,000 people were killed annually by distracted drivers, often people busy on their phone texting, reading or streaming.[7] That figure amounts to the death toll of the 9/11 attack, but for every year.

Most Americans are also more afraid of terrorism than of guns, even though they are less likely to be shot by a terrorist than by a child playing with a gun in their household. Unless you live in Afghanistan or Nigeria, you will much more likely be killed by a distracted driver, possibly yourself. And it is not difficult to understand why. When twenty-year-old drivers use a phone, their reaction times decline to that of a seventy-year-old without one.[8] That's known as instant brain ageing.

Why do people text while driving? They might not be aware of how dangerous it is. However, in a survey, I found that most are well aware that a hazard exists.[9] At issue is not lack of awareness. It is lack of self-control. 'When a text comes in, I just have to look, no matter what,' one student explains. And self-control has been made more difficult ever since platforms introduced notifications, likes and other psychological tricks to keep users' eyes glued to their sites rather than their surroundings. Yet so much damage could be avoided if people managed to overcome their urge to check their phone when they should be paying attention to the road. And it's not just young people. 'Don't text your loved ones when you know they are driving' – so said a devastated mom who found her badly injured daughter in intensive care, face scarred and one eye lost, after having sent her child 'a stupid text'.[10] A smartphone is an amazing piece of technology, but it requires smart people who use it wisely. Here, the ability to stay in charge and control technology protects the personal safety of yourself and your loved ones.

Mass Surveillance Is a Problem, Not a Solution

Part of the reason why we fear a terrorist attack rather than a driver glued to a smartphone is that more media attention is devoted to terrorism than to distracted driving, and politicians have followed suit. To protect their citizens, governments all around the world experiment with face recognition surveillance systems. These systems do an exceptional job of recognizing faces when tested in a lab using visa or job application photographs, or other well-lit photos with people's heads held in similar positions. But how accurate are they in the real world? One test took place close to my home.

On the evening of 19 December 2016, a twenty-four-year-old Islamist terrorist hijacked a heavy truck and ploughed into a busy Berlin Christmas market packed with tourists and locals enjoying sausages and mulled wine, killing twelve people and injuring forty-nine. The following year, the German Ministry of the Interior installed face recognition systems at a Berlin train station to test how accurately they recognized suspects. At the end of the year-long pilot test, the ministry proudly announced in its press release two exciting numbers: a hit rate of 80 per cent, meaning that of every ten suspects, the systems identified eight correctly and missed two; and a false alarm rate of 0.1 per cent, meaning that only one out of every 1,000 innocent passers-by was mistaken for a suspect. The minister hailed the system an impressive success and concluded that nationwide surveillance is feasible and desirable.

After the press release, a heated debate arose. One group had faith that more security justifies more surveillance, while the other group feared that the cameras would eventually become the 'telescreens' in George Orwell's *Nineteen Eighty-Four*. Both, however, took the accuracy of the system for granted.[11] Instead of taking sides in that emotional debate, let's consider what would actually happen if such face recognition systems were widely implemented. Every day, about 12 million people pass through train stations in Germany. Apart from several hundred wanted suspects, these are normal people heading for work or out for pleasure. The impressive-sounding false positive rate of 0.1 per cent translates into nearly 12,000 passers-by per day who would be falsely mistaken as suspects. Each one would have to be stopped, searched for weapons or drugs and be restrained or held in custody until their identity is proven.[12] Police-related resources, already strained, would be used for scrutinizing these innocent citizens rather than for effective crime prevention, meaning that such a system would in fact come at the cost of security. Ultimately, one would end up with a surveillance system that infringes on individual freedom and disrupts social and economic life.

Face recognition can perform a valuable service, but for a different task: *identification of an individual* rather than *mass screening*. After a crime happens at a subway station, or a car runs through a red light, a video recording can help to identify the perpetrator. Here we know that the person has committed a crime. When screening everyone at the station, in contrast, we do not know whether the people being screened are suspects. Most of them aren't, which – like mass medical screenings – leads to the large number of false alarms. Face recognition is even better at another task. When you unlock your phone by looking at the screen, it performs a task called *authentication*. Unlike a perpetrator running away in the subway, you look directly into the camera, hold it close to your face and keep perfectly still; it's virtually always you who tries to unlock your phone. This situation creates a fairly stable world: you and your phone. Errors rarely occur.

To discuss the pros and cons of face recognition systems, one needs to distinguish between these three situations: many-to-many, one-to-many and one-to-one. In mass screening, many people are compared with many others in a data bank; in identification, one person is compared with many others; and in authentication, one person is compared with one other. Once again, the smaller the uncertainty, as in identification as opposed to mass screening, the better the performance of the system. Recall the storming of the Capitol in January 2021, where face recognition systems speedily identified some of the intruders who had forced their way into the building. The general point is that AI is not good or bad, but useful for some tasks and less so for others.

Last but not least, the concerns about privacy fit in with this analysis. The general public is most concerned about mass surveillance by governments, not identification of perpetrators and authentication. And mass surveillance is exactly what face recognition systems are most unreliable at doing. Understanding this crucial difference helps protect the individual freedoms valued in Western democracies against the surveillance interests of their own governments.

I Have Nothing to Hide

This phrase has become popular in discussions about social media companies that collect all of the personal data they can get their hands on. You might hear it from users who prefer to pay with their data, not with their money. And the phrase could well hold true for those of us who live uneventful lives without any serious health issues, have never made any potential enemies and wouldn't speak up on civil rights denied by a government. Yet the issue is not about hiding or the freedom to post pictures of adorable kittens at no cost. Tech companies don't care whether or not you have something to hide. Rather, because you don't spend any money for their services, they have to employ psychological tricks to get you to spend as much time as possible on their apps. You are not the customer; the customers are the advertisers who pay tech companies to grab your attention. Many of us have become glued to our smartphone, get too little sleep because of our new bed partner, find hardly any time for anything else and eagerly await another dopamine shot via each new 'like'. Jia Tolentino, a writer at the *New Yorker*, wrote about her struggle with her mobile phone:[13] 'I carry my phone around with me as if it were an oxygen tank. I stare at it while I make breakfast and take out the recycling, ruining what I prize most about working from home – the sense of control, the relative peace.' Others are hurt after destructive online comments from strangers about their looks or wits. Others again drift into extremist groups that fall prey to fake news and hate speech.

The world is split between those who don't worry much about being affected by digital technology and those like Tolentino who believe it makes them addicted in the same way that compulsive gamblers cannot stop thinking about gambling. Yet technology, and social media in particular, could well exist without being designed to rob people of time and sleep. It is not the social media per se that make some of us addicted, it is the personalized ad-based business model. The damage to its users flows from that 'original sin'.

The Free Coffeehouse

Imagine a coffeehouse that has eliminated all competitors in town by offering free coffee, leaving you no choice but to go there to meet your friends. While you enjoy the many hours you spend there chatting with your friends, bugs and cameras wired into the tables and walls closely monitor your conversations and record whom you are sitting with. The room is also filled with salespeople who pay for your coffee and constantly interrupt you to offer their personalized products and services on sale. The customers in this coffeehouse are in effect the salespeople, not you and your friends. This is basically how platforms like Facebook function.[14]

Social media could function in a healthier way if they were based on the business model of a real coffeehouse or of TV, radio or other services where you as the customer pay for the amenities you want. In fact, in 1998, Sergey Brin and Larry Page, the young founders of Google, had criticized ad-based search engines because these are inherently biased towards the needs of advertisers, not the consumers.[15] Yet under the pressure of venture capitalists, they soon caved in and built the most successful personalized advertisement model in existence. In this business model, your attention is the product being sold. The actual customers are the companies who place ads on the sites. The more often people see their ads, the more the advertisers pay, leading social media marketers to run experiment after experiment in order to maximize the time you spend on their sites and to make you want to return as quickly as possible. The urge to grab the phone while driving a car is a case in point. In short, the quintessence of the business model is to capture users' time and attention to the greatest extent possible.

To serve advertisers, tech companies collect data minute by minute on where you are, what you are doing and what you are looking at. Based on your habits, they make a kind of avatar of you. When an advertiser places an ad, say for the latest hand guns or expensive lipsticks, the ad is shown to those who most likely will click on it. Typically, advertisers pay the tech company for every time a user clicks on the ad, or for every impression. Therefore, to increase the chance that you click on an ad, or just see it, everything is done to influence you to stay as long on the page as possible. Likes, notifications and other psychological tricks work together to make you dependent – day and night. Thus, it's not your data that are being sold, it's your attention, time and sleep.

If Google and Facebook had a fee-for-service model, none of that would be necessary. The armies of engineers and psychologists who run experiments on how to keep you glued to your smartphone could be working on more useful technological innovations. Social media companies would still have to collect specific data for improving recommendations in order to meet your specific needs, but they would no longer be motivated to collect other superfluous personal data – such as data that might indicate that you are depressed, have cancer or are pregnant. The main motivation behind collecting these data on you – personalized advertisements – would disappear. Netflix is a good example of a company that has already implemented this fee-for-service model.[16] From the user perspective, the small disadvantage would be that we all would have to pay a few pounds every month to use social media. For the social media companies, however, the big advantage of the more lucrative pay-with-your-data plan is that the men – yes, virtually all men – at the top of the ladder are now among the wealthiest and most powerful people on earth.

STAYING ON TOP OF TECHNOLOGY

These examples provide a first impression of what staying on top of technology is about. Resisting the siren call to text while driving entails the ability to stay in charge and control a technology. The possibilities and limitations of face recognition systems show us that the technology is excellent in fairly stable situations, such as unlocking your phone or for border control, where your passport photo is compared with another photo taken of you. But when screening faces in real-world conditions, the AI stumbles and creates too many false alarms, which can lead to huge problems when masses of innocent people are stopped and searched. Finally, the problems caused by social media – from loss of time, sleep and the ability to concentrate to addiction – are not the fault of social media per se, but of the companies' pay-with-your-data business model. To stamp out these severe problems, we need to go beyond new privacy settings or government regulations of online content and tackle the root of the problem, such as by changing the underlying business model. Governments need more political courage to protect the people they represent.

One might think that helping everyone to understand the potentials and risks of digital technology is a primary goal of all education systems and governments worldwide. It is not. In fact, it is not even mentioned in the OECD's 'Key Issues for Digital Transformation in the G20' of 2017 and the European Commission's 2020 'White Paper on Artificial Intelligence.'[17] These programmes focus on other important issues, including creating innovation hubs, digital infrastructures and proper legislation and increasing people's trust in AI. As a consequence, most digital natives are woefully unprepared in telling facts from fakes, and news from hidden ads.

Solving the problems, however, entails more than infrastructure and regulation. It requires taking time to reflect and do some serious research. Did you have to wait for a long time on a service hotline? It could be that your address or a prediction algorithm indicated that you are a low-value customer. Have you noticed that the first result in a Google search is not the most useful one for you? It is likely the one for which an advertiser paid most.[18] Are you aware that your beloved smart TV may record your personal conversations in your living room or bedroom?[19]

If none of this is new to you, you might be surprised to learn that for most people it is. Few know that algorithms determine their waiting time or analyse what smart TVs record for the benefit of unnamed third parties. Studies report that about 50 per cent of adult users do not understand that the marked top search entries are ads rather than the most relevant or popular results.[20] These ads are in fact marked, but over the years they have come to look more like 'organic' search results (non-ads). In 2013, Google's ads were no longer highlighted with a special background colour, and a small yellow 'Ad' icon was instead introduced; since 2020, the yellow colour has also been removed, and the word 'Ad' is in black and white, blending into the organic search results. Google gets paid by advertisers for each click on their ads, so if people mistakenly believe the first results are the most relevant for them, that is good for business.

As mentioned, many executives and politicians are excessively enthusiastic about big data and digitalization. Enthusiasm is not the same as understanding. Many of the overly zealous prophets do not appear to know what they are talking about. According to a study of over 400 executives in eighty large publicly listed companies, 92 per cent of the executives have no recognizable or documented experience with digitalization.[21] Similarly, when Mark Zuckerberg had to testify on Facebook's latest privacy controversy to politicians from the US Senate and the House, the most stunning revelation was not what he said in his rehearsed responses, it was how little US politicians seemed to know about the opaque ways in which social media companies operate.[22] When I served on the Advisory Council for Consumer Affairs at the German Ministry of Justice and Consumer Protection, we looked at how the secret algorithms of credit-scoring companies are supervised by the data protection authorities, who are there to ensure that the algorithms are reliable indicators of creditworthiness that do not discriminate on the basis of gender, race or other individual features. When the largest credit-scoring company submitted its algorithms, the authorities admitted to lacking the necessary expertise in IT and statistics to evaluate them. In the end, the company itself bailed them out by selecting the experts who wrote the report, even paying their fees.[23] Ignorance appears to be the rule rather than the exception in our smart world. We need to change that quickly, not in the distant future.

Technological Paternalism

Paternalism (from the Latin word *pater*, for father) is the view that a chosen group has the right to treat others like children, who should willingly defer to that group's authority. Historically, its justification has been that the ruling group has been chosen by God, is part of the aristocracy or owns secret knowledge or splendid wealth. Those under their authority are considered inferior because they are women, people of colour, poor or uneducated, among others. During the twentieth century, paternalism was on the retreat after the vast majority of people finally had the opportunity to learn to read and write, and after governments eventually granted both men and women freedom of speech and movement, along with the right to vote. That revolution, in the name of which committed supporters were imprisoned or gave their lives, enabled the next generations, including us, to take matters into our own hands. The twenty-first century, however, is witnessing the rise of a new paternalism by corporations that use machines to predict and manipulate our behaviour, whether we consent or not. Its prophets even announce the coming of a new god, an omniscient superintelligence known as AGI (Artificial General Intelligence) that is said to surpass humans in all aspects of brainpower. Until its arrival, we should defer to its prophets.[24]

Technological solutionism is the belief that every societal problem is a 'bug' that needs a 'fix' through an algorithm. Technological paternalism is its natural consequence, government by algorithms. It doesn't need to peddle the fiction of a superintelligence; it instead expects us to accept that corporations and governments record where we are, what we are doing, and with whom, minute by minute, and also to trust that these records will make the world a better place. As Eric Schmidt explains, 'The goal is to enable Google users to be able to ask the question such as "What shall I do tomorrow?" and "What job shall I take?"'[25] Quite a few popular writers instigate our awe of technological paternalism by telling stories that are, at best, economical with the truth.[26] More surprisingly, even some influential researchers see no limits to what AI can do, arguing that the human brain is merely an inferior computer and that we should replace humans with algorithms whenever possible.[27] AI will tell us what to do, and we should listen and follow. We just need to wait a bit until AI gets smarter. Oddly, *the message is never that people need to become smarter as well.*

I have written this book to enable people to gain a realistic appreciation of what AI can do and how it is used to influence us. We do not need more paternalism; we've had more than our fair share in the past centuries. But nor do we need technophobic panic, which is revived with every breakthrough technology. When trains were invented, doctors warned that passengers would die from suffocation.[28] When radio became widely available, the concern was that listening too much would harm children because they need repose, not jazz.[29] Instead of fright or hype, the digital world needs better-informed and healthily critical citizens who want to keep control of their lives in their own hands.

This book is not an academic introduction to AI, or to its subfields such as machine learning and big data analytics. Rather, it is about the human affair with AI: about trust, deception, understanding, addiction and personal and social transformation. It is written for a general audience as a guide to navigating the challenges of a smart world and draws, among others, on my own research on decision making under uncertainty at the Max Planck Institute for Human Development, a topic that continues to fascinate me. In the course of the book, my personal take on freedom and dignity is not disguised, but I do my best to stick to the evidence and let the readers make up their own minds. My deeply held conviction is that we human beings are not as stupid and incapable of functioning as is often claimed – so long as we continue to remain active and make use of our brains, which have developed in the intricate course of evolution. The danger of falling for the negative *AI-beats-humans* narrative and passively agreeing to let authorities or machines 'optimize' our lives on their terms is growing by the day, and has particularly motivated me to write this book. As in my previous books *Gut Feelings* and *Risk Savvy*, *How to Stay Smart in a Smart World* is ultimately a passionate call to keep the hard-fought legacies of personal liberty and democracy alive.

Today and in the near future, we face a conflict between two systems, autocratic and democratic, not unlike the Cold War. Yet, different from that era, where nuclear technology maintained an uneasy balance between the two forces, digital technology can easily tilt the scales towards autocratic systems. We have seen this happen during the Covid-19 pandemic, when some autocratic countries successfully contained the virus with the help of strict digital surveillance systems.

I cannot deal with all aspects related to the vast field of digitalization but will provide a selection of topics explaining general principles that can be more widely applied, such as the *stable-world principle* and the *Texas sharpshooter fallacy* discussed in Chapter 2, and the *adapt-to-AI principle* and the *Russian-tank fallacy* discussed in Chapter 4. As you may have noticed, I use the term AI in a broad sense, including any kind of algorithms that are meant to do what human intelligence does, but will differentiate whenever necessary.

In each culture, we need to talk about the future world in which we and our children wish to live. There will be no single answer. But there is a general message that applies to all visions. Despite – or because of – technological innovation, we need to use our brains more than ever.

Let's begin with a problem dear to our heart, finding true love, and with secret algorithms that are so simple that everyone can understand them.

PART ONE

The Human Affair With AI

I

Is True Love Just a Click Away?

> 'For one human being to love another: that is perhaps the
> most difficult of all our tasks, the ultimate, the last test and
> proof, the work for which all other work is but preparation.'
>
> Rainer Maria Rilke[1]

> 'Dating is just for other people to know that you're dating,
> people post about it all the time. Like kissing photos.'
>
> Sophia, thirteen-year-old, Montclair, New Jersey[2]

Money can't buy me love, the Beatles tell us. But can algorithms? A couple of hundred dollars will buy you a six-month premium membership to online dating sites around the globe. The sites advertise secret love algorithms that may get you the perfect date. Every year, millions of hopeful customers, young and old, use online dating sites or mobile dating apps, and the trend is increasing.[3] Despite this popularity, many are unaware that algorithms are behind the selection of potential romantic partners.[4]

AI FINDS YOU LOVE

An attractive young woman with long windswept hair smiles at you from a website. Next to her is a handsome young man sporting a trim three-day beard, looking equally blissful. Close to their faces is the name of one of the largest online dating sites, Parship. Millions of singles in London, Paris, Berlin, Mexico City, Vienna and Amsterdam embark on their quest to find true love and long-term happiness via its services.[5] Like EliteSingles, OKCupid and a host of others, Parship is a serious agency for singles seeking a partner for life. It attracts people hoping the day will come when they won't have to date any more. Unlike Tinder and similar dating apps, where users see little more than looks and location, Parship uses a matching algorithm based on personality and interests. Its websites and posters prominently display the same catchphrase:

Every 11 Minutes, a Single Falls in Love.

That sounds like a very attractive deal: sign up, pay the fee and wait for eleven minutes! Happiness is just a click away. Millions of people have signed up, hoping to be one of those who fall in love quickly.

Yet think for a moment. Every eleven minutes, a single falls in love. That would be great news if the site had only a hundred customers. But Parship has millions of customers. Let us look more closely. One person falling in love every eleven minutes translates into about six per hour, which makes 144 per day – assuming that singles are active day and night on the website. In an entire year, that makes 52,560 enamored clients (144 × 365). It means that if the site has one million customers, only about 5 per cent of the singles fall in love within a year. After searching for ten years, about half of the customers can therefore be expected to have found true love. And if the site has even more than one million paying customers, the expected waiting time is even longer. In other words, there is a real chance that you will be looking (and paying) until old age; by that time, it's indeed money that bought you love.[6] This simple check reveals a sobering truth about the success of the matching algorithm behind the persuasive slogan.

Now we know what 'every 11 minutes' means. What about the second part of the catchphrase: 'a single falls in love'? After all, it takes two to fall in love to make a couple. It turns out that every eleven minutes a premium member quit, and when asked why, clicked the 'fell in love' button. Whether true love was in play, whether it was found online or offline or whether it was just a handy excuse to stop paying for the service remains unknown.

Customer evaluations are consistent with this back-of-the-envelope calculation. In 1,500 evaluations of five online dating sites that Germans use, including Parship, none received an average rating of good. Only 7.7 per cent said that their search was successful; the rest had quit or were still looking.[7]

In other countries and sites, chances appear to be on par for similar services that target highly educated singles in New York, Toronto or Seoul. For instance, the EliteSingles website advertises that 381,000 new members joined per month in 2018 and that 1,000+ singles find love through the service every month.[8] Once again, these figures sound impressive – so many happy people! But the question remains, what are your actual chances of finding love? If the figures are correct, then this amounts to roughly one in every 381 singles per month, which is about one out of thirty per year, or 3 to 4 per cent. This figure is in the ballpark of the 5 per cent estimated before for Parship. These calculations are rough estimates based on the numbers the online services themselves provide. Just to make sure, I checked another online dating site. JDate (for Jewish singles) reports that it has hundreds of thousands of members worldwide and that 'each week, hundreds of JDaters meet their soul mates.'[9] If we put these two numbers together, the result is about one soulmate among 1,000 singles per week, which translates into some 52 in 1,000 per year and once again a chance of about 5 per cent per year. This long waiting time fits well with one of the site's advertised 'success stories': the case of Ryan, who spent fifteen years scrolling and clicking on faces until he finally found his soulmate through the site.[10]

Love algorithms can deliver three kinds of services: access, communication and finding true love. Access enables customers to meet potential partners whom they are otherwise unlikely to meet. It is particularly helpful for people who live socially or physically isolated lives or do not meet current social norms, such as those with disabilities or strict religious beliefs. Communication via computer-mediated interaction before meeting face to face is another service. Together, access and communication are the true feat of online dating. But increased access also comes with a downside when the chances of finding true love are slim, as we have just seen. After experiencing twenty-two *meh* dates instead of a single one that went wrong, you might well feel worse with that amount of misfortune and choice overload. A review of studies on online dating concluded that 'no compelling evidence supports matching sites' claims that mathematical algorithms work – that they foster romantic outcomes that are superior to those fostered by other means of pairing partners'.[11]

To check these results, I contacted major reputable online dating agencies. After all, several dating agencies – including eHarmony.com, perfectMatch.com and Chemistry.com – claim to have powerful 'scientific' algorithms, even though none of them have been shown to be reliable and valid by standard scientific methods.[12] When I enquired about the actual number of paying customers, the success rate and how they determined it, I received friendly but firm refusals to answer these questions.[13]

Finally, let us look beyond online dating agencies. Do couples who met online – via social networks, chat rooms, dating agencies or others – break up less often and are they more satisfied with their relationship than those who met offline? A classic representative study with over 19,000 married US residents found that those who met online had fewer marital break-ups than those who met offline and also reported slightly higher satisfaction with their marriages. Note that those who met through online dating agencies using love algorithms were not more satisfied than those who met on other online sites.[14] On the other hand, more recent studies in the US reported that break-up rates (both marital and non-marital relationships) were higher for couples who met online, and representative studies in Germany and Switzerland reported no difference in couples' satisfaction with their relationships, whether they met online or offline.[15] While these results are inconsistent, several studies consistently report that the proportion of couples who met online is higher among same-sex couples, and that online dating brings together people from more diverse backgrounds in education, race and ethnicity, which can still be barriers offline.[16] This increase in diversity, however, appears to be largely due to the fact that couples who met online tend to be younger.

Thus, the jury is still out on whether online search leads to more satisfaction and fewer break-ups than offline search. All in all, unless you belong to the lucky 5 per cent every year, you might as well spend your time and money on meeting colleagues after work, going to parties, travelling or walking a dog, or participate in a local online community that shares one of your personal passions – that is likely to be a faster route to happiness. Cupid's arrow might strike in un-expected places.

HOW DO LOVE ALGORITHMS WORK?

Love algorithms are big secrets. Like algorithms for credit scoring, predictive policing and page ranking, they are proprietary. And every agency uses different algorithms. That makes it difficult to find out exactly how they work. Nevertheless, we know the basic procedure, which is one of the simplest versions of algorithms. On serious dating sites, customers have to fill out a survey about their values, interests and personality. A survey may consist of more than a hundred questions. The answers are then transformed into a profile of the customer.[17] To make it simple, consider two profiles with only three features (figure 1.1). Adam wants children, enjoys being the centre of attention and does not like to cook. Eve also wants children, does not enjoy being the centre of attention and also does not like to cook.

The first principle on which the match between Adam and Eve is calculated is *similarity*. In the case of wanting children, similarity is crucial. The simplest algorithm would just count the number of times both agree, which would be two out of three, or two-thirds. But looking at similarity alone wouldn't work. What matters is not only *similarity* but also *complementarity*. For instance, Adam is keen to be the centre of attention. He might not be thrilled by a partner sharing that desire, with the prospect of eternally fighting over who gets to be in the limelight. A partner with complementary interests, that is, someone who dislikes being the centre of attention, is a better fit for Adam. In the same way, if both hate cooking, they are similar but

Feature	Adam	Eve
Wants children	Yes	Yes
Centre of attention	Yes	No
Likes to cook	No	No

FIGURE 1.1: Two profiles with three features.

likely not the best match. To find out whether a customer wants a similar or a complementary partner, some agencies ask them in the survey what they expect from their ideal partner.

Finally, there is a third principle, *importance*. Not all features are equally important. Some dating services estimate the importance themselves, while others ask their customers to indicate how important an attribute is for them: irrelevant, a little important and so on. The algorithm, however, needs numbers as inputs instead of verbal answers. The dating app OK Cupid, one of the few that have made their algorithms fairly transparent, uses irrelevant = 0, a little important = 1, somewhat important = 10, very important = 50 and mandatory = 250.[18] Now we can put all three principles together and answer the question, how satisfactory is Eve for Adam?

On the first two attributes, Eve matches Adam's ideal partner (figure 1.2). Because the importance he sets on these is 10 and 50 respectively, the result is 60 out of 60 points. The fact that Eve doesn't enjoy cooking is of little importance to Adam, so she gets 0 out of 1 point for the third attribute. In total, Eve gets 60 out of 61 points, which is about 98 per cent.

In the same way, the algorithm calculates how satisfying Adam is for Eve (figure 1.3). Adam wants children and so does Eve's ideal partner. Because, for Eve, children are mandatory, this similarity results in 250 out of 250 points. Yet there is no match for the other two attributes. The algorithm calculates a total of 250 out of 310 points, which is 81 per cent.

Features	Adam's Ideal Partner	Eve	Importance for Adam	Points
Wants children	Yes	Yes	10	10/10
Centre of attention	No	No	50	50/50
Likes to cook	Yes	No	1	0/1
				Score: 60/61

FIGURE 1.2: Adam's point of view. How satisfying is Eve for Adam? The answer is 60 out of 61 possible points, or 98 per cent, which is extremely good.

Features	Eve's Ideal Partner	Adam	Importance for Eve	Points
Wants children	Yes	Yes	250	250/250
Centre of attention	No	Yes	50	0/50
Likes to cook	Yes	No	10	0/10
				Score: 250/310

FIGURE 1.3: Eve's point of view. How satisfying is Adam for Eve? The answer is 250 out of 310 possible points, or 81 per cent, which is not as good.

In a last step, the algorithm calculates the total match between Adam and Eve by taking an average between their scores, which would be 89.5 per cent in our example.[19]

The reality of profile matching is more complicated than in this simple example, but the basic logic remains the same. There are more features, and the features may be quantitative, such as age and income. Similarity tends to count for hobbies and values, while complementarity is surprisingly often desired when it comes to education and age, especially for heterosexual couples. Women who subscribe to dating services in Boston, Chicago, New York and Seattle desire men with a higher level of education: the higher the better. But men in those same cities do not want the most educated women. On average, they prefer women with undergraduate degrees and find anyone above that level, with a Master's or PhD, less attractive. Similarly, the average woman's desirability drops from age eighteen until she is sixty, while the desirability of men peaks around age fifty.[20] This striking discrepancy was also observed among OK Cupid's customers. Women find men most attractive if they are about as old as they are, give or take two to three years. The average man, however, always prefers women in their early twenties, no matter what his age.[21] These men never grow up. Their preferences follow a basic insight of evolutionary psychology: men tend to be attracted by cues that indicate high fertility, such as youth and smooth skin, while women tend to be more interested in cues that indicate a man's ability to support a family, such as wealth and a good education.

All in all, it is not that difficult to understand the basics of algorithms that match two profiles, even if they are guarded as top secret. In general, an algorithm transforms input numbers into output numbers, such as profiles into probabilities of matches.

A Profile Is Not the Person

If love algorithms can use profiles, similarity, complementarity and ratings of importance, why can't they quickly find the ideal partner for life? Understanding these four principles helps us acquire a realistic understanding of what these algorithms can and cannot do. Let us begin with the profiles. In a face-to-face meeting, the 'data' are rich and complex: a smile and a gesture, the humour reflected in someone's eyes, the tone of voice, the way the other asks questions, the intensity or superficiality with which a person listens. And then there are touch and scent, which can be crucial to mating compatibility, especially for women.[22] Profiles, in contrast, are based not on real interactions but on the responses given in the initial survey. A profile is not the person, it is a self-presentation, not necessarily of true interests and values. Even when 'personality traits' are used in the profile, the algorithm infers these from self-reports. For instance, some sites ask whether attributes such as 'sexy' and 'plain' apply to you, and how 'rational', 'opinionated' and 'selfish' you are. What would you say? Few people are realistic and candid when yearning for the perfect date. When you are asked for your interests, should you admit to being a couch potato with no special interests? Or acknowledge that you are a first-rate dancer, which might intimidate most candidates? As a consequence, self-reported interests and personality predict romantic love only weakly.[23] The same result is known from speed dating.[24] What people say they prefer does not match with the actual choices they make.[25]

Now consider the principles of similarity and complementarity. There is a saying that birds of a feather flock together, and yet another that opposites attract. Whatever the truth, love algorithms can compare similarity and complementarity only by looking at people's profiles, not their actual behaviour. And this turns out to be a crucial limitation. A review of 313 laboratory and field studies on the topic showed something striking:[26] if people did not know each other, higher similarity between their profiles (attitudes and personality traits) clearly went along with higher mutual attraction. After a short interaction of only a few minutes or hours, however, that attraction largely faded away when people met face to face. This means that similar profiles do spark initial attraction but appear to be irrelevant for a real relationship. It may also explain why people find partners with a highly matching percentage attractive, and why at the same time the match percentage contributes little to finding true love. In fact, a study of over 23,000 married persons in Australia, Germany and the UK found that the degree to which partners were satisfied with their relationship had very little to do with how closely their personality trait profiles resembled each other.[27] Instead, a person's own personality – such as being agreeable, conscientious and emotionally stable – was related to how satisfied they were with a relationship. Some individuals will mess up any relationship, no matter how suitable their partner is. Online dating sites such as eHarmony have recognized this finding and reject customers who do not appear to be emotionally healthy.[28]

Finally, consider the principle of importance. You may have wondered why OK Cupid uses the numbers 1 to 250. As mentioned above, the ultimate reason is that algorithms need numbers to calculate matching percentages. Like other algorithms, love algorithms take numbers as inputs and transform them into output numbers. Dating services either intuitively assign numbers to their customers' importance statements, as OK Cupid does, or else try to estimate them from data. For the latter, the service would need reliable data about which combinations of profiles led to lasting love. I am not aware of any service that bothers to follow up their customers and systematically collect these statistics. Fixed numbers also assume that customers' ratings of importance are stable. However, some judgements may well change in the course of a relationship, such as when a partner learns to appreciate the other's interests and values that were considered of little importance beforehand. Whether these numbers capture the true importance therefore remains uncertain.

All in all, the big feat of dating platforms is access, not the ability to find true love. That may come when people meet face to face. Self-presentation in profiles and the principles of similarity, complementarity and importance calculated from these profiles are the basics of matching algorithms, but not necessarily the main ingredients for a successful relationship. This can explain why love algorithms often flop. But, as we will see in the next chapter, a more general reason exists: unlike chess, finding true love is a game riddled with uncertainty, and that is where algorithms run into problems.

COURTSHIP ADAPTS TO SOFTWARE

It's easy to think of algorithms as 'neutral' tools to speed up access to the best romantic partners. Yet they are not. As algorithms increasingly populate our world, they have the power to influence our values – even when they don't work very well. That power extends to courtship as well. For instance, a blind date is hardly possible today; each party will look the other one up on social media. Like other technologies, algorithms change behaviour and ultimately our desire. To begin with, software can turn courtship into an optimal search problem and decrease commitment.

Always Looking for Someone Better

As the story goes, a young woman has found the man of her dreams, and they are together in bed. When he leaves for a minute to go to the bathroom, she automatically reaches for her smartphone, opens Tinder and begins browsing and swiping for other men. Surprised at what she is doing, she cannot really explain it. She just can't stop. Stories like this illustrate how software can take over and control behaviour.

Easy access to numerous partners can turn a happy 'satisficer' into a restless 'optimizer'. *Satisficing* is a term from decision theory that, in the context of dating, means choosing a partner who is satisfactory. To do so, you need to develop a desirable standard (an *aspiration level*), pick the first partner who meets it and stop looking any further. Stopping the search is a prerequisite for committing to a happy long-term relationship. *Optimizing*, in contrast, means looking for absolutely the best partner and nothing less. Since there are plenty of fish in the sea and it is impossible to know what other alternatives might pop up, optimizing leads to disenchantment and a culture of 'always looking for someone better'. Even after accidentally stumbling across the very best partner (if such a person exists), an optimizer would not know and would continue searching for a better one, openly or secretly. Dating sites that do not limit the number of viewable candidates per day prompt this behaviour. A satisficer, by contrast, would cancel the online dating service immediately and embark on a serious relationship.

Yet it is in the very interest of dating agencies that customers stay on board as long as possible. They would make little profit if everyone found true love in eleven minutes and quit. That is why many agencies emphasize providing access over brokering true love. Access to large numbers of potential partners is one way to keep users on the app, just as supermarkets offer a hundred varieties of mustard and jams to keep customers looking and buying. Accordingly, many users design their dating profiles as if these were product descriptions in online shopping and dispose of other products with a swipe. In their world, true love means searching non-stop for the best deal.

Optimize Your Profile, Not Your Person

The second epigraph to this chapter cites Sophia, a thirteen-year-old from New Jersey, who gave her own view on dating. Many girls like Sophia spend large parts of their time competing on social media and, later, on the online sexual marketplace, managing their selfies and reputation. 'I feel like I'm brainwashed into wanting likes,' she explained.[29] Self-presentation is of course nothing new, but digital media offer handy tools to edit one's self. The psychologist Robert Epstein described an online date he had with a woman.[30] When they finally met for coffee, the woman did not look anything like the woman in the pictures she had posted. She was in marketing and thought it a good strategy to post photos that attract 'customers'. Later, Epstein noticed that she'd replaced the photos with those of yet another woman.

The life blood of advertising is appearance and duplicity to attract attention. In their online profiles, people lie about their age, marital status, income, height and weight. Researchers from Cornell measured and weighed people and then checked the numbers against their online profiles. On average, people were one inch shorter and five pounds heavier than what they'd posted.[31] And the shorter and heavier people were, the bigger the discrepancies. A study of over 5,000 subscribers to online dating services in Boston and San Diego found that women in their twenties listed their weight on average as 5 pounds lower than the corresponding weight in the general population, which increased to 17 pounds for women in their thirties and to 19 pounds for women in their forties.[32] No such discrepancies in weight were found for men. Women also prefer to list their age as twenty-nine, thirty-five and forty-four more often than other ages.[33] Men, in contrast, tend to overstate their income, and there is a reason why. When men claimed to have an income of $250,000 rather than less than $50,000, three times as many women replied. Men also lie about their marital status: likely one out of eight male online suitors is married.[34] The researchers who measured and weighted people used hard facts to determine the extent of cheating. But even when asked in surveys, more than half of US participants openly admitted to lying on their dating profile, a higher number than that of their British counterparts.[35]

Some online dating services appear to resort to tricks themselves. They claim to have more customers than in reality and maintain that these are highly satisfied.[36] When asked about the actual numbers, the agencies become highly secretive.

FEMALE BOTS

Have you ever been contacted by a distraught widow in Somalia seeking to transfer her multi-million heritage to your safe bank account? If you reply, she might soon ask you to send money to cover customs and taxes in return for a promised $10 million. Did you ever receive an email that you are the lucky winner of $250,000 in an overseas lottery? One might believe that nobody with any brains would fall for such scams. Yet some people are taken in hope. As one British victim explained: 'That amount of money gives you dreams, and you don't want them taken from you.'[37] Finding potential victims was once a trial-and-error operation, but the AI tools behind Facebook have made it easier. As they do for every advertiser, Facebook's machine learning algorithms help identify those users who are most likely to click on the fraudulent ad. Companies behind such scams, after camouflaging their ad content, pay Facebook on average $44,000 in advertising fees and make a return of $79,000 from the victims.[38] In the UK alone, around 1 million adults fall victim to mass-marketed scams per year and together lose about £3.5 billion.[39]

Romance Scams

Still, most people resist the temptation because the messages are unsolicited and from strangers. To widen their circle of victims, international criminal groups therefore search for people on dating websites, which are designed for connecting strangers. They set up false user profiles, typically with edited pictures of stolen photographs, preferably army officers, engineers and attractive models. Then the crooks start a romantic relationship online, declare their love for the victim and ask that they move from the dating site to Instant Messenger or email to start an exclusive relationship. During the grooming stage, many a victim falls in love.[40] Some weeks or months later, after trust and love are gained, the criminals first ask for small amounts of money, and then for more. The plot may involve other criminals in the group who pretend to be doctors and inform the victim that their loved one has been rushed to a hospital, requesting money to pay the hospital bills. The game ends when the victim finds out about the scam, or has no money left. According to the FBI, victims lose an average of $14,000.[41] Online dating scams are now commonplace, and many victims are too embarrassed to go public. But there is an easy way of detecting scams. If your online sweetheart begins to ask for money, for whatever reason, you can guess why. If you do an image search and the person's photo appears under other names, you know. There is a simple rule to avoid heartbreak and an empty bank account: never ever send money to someone you met online and don't know in person.

Besides the financial loss, victims experience the loss of a relationship. For most, the loss of the object of love is more upsetting. As one victim explained, 'I'd been talking to this guy for so long and how could one day you get up and be told it's a scam, how can that go away? I mean your feelings don't change.' Many are embarrassed and shocked on learning that they have fallen prey to a scam: 'Well you are mentally raped. Because they've totally picked your brains and everything else', and 'God, how can I be so stupid!'[42]

The high-tech version of these human swindlers are bots. Bots are autonomous software agents that make decisions without human intervention. Unlike benevolent bots, such as editing bots on Wikipedia and web crawlers, which are designed to support human users, malevolent bots are designed to exploit us. Consider the Canadian online dating service Ashley Madison, a cheater dating site that was founded with the slogan 'Life is short. Have an affair.' Not surprisingly, there was a shortage of female customers. The business model was that male customers had to pay a fee to initiate a conversation with a female. When hackers stole all of the site's customer data – including emails, names, addresses and sexual fantasies – it turned out that Ashley Madison had 'employed' over 70,000 'female' bots to send over 20 million fake messages to male cheaters.[43] The hackers threatened to leak this data if Ashley Madison did not immediately shut down its services. When the infidelity dating site refused, the hackers released the personal data of 32 million customers, including those who had paid a $19 fee to be deleted, which was yet another fake service. 'This will wreck my marriage,' a Kentucky man said who had used the site for years to cheat on his wife.[44] Others were angry about their exposure after only receiving fake profiles of potential partners. And some 1,200 of the email addresses ended with .sa, indicating customers from Saudi Arabia, where adultery can mean the death penalty.

You Caught His Eye

The most unexpected part of this sad story is that dating sites themselves take advantage of scammers to lure customers into purchasing subscriptions. In the US, the Federal Trade Commission (FTC) sued the online service Match for using fake love interest advertisements to trick hundreds of thousands of consumers.[45] Match owns Match.com, Tinder, OKCupid, PlentyOfFish and other dating sites.

Assume you are looking for 'the one'. Most online services offer to create a profile for you free of charge, in addition to the option of purchasing a subscription. So you might just sign up because it's free and see what happens. To your surprise, your profile quickly attracts attention, and the dating service reports that someone has expressed an interest in you (figure 1.4). But, because you didn't subscribe, you cannot respond. That persuades you to purchase a subscription and write back to the person. Too late; the profile is now 'unavailable'. Oh no, you waited too long and should have subscribed directly in the first place. Now you may well have missed 'the one'.

But don't worry, it's not what you think. Millions of the interested 'eyes' are scammers who want you to become their romance scam victim. According to the FTC, the dating service was well aware of the scammers and had flagged their accounts as fraudulent, yet

---

match.com

He just emailed you!

You caught his eye and now he's expressed

interest in you... Could he be the one?

READ HIS EMAIL >>

You will be notified when other Match.com members express interest in you.

Please note: This email may contain advertisements.

Match.com P.O. Box 25472, Dallas TX 75225

FIGURE 1.4: 'You caught his eye'. A message sent to people who have put up a profile on a dating service for free in order to lure them into a paid subscription. Only by paying can they respond to the person who expressed interest. The Federal Trade Commission sued the dating service Match, which owns Match.com, Tinder, PlentyOfFish and other dating sites, because Match knew that many of these contacts were scammers, having flagged their accounts as fraudulent. It nevertheless forwarded these contacts, but only to their non-subscribing customers to nudge them into subscribing.

nevertheless forwarded their messages to make their non-paying customers curious and subscribe. In this way, the dating services exploited the scammers to get subscriptions, deceiving their own customers and profiting from fraud. And the ploy works. The FTC reported that within two years, about 500,000 curious customers purchased a subscription within twenty-four hours after a receiving a fraudulent message such as 'You caught his eye.' Those who received the disappointing response 'unavailable' were actually the fortunate ones. Match does try to prevent contact with scammers, but only for their subscribers. For the non-subscribers, they used scammers as bait. That may explain why customers are often puzzled that the number of notifications of interest faded away the moment they subscribed.

ARRANGED MARRIAGES GO ONLINE

In the Western world, dating happens between two individuals. Marriage usually comes last. That is not so in all cultures. In the traditional Indian system, parents decide on the choice set. Marriage comes first, then sex, then love.

The Indian Institute of Management in Bangalore, with its landscaped gardens, provides an idyllic environment for learning. Its motto is *Let our study be enlightening*. While teaching there at a winter institute on decision making, I was approached by Sanjey, an assistant professor. He told me his story about finding true love. In the traditional Indian system, the family of a prospective bride or groom searches for a match, not the individual. In the digital age, marriage advertisements are typically placed in the Wanted section of a matrimonial website, not unlike in the West, but it is often the family who advertises, not the individual. The ads typically provide the age and height of the young man or woman, and some of the following: their profession and salary, the expected salary of the partner, the profession of the father, the caste, and whether a dowry is required. From the responses on the website, the family might select three to six possible partners. Then the parents pick one of the candidates and arrange a meeting at a restaurant, where the young people meet for the first time and have a chance to talk to one another – in the presence of their parents. After returning home, the parents of each ask their child whether he or she would accept the candidate as a partner for life. If both young people accept, the wedding preparations go ahead. If one of them rejects the other, then the process is repeated with the next candidate on the list.

Sanjey disliked this procedure. But not, as one might think, because he wanted to do it the Western way and have more choice. Rather, he did not want to have any choice at all. He asked his parents to decide for him, trusting their experience, and simply hoped that they would select an attractive, loveable wife. When I asked him why he did not want to see at least a few of the women, he explained that he did not want to hurt a woman's feelings by rejecting her. That was a remarkable statement, so unlike the spirit of casually rejecting candidates online literally with a swipe of a hand. Sanjey married the woman his parents selected, and both of them told me they had since fallen in love and have been happy together for years. In the world of Tinder, access is an asset. In Sanjey's world, access implies rejecting and hurting others' feelings.

Trusting one's parents and their experience is unthinkable, even irrational, for most Westerners. But as Sanjey and other researchers at the Indian Institute of Management politely pointed out, why would Americans and Europeans consider it 'rational' to seek a partner by randomly meeting someone in a disco, where they can hardly hear each other and have had a drink too many? Will parents' choices or love marriages be the future? There is a third option. The increasing faith in the omnipotence of AI may well put an end to both systems.

THE ULTIMATE CONVENIENCE: LET THE AI ARRANGE OUR MARRIAGES

We dream of autonomous cars because they are purportedly safer than human drivers. Why not autonomous partner algorithms? The argument in favour of both is similar. Almost all deadly car accidents are due to human failure: drunk driving, drugs, fatigue or distraction by one's cell phone. Self-driving cars would protect people from their own errors. Similarly, every other first marriage and two-thirds of second marriages end in divorce in the US, leading to regret for having married the wrong partner as well as to emotional issues for the children. Why not put an algorithm 'in the driver's seat' that protects people from making bad decisions? An autonomous AI would match the right people before they go astray.

One philosopher of AI advises: 'We should defer to the superintelligence's opinion whenever feasible.'[46] In this vision of rational choice, you trust an algorithm, not yourself or your family, to choose your romantic partner. Taken to the extreme, the result would be an autonomous AI that arranges marriages without any interference from humans. All you have to do is to turn up in time at the location you are told.

Such an AI is science fiction, but the science fiction exists. 'Hang the DJ', an episode of the British TV series *Black Mirror*, named after the dark display of a smartphone, projects us into such a future world where romantic relationships are no longer individual decisions. In this world, a love algorithm matches people into relationships, and everyone follows the algorithm's choice without hesitation. Moreover, each relationship comes with an expiration date, upon which the lovers dutifully separate. After separation, the algorithm pairs each individual with a new partner until the next expiration date.

Today we are already told that algorithms can predict personality better than humans can.[47] Wouldn't it be foolish not to follow the AI? For some, to defer to its selection may be the ultimate convenience: no flirting necessary, no rejection possible, no feelings ever hurt. Everything is optimized and no one wastes time and money finding a partner on their own or through dating agencies. For others like me, that vision is the final romantic nightmare. The protagonists in the *Black Mirror* episode, where everyone believes and obeys the matching AI, are a couple who take their lives back into their own hands. They fall in love and decide, against the will of the algorithm, to stay together. But this romantic couple is the odd one out.

2

What AI Is Best At:
The Stable-World Principle

*'If one could devise a successful chess machine, one would
seem to have penetrated to the core of the human intellectual
endeavor.'*

Allan Newell, J. C. Shaw, and Herbert A. Simon[1]

*'Imagine how much harder physics would be if electrons had
feelings.'*

Richard Feynman[2]

Why can AI win at chess but not find the best mate? After all, the
goal appears to be similar: to assign a score to each move or candidate and then pick the best one. Chess algorithms such as Deep Blue
assign scores to billions of possible positions it can foresee, just
as love algorithms assign matching scores to millions of potential
partners. It works out marvellously for chess. Why not for everything else?

Herbert Simon was one of the founders of artificial intelligence, and
the only recipient to date of both the Nobel Memorial Prize in Economics and the Turing Award, which has been dubbed 'the Nobel
Prize in Computing'. Simon firmly believed that once a machine can
beat the best chess player, it has reached the essence of human intelligence. In 1965, he predicted that, within twenty years, machines
would be capable of doing any work that humans can do.[3] The belief
that chess is the pinnacle of the human intellect was so self-evident
(and still is to some) that it was shared by both early enthusiasts such

as Simon and critics of AI as well. For instance, when the philosopher Hubert Dreyfus slated Simon's enthusiasm in his widely read book *What Computers Can't Do* of 1979, he nevertheless referred to chess as the core of general intelligence, only to point out that computers have been unable to win.[4]

When, finally, Deep Blue beat the world champion Garry Kasparov in 1997, AI therefore appeared to be far along the path to acquiring human-like intelligence. All that is missing appears to be more computational power and more data for AI to outsmart us in every respect. And no longer is computational power a scarce resource. According to Moore's law, computing power – the number of transistors in integrated circuits – doubles every two years or so. This exponential increase was indeed essential for the victories of AI in chess and Go. Simon's equation of this success with reaching human intelligence underlies the *AI-beats-humans* argument in the introduction of this book. Following Simon, popular writers now argue that it will not take long until we succeed in building an awe-inspiring superintelligence that will exceed us in everything we know and everything we do.

I am a great admirer of Simon's work, but here he overlooked a fundamental issue, which others have also ignored.

THE STABLE-WORLD PRINCIPLE

There is a crucial difference between games such as chess and problems such as finding a romantic partner. In chess, each position can be represented by a profile that specifies the location of each figure, from pawn to king. A chess computer does not need to make an inference about what the true position is because the profile *is* the position. There is no uncertainty. In many other situations, such as in online dating, uncertainty abounds. Although each person has a profile, as we have seen, the profile is not the person. People tend to edit their profiles, and, even when they do it scrupulously, a profile does not capture the rich dimensions of a human being.

This insight is expressed more generally in the *stable-world principle*:[5]

Complex algorithms work best in well-defined, stable situations where large amounts of data are available. Human intelligence has evolved to deal with uncertainty, independent of whether big or small data are available.

The rules of chess and Go are well defined and are stable in the sense that they hold today and tomorrow. There is no uncertainty about the nature of the rules and whether they may unexpectedly change in the future. Between romantic partners, in contrast, the rules of conduct need to be negotiated and can be violated.

The stable-world principle applies to forecasting the future as well. To successfully predict the future, one needs a good theory, reliable data and a stable world. In August 2004, NASA launched the probe Messenger, which entered its orbit of the planet Mercury in March 2011, at exactly the location NASA had predicted more than six years beforehand. This incredible feat was possible because a good theory of movements of the planets exists, astronomical data are highly reliable and the movement of Mercury remains stable over time, without being significantly influenced by human behaviour. Accordingly, AI is superb at dealing with such stable situations, from using face recognition for unlocking your phone to finding the fastest route to your destination to sorting and analysing large data in accounting.

But tech companies often try to predict human behaviour without a good theory, reliable data or a stable world. If you apply for a job, an algorithm may screen your application and recommend whether you should be invited for a job talk. If you ever get arrested, the judge may consult a risk assessment tool to calculate the probability that you will reoffend before your court date and then decide whether you should be bailed or jailed. If you get cancer, the hospital may rely on a big data algorithm to design personalized treatment for you. If you are a social worker, you might be sent to families in your community whom an algorithm deems to be at the highest risk. In all of these situations, there is a lack of good theory, reliable data or a stable world. Hence, AI's miraculous power is often a mirage.

The distinction I make corresponds to that between *risk* and *uncertainty* originally made by the economist Frank Knight. In situations of risk, such as roulette, we know all possible outcomes (the numbers o to 36) in advance, along with their consequences and probabilities. In situations of uncertainty, in contrast, we cannot know all possible outcomes or their consequences in advance. That is the case when hiring an employee, forecasting an election, or predicting infection rates of the flu or Covid-19. Finance experts use the terms *radical uncertainty* and *black swans* to characterize a world where the future is unknowable and surprises happen.[6] In these situations, Knight argued, calculation is not enough; instead, we need judgement, intelligence, intuition and the courage to make decisions. Many situations are a mixture of risk and uncertainty, which means that both machine calculation and human intelligence have a role to play.

The stable-world principle clarifies that with increasing computing power, machines will soon solve all problems in *stable* situations better than humans. For instance, we may see a program that outperforms humans in all games with well-defined rules. Yet the same does not hold for unstable situations. If the future is unlike the past, collecting and analysing big data – which is always from the past – can lead to false conclusions. With this insight, we can better understand where complex algorithms fed with big data are likely to be successful, and where humans are indispensable.

SUCCESSES OF AI

'I, for one, welcome our new computer overlords,' said Ken Jennings, acknowledging his defeat in the quiz show *Jeopardy!* by IBM's supercomputer Watson in 2011.[7] The new overlord was room-size and came with 20 tons of air-conditioning equipment. Watson is named after IBM's founder, Thomas J. Watson. It has a DeepQA (question-answering) algorithm that was trained on thousands of question-and-answer pairs from the show to learn which answer matched with which question. There is no question that Watson's performance in the game show was truly impressive.

The stunning victories of AI over human experts to date have all been in well-defined games, from draughts to backgammon to Scrabble. *Jeopardy!* already has strict rules, but, for Watson to win, even these had to be adapted by excluding certain types of questions.[8] In May 2017, the computer program AlphaGo won against the world's top-ranked Go player at the time, Ke Jie. The games drew 280 million viewers in China, where Go champions are national heroes with the status of rock stars.[9] Like chess, Go is a well-defined game with fixed rules that cannot be negotiated by the players. In December 2017, its descendant, AlphaZero, was introduced, which beat AlphaGo. Both use deep neural networks, whose algorithms are not designed by humans but learned by machines. AlphaGo learns from games played by human experts, while all that AlphaZero needs to know are the rules of the game, without any further human input. It just uses computing power to play millions of games against itself and learn how to win by trial and error.

AlphaZero also beat the best human players at chess and shogi (Japanese chess). Yet it would be an error to believe that AlphaZero is capable of doing everything. It is specialized to play games for two players that have known and unchangeable rules. It does not work for driving a car, teaching children, finding true love, taking over the world or other practical matters fraught with uncertainty.[10] Similarly, the recommender algorithm in Google's search engine is highly specialized and cannot play Go. In fact, AlphaGo and Google's search engine have very little in common.

Another example of successful AI is face recognition systems used not only for border controls and unlocking phones but also for identifying one's friends in photos on online social networks, verifying identities at ATMs and checking into hotels. In an experiment, Google's automated face recognition system was fed a huge number of pictures, using more than 1,000 hours on a network of powerful computers. When it was then given the task to determine whether two photographs show the same person, it was accurate in 99.6 per cent of the cases, which is the level at which humans perform the same task.[11] These systems work best if you hold your face still in front of the border-control camera or your smartphone, that is, in controlled authentication tasks, where one face is compared with one photo. As noted in the Introduction, face recognition systems perform substantially less well in mass screening, that is, in less controlled situations, where many individuals are compared with many other individuals.

For instance, when the Cardiff police screened the faces of 170,000 soccer fans in the 2017 UEFA Champions League final between Real Madrid and Juventus, the system reported 2,470 matches with a criminal database of half a million images, 2,297 (93 per cent) of which were false alarms.[12] Similarly, when Amazon's facial recognition system compared photos of the 535 members of the US Congress with a criminal database, it reported 28 members that matched, all falsely.

As a final example, consider fraud control. One of the reasons why you may pay too much into health insurance is a form of fraud practised by corrupt doctors and pharmacies. Here is how it works. If a drug costs £100 and the reimbursement rate is 90 per cent, then the pharmacy gets £90 back from the insurer. If the pharmacy presents prescriptions written by a doctor without actually having sold the medication, it can make an illegal profit. In Portugal, for instance, one doctor wrote 32,000 prescriptions for expensive drugs in one year – which boils down to one fake prescription every three minutes.[13] The prescriptions bore the names of deceased patients or the faked signatures of deceased doctors. These doctors and pharmacies caused some 40 per cent of all public expenditure fraud in the country. To put a stop to this, the Portuguese National Health Service introduced an electronic prescription programme requiring doctors to complete the prescription and send it to their patients by text message or email, and reported that the system could reduce fraud by 80 per cent. In this case, the surveillance potential of software has been clearly used for the benefit of the health system.

There are countless examples for successes of AI surpassing human capability, from industry robots that tirelessly and precisely repeat the same movements to search engines that can find words and phrases in large bodies of text. In general, my thesis is that the better defined and more stable a situation is, the more likely it is that machine learning will outperform humans.

The moment human behaviour enters the field, uncertainty appears, and predictions get difficult. AI can get into trouble if either problems are not well defined or situations are unstable, or both. That holds not only for the success of romantic relations, but also for anticipating the next large financial crisis, which we may likely miss as we did the crisis of 2008.

The distinction between stable, well-defined problems and unstable, ill-defined ones is reminiscent of that between 'known unknowns' and 'unknown unknowns' in the NASA terminology popularized by former US Secretary of Defense Donald Rumsfeld. Yet the distinction is not carved in stone: most situations are a mix of both. For instance, translating from one language into another is regulated by a stable set of grammatical rules but also involves mastering ambiguous terms, phrases with multiple meanings, irony and other sources of uncertainty.

PSYCHOLOGICAL AI

In 1957, Simon predicted that, within ten years, a computer would beat the world's chess champion.[14] And he was right, apart from the timing. But that victory did not happen in the way Simon imagined.

For Simon, AI meant *teaching computers how human experts solve a problem*. The computer is the student, the human the teacher. Researchers extract the heuristics (rules of thumb) of strategic thinking used by experts and program these into a computer, which then can process the rules faster and without errors. Let's call this teacher-student vision *psychological AI*. It is the original meaning of AI, where the 'I' refers to the intelligence of humans mimicked by a machine. Simon and his students went a long way to extract the rules by observing chess masters and asking them to think aloud while playing. It worked for some problems, yet never succeeded in beating a world champion in chess.

The program that beat Kasparov in 1997, IBM's Deep Blue, was not based on the idea that human intelligence and machine intelligence are two sides of the same coin. Instead, it relied on massive computing power to examine 200 million positions per second. The machine calculates: if I do A, and he does B, then I do C, and he does D, and so on, where will I end up? Kasparov, by contrast, could evaluate perhaps three positions per second. When Joe Hoane, one of Deep Blue's programmers, was asked how much of his work was devoted specifically to artificial intelligence in emulating human thought, he responded dismissively: 'It is not an artificial intelligence project in any way. It is a project in – we play chess through sheer speed of calculation and we just shift through the possibilities and we just pick one line.'[15]

Simon tried to build a machine in the image of a human. IBM did not. Nor did Google when building AlphaZero. Their engineers relied on *machine learning*, which is another branch of AI that includes deep neural networks and other algorithms, without trying to mimic human intelligence. The 'I' in machine learning AI has no relation to intelligence as we know it, which is why the term automated decision making (ADM) is often used instead. Psychological AI turned out to be a bust for chess, while machine learning using brute-force calculation succeeded. That success was also perceived as relinquishing the dream of building an artificial intelligence that resembles human intelligence. And there is a fundamental difference between human intelligence and machine learning. The chess program using brute force doesn't know it is outsmarting a player. In fact, it doesn't even know it is playing something called chess; it is simply good at it. Brute computational power is high-speed calculation, not intelligence.

Is psychological AI a bad idea? Not at all. It has its place, although not, as Simon believed, in games like chess and other well-defined situations. The stable-world principle provides a different perspective: psychological AI is likely to be successful instead in situations of uncertainty, such as predicting the future. After all, humans evolved heuristics to deal with uncertainty, and psychological AI aims to program these heuristics into a computer.

It is interesting that Simon was also one of the fathers of research on heuristics, and is known for the insight that, under uncertainty, it makes no sense to seek the optimal solution; instead, it's more effective to look for a satisfactory one. In my own research, I have extended his work on psychological AI to a wide range of situations of uncertainty.

Fast-and-frugal Trees

When making decisions, experts tend to use fewer pieces of information than novices; they know what is relevant and ignore the rest. And if some cues (features) are more important than others, experts consider these first and may base their decision on the most important cue only. My research team and I have programed these intuitions into simple algorithms called *fast-and-frugal trees*, named for their speed and frugal use of information.

In conflict-ridden countries across the world, innocent civilians are frequently wounded or killed after being mistaken for terrorists at military checkpoints. The main problem is that checkpoint personnel, who have to infer whether an approaching vehicle contains civilians or suicide attackers, typically get no systematic training in how to make these life-and-death decisions. Together with armed forces instructors, some of my research colleagues designed a fast-and-frugal tree that helps make more reliable decisions.[16] The first question in the tree is whether an approaching vehicle contains more than one occupant (figure 2.1, left). If yes, the inference is that the occupants are non-hostile civilians (because assigning multiple suicide attackers to one car would be a waste of scarce resources). If not, the next question is whether the vehicle slows down or stops at the checkpoint. If not, the inference is that the occupant is hostile. If yes, the third and final question is whether

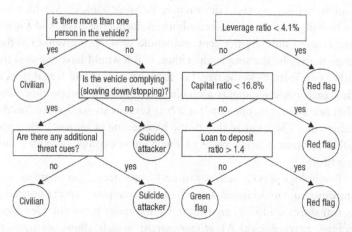

FIGURE 2.1: Psychological AI. Fast-and-frugal trees are examples of psychological AI, which constructs decision aids based on psychological principles. Left: A fast-and-frugal tree for checkpoint decisions that reduce civilian casualties. Right: A fast-and-frugal tree for identifying banks that are in financial distress. In general, a fast-and-frugal tree has a small number of cues (or questions) and allows for a decision after each cue.

further threat cues exist (such as an intelligence report about a suspicious green Honda Civic in the area). The tree is easy to memorize and execute and can reduce civilian casualties by more than 60 per cent.

Another risky venture is to identify failing banks. Traditional finance bets on highly complex 'value-at-risk' models that purport to safely estimate the capital a bank needs to avoid bankruptcy with a high probability, say 99.9 per cent. Yet these models did not prevent 42 of the 116 large global banks (with more than $100 billion assets at the end of 2006) from failing during the financial crisis in 2008. Part of the problem is that these models are too complex and fragile for the uncertain world of banking – they need to estimate millions of risk factors and their correlations on the basis of often unreliable data. Together with experts at the Bank of England, my colleagues and I developed a fast-and-frugal tree that matches or outperforms complex methods in predicting bank failure (figure 2.1, right).[17] The first branch of the tree asks for the leverage ratio (roughly, the ratio of a bank's capital to its total assets) of each bank and is placed first because this ratio discriminated best between the banks that failed and those that survived. For instance, the Swiss bank UBS, which had to be bailed out by the Swiss authorities during the crisis, had a leverage ratio of only 1.7 per cent and would have been given a red flag immediately by the simple algorithm. U B S would have satisfied the other two features in the tree, but the logic of fast-and-frugal trees is that each question stands alone in the order of its importance and that one cannot compensate for a bad value with good values on the other cues. This logic is akin to the functioning of human bodies and other complex systems: perfect kidneys cannot compensate for a failing heart.

Psychological AI, such as fast-and-frugal trees, can augment and improve human decisions. In each of the examples, expert knowledge is transformed into an algorithm. Unlike many more complex algorithms, psychological AI is transparent, which allows its users to understand and adapt an algorithm when situations change. In situations of uncertainty, both human judgement and transparency are indispensable.[18] In the case of banks, transparent algorithms that make no room for estimating millions of risk factors can help authorities more readily detect when banks are trying to game the rules.

GAMING AI

The stable-world principle helps us to understand what problems an AI application is likely to be more successful at solving than others. We need to know more than that, however, in order to evaluate whether it is likely to be successful in the real world. Much of AI is commercial or military, not scientific. Commercial organizations may have goals that conflict with what their product is officially supposed to do. Even in a stable world, where an AI product could be delivered to the benefit of society, the AI may be gamed to serve a hidden interest. The problem is not the technology, but rather who is behind it. I illustrate three ways customers are taken in, in both situations where AI works and ones where it does not: how a potentially useful AI application is exploited for profit, how a mediocre algorithm is made to look impressive, and how ineffective technological solutions are marketed even when investing in people would be more effective.

How Electronic Health Records Were Gamed

A medical record contains all relevant information about a patient's medical history, such as test results, diagnoses and treatment results. These confidential files have been traditionally kept on paper. One problem with paper is that when patients visit new doctors, it is difficult to access the patient's history in the time available, and many tests are unnecessarily repeated. That raises costs and takes away doctors' valuable time from listening and talking to the patient. Moreover, if a new doctor is not aware of relevant aspects of a patient's medical history, the patient may be given unintentionally harmful treatment. To avoid this, electronic health records, also called electronic medical records or electronic patient records, promise to be fertile tools for fast access to the information that doctors need. These records have algorithms for recording and storing information, including images, which the doctor can access quickly, unless the file is hundreds of pages long. Keeping records and making these readily accessible is an ideal task for basic AI programs that involves sorting past data in a (hopefully) reliable way.

At a summit meeting in 2003, the British prime minister, Tony Blair, boasted to the US president, George W. Bush, about his new multi-billion investment 'Connecting for Health' to wire the entire British healthcare system. Back in Washington, Bush pressed for a similar programme to computerize health records.[19] Researchers at the RA ND Corporation estimated that the US healthcare system could save $81 billion per year by adopting it rapidly.[20] That estimate led to the US surpassing the UK's investment, with a $30 billion federal incentive programme and an explosive growth of the industry. Finally, a case where investment in a database paid for patients, we might think. However, when the RAND Corporation reviewed the situation in 2013, their optimism had faded. Hospitals with electronic record systems had *increased* their billing. Costs had gone up instead of down, from about $2 trillion aggregate expenditures in 2005 to $2.8 trillion in 2013.[21] Moreover, RAND reported that the quality and efficiency of healthcare were only marginally better, if at all.

Why did such a good idea not pan out? The answer is that the system was gamed.

Consider the hope of saving costs. The plan was that easy access to past tests would reduce unnecessary duplicate testing. In fact, when a doctor entered data into the record, the software automatically recommended new procedures to consider. After being prompted, just to be on the safe side, doctors using electronic records ended up performing more, not fewer, tests.[22] Almost all of these alerts appear to have been false alarms.[23] Companies were gaming the software for sales pitches to increase profit and inflate medical bills.

Consider the hope of better access. The plan was that electronic records would allow doctors and patients to access all needed health information quickly and at any time. The generous funding, however, led to competition between companies, and the systems installed by hospitals and doctors were proprietary, employing incompatible formats and secret algorithms that were not designed to communicate with one another.[24] Thus, access was in fact limited, not universal – just as you can't use the charging cable of a Mac for a PC or even for your previous-generation Mac. The competing software companies had used the governmental subsidies to increase their own gains. Their primary goal was brand loyalty, not patient safety.

Consider the hope of improving patients' health. As mentioned, there is lack of evidence that patients benefit from their electronic health records.[25] Some software systems even prompt doctors to 'upcode' the diagnosis of a patient to more severe ones, which increases billing and profit and leads to more tests and treatments. All this happens at the expense of increased anxiety among patients, who are oblivious to the fact that their severe diagnosis may have been made in the interest of the billing system. Not all doctors are aware of these issues. One reason is that the vendors of electronic health reports can protect themselves from liability by non-disclosure agreements in their contracts, meaning that doctors and clinics who experience flaws in the software are prohibited from discussing these in open forums.[26] Doctors who have spoken up on safety issues, serious injuries and deaths related to problems with the software later requested that their names not be disclosed for fear of being sued.[27]

The sad fact is that electronic health records were developed by software companies for maximizing billing, not patient care. Hospitals and doctors have used the governmental subsidy provided by Medicare HITECH to buy electronic systems that allow them to charge Medicare even more for their services. Discussions on electronic health records, however, rarely recognize this issue and instead mostly revolve around issues of privacy and doctors' time. Privacy is indeed a legitimate concern when hundreds of thousands of doctors, health administrators and insurance personnel have access to personal files of patients. Clinics have been hacked, records have been stolen, surgeries have had to be cancelled, and clinics have been blackmailed into paying to get their records back. Recently even patients have become the target of hackers: tens of thousands of patients from psychotherapy centres in Finland were blackmailed with the threat of having their intimate conversations with their therapists published online.[28]

These issues and the fact that managing electronic health records decreases doctors' time with patients are serious problems.[29] Yet solving them requires first solving the more fundamental problem that the potential benefit of electronic patient records for the patient is eaten up by a primarily profit-driven system. There are too many players – clinics, administrators, lobbyists, big pharma, insurers – who pursue interests conflicting with those of patients and their health. Such interests do not provide a fertile ground for using AI to serve patients. To reap the fruits of digital health, we need health systems that first and foremost serve patients.[30] Otherwise, digital health will become a band-aid solution or will even amplify the problems.

THE TEXAS SHARPSHOOTER FALLACY

Electronic health records could be beneficial for patients; the data are known and only need to be made accessible. Now consider a situation of uncertainty rather than relative stability: predicting divorce. The stable-world principle indicates that algorithms are here unlikely to perform well. Yet there is a clever way to make these predictions look much better than they are. This procedure is sometimes a fallacy, that is, an unintentional result out of ignorance, but also can be a deliberate trick to persuade people.

Predicting Divorce

Assume you are newly married. Would you like to know whether your marriage will end in divorce? One might object that this is a hypothetical question because whether a couple will split is hard to know in advance. Yet in a series of studies, clinical researchers reported to have found an algorithm that predicts with about 90 per cent accuracy whether a couple would divorce in the following three years.[31] Study after study suggested the algorithm had high levels of accuracy, varying between 67 and 95 per cent.[32] These impressive findings attracted wide attention in the media, and love labs and marriage institutes worldwide advertised 'science-based predictions' of relationship stability and therapy.[33] Unlike in online dating agencies, the algorithm in these clinical studies is transparent. It uses features such as education, the number of young children, violence, binge drinking and drug abuse.

Who would have thought that an algorithm can tell whether a young couple will divorce? In the future, you can drive up to the love lab with your partner, get interviewed and then be told whether the two of you will likely get divorced or not. If the answer is yes, you might as well contact a lawyer before wasting any more time together.

Or, better still, consult the love lab before even tying the knot. But think for a moment. When it comes to marriage, we are not dealing with a stable world. Whether a couple stays together depends on so many factors, loaded with plenty of uncertainty. That alone is reason for scepticism about the algorithm's level of accuracy. There is indeed a delusion behind these numbers. And it can be found in many a study in the social sciences, not only in predicting divorce. Let me explain.

The Sharpshooter

A Texan cowboy shoots at a barn wall with a revolver from quite a distance. He proudly shows his amazing performance: The bullet holes are grouped around the bull's-eye of the target. How did he do that? Years of hard training? A miraculous revolver?

None of that; the strategy is much easier. What the sharpshooter in fact did was shoot first and then paint the circles of the target around the bullet holes so that the bull's-eye was in the middle (figure 2.2). Clearly this procedure guarantees better results than if the cowboy had painted the target first before shooting. If one counts all shots that 'hit' the target, then fitting the target to the shots produces nine out of ten possible hits, or a 90 per cent accuracy. Doing it the right way, that is, by painting the target first, say at the centre of the barn, would have likely led to fewer hits. You might think of this trick as cheating, and it is. In science it is called *data fitting*, which by itself is nothing immoral. But to use the eye-catching results and sell them as *prediction* is clearly deceptive.

FIGURE 2.2: Shoot first, paint target later. The Texas sharpshooter shoots first (left) and then draws the target around the bullet holes so that the bull's-eye is in the centre (right). The sharpshooter's accuracy looks impressive if one doesn't know that the data (the bullet holes) were obtained first and then the algorithm (the target) was fitted to the data.

In our analogy, the sharpshooter is the algorithm, the target is the prediction the algorithm makes and the bullet holes are the data. To shift the target into the optimal position, the sharpshooter has two degrees of freedom: move it left or right and up or down on the barn wall. With these two options, he can centre any possible set of shots miraculously around the bull's-eye. These degrees of freedom are called the *free parameters* of an algorithm. Algorithms can have more than two free parameters. Financial models, for instance, have considerably more, which gives them huge flexibility to account for almost anything – after the fact.

If the sharpshooter had first painted the target on the barn and then neatly shot around the bull's-eye, he would indeed deserve admiration. Along these lines, real prediction occurs when predictions are made first, and then the data are obtained. The distinction between fitting and predicting is the life blood of every student in machine learning and should be evident to scientists in every field. But in the social sciences or in commercial enterprises, algorithms are often merely fitted to match the data, and the result is sold as prediction.[34] Here is a useful principle:

Always check whether an algorithm's impressive performance was obtained by prediction or mere fitting.

Let's go back and apply this principle to the notable levels of accuracy in 'predicting' divorce. In fact, none of these studies had actually predicted anything at all. The authors always knew already which couples were still together and which had divorced, and then, like the Texas sharpshooter, fitted their algorithm to the data.[35] What they should have done instead is a two-step procedure: take one group of couples and fit (develop) the algorithm, and then test the predictions for a new group of couples.

Independent researchers did precisely this with a new group of 528 persons.[36] When they fitted the algorithm to the data, it 'predicted' a similarly high percentage (65 per cent) of the divorced couples correctly as 'divorced.' When the algorithm was tested on a new group of couples and *did not already know* whether any of their marriages had ended up in divorce, everything changed. The algorithm correctly predicted only 21 per cent of those who would get divorced.[37] That is its true accuracy.

And there is another question: how good is 21 per cent? Is it better than a blind guess? Among the couples studied, 16 per cent got divorced in the first three to six years of marriage. That means if you close your eyes and simply predict that each couple will get divorced, you can already expect to get 16 per cent right. That is the benchmark. Any algorithm worth its salt must therefore predict substantially better than that. In the study we've been looking at, the algorithm does a bit better, but not by much. The true performance of the algorithm was 5 percentage points above chance; all the rest was hot air.

Beware of the Texas sharpshooter fallacy. Even when the term 'prediction' is used, as in the studies on the divorce algorithm, it may be falsely employed. To find out, one needs to check whether the algorithm has been first trained on one sample of data and then tested on a different sample. This two-step process is called *cross-validation*. Many neuroscientists, psychologists, sociologists, economists and educational researchers just fit their algorithms to data, then stop and report the big numbers.[38] You might wonder why. One reason is that this produces more impressive numbers. Reporting these electrifies audiences unaware of the Texas sharpshooter fallacy and persuades them of the magical powers of an algorithm. There is also a more charitable but even more alarming explanation. Quite a few social scientists do not appear to understand that fitting is not prediction, a confusion that has a long history and has been documented in many other studies.[39] At the beginning of the twenty-first century, merely fitting data was the rule in psychology.[40] Today, social scientists are increasingly beginning to recognize the importance of making true predictions.

Financial charlatanism is another instance of the sharpshooter fallacy. You may have heard great news like this: 'Our backtesting shows: this innovative strategy beat the market over the last ten years on average by 5 per cent.' Backtests are historical simulations of an investment strategy. As in the case of the divorce algorithm, all the data are known, and large numbers of investment strategies are fitted to the data; the one with the highest fit is then advertised as the best investment strategy – similar to the Texas sharpshooter's strategy. This problem has been exposed many times, but many in the world of finance proceed by fitting their algorithms to data, without always reporting how many algorithms they tried.[41] Being honest would not produce attention-grabbing numbers, and customers might prefer to invest in the algorithms of the competition. The solution is not to install a code of honesty, which would put the honest ones out of business. Instead, it would be to have informed citizens who ask whether there was a Texas sharpshooter strategy involved.

The physicist Niels Bohr liked to say, 'Prediction is hard, especially about the future.' This remark has been attributed to Mark Twain, Yogi Berra and a host of others known for their witty sayings.[42] But it is in fact quite serious. As we have seen, what is called prediction may have nothing to do with the future. Hindsight is easy, but prediction is difficult, particularly in matters of love and divorce.

THE MOONSHOT

You may have already seen IBM's commercials where what looks like a sentient box interacts with Bob Dylan, Serena Williams and other celebrities. Watson's claim to fame began in 2011, after winning the TV quiz show *Jeopardy!* against two of its best contestants. After this spectacular success, the value of IBM's stocks increased by $18 million.[43] Ginni Rometty, IBM's CEO, announced that the 'next moonshot' would be healthcare – not because Watson knew anything about health, but because that is where the big money is. To adapt Watson to healthcare, it was fed medical data, such as patients' case histories and treatments. Before it was clear whether Watson could actually learn to diagnose and recommend treatments like a doctor, high expectations were raised. Rometty announced a medical 'golden age' in which AI 'is real, it's mainstream, it's here, and it can change almost everything about health care'.[44] IBM's PR department created the impression that Watson would revolutionize healthcare, or had already, and the Watson team came under pressure to quickly commercialize their product.[45] The first application was oncology.

Watson for Oncology became marketed around the world as recommending treatments for cancer patients. From MD Anderson, one of the most respected cancer centres in the US, to Manipal Hospitals in India, clinics purchased the services and paid a per-patient fee ranging between $200 and $1,000. Yet Watson could not even deliver the performance of a capable human doctor, let alone the moonshot. Many of the program's treatment recommendations proved to be incorrect, and some unsafe, endangering the lives of patients.[46] IBM's messages eventually faded from hype to modesty, announcing that Watson's medical knowledge was at the level of a first-year medical student.[47] MD Anderson annulled their contract, realizing that the software could not live up to what the marketing department of IBM suggested. The cancer centre had spent $62 million, which made Watson the best-paid med student ever. Major German clinics also fired Watson after realizing that its treatment recommendations bore more resemblance to artificial stupidity than intelligence. In the words of the CEO of Rhön-Klinikum, a network of hospitals and clinics, to carry on with Watson would be the equivalent of 'investing in a Las Vegas show'.[48] Other IBM partners have also halted or shrunk Watson's oncology-related projects. IBM has yet to publish any scientific papers demonstrating how well the technology affects physicians and patients.

The moral of this story is not about Watson or AI in general. It is about aggressive marketing that cannot fulfil the expectations raised and about the uncritical faith in the marketing hype by journalists, unlike among AI scientists. In the words of Oren Etzioni, CEO of the Allen Institute for AI and former computer science professor, 'IBM Watson is the Donald Trump of the AI industry – outlandish claims that aren't backed by credible data.'[49] In more polite terms, Watson is just a computer program that could morph into an assistant for routine medical tasks, but not the brilliant doctor advertised.

IBM also markets Watson as a general-purpose intelligence in espionage, law and finance. Naive bankers buy Watson's services to make better investment decisions. But if Watson is such a crack at predicting the stock market or simply making smart investments, IBM should not be in the financial difficulty it is.

Make People Smarter

Why not invest more money and keep trying? That is a legitimate question – except that too much trial and error eats up the attention and resources that could better be spent on effective measures that truly save lives from cancer.

Robert Weinberg, a world-renowned cancer biologist at MIT, has devoted his professional life to seeking causes of and cures for cancer. Yet cancer drugs may prolong life by only a few weeks or months, while massively decreasing its quality. Moreover, they are so expensive that no country in the world can afford them for all of their citizens. At a 2011 conference in Amsterdam hosted by the Dutch Royal Academy of Sciences and the Dutch Central Bank, Weinberg gave a keynote address with a surprising message for a cancer biologist. Despite having spent his life unravelling the biological conditions of cancer, he views the real promise in fighting cancer today outside of biological science: in making children and teenagers health literate. The argument is this:

- About half of all cancers have their roots in behaviour. Smoking, diet and lack of movement leading to obesity are the key factors.
- These habits are set early in childhood or adolescence.
- Thus, we need to start early in making children and teenagers health literate to prevent these habits that cause cancer from being formed.

Weinberg and I joined forces and designed an experimental programme in schools, where young people are not told what and what not to do but instead learn what the health risks are and how they will be lured by advertising and their peers into unhealthy behaviour. The programme teaches skills such as the joy of cooking, knowledge of how one's body functions, healthy activities, basic scientific attitudes such as asking questions and finding out answers by doing experiments, and awareness of where to look up trustworthy information. Rejecting compulsion or nudging, it provides young people with tools for taking control of their health. We featured this risk literacy programme in two subsequent conferences on preventing cancer in Amsterdam. The head of the Dutch Cancer Society had visited me in Berlin and told me he was interested in funding the programme in schools in areas of the Netherlands where obesity is on the rise among children.

At the third conference on reducing cancer incidence, the very same head of the Cancer Society gave a talk. We had expected to hear him speak on the programme for preventing cancer. Instead, he spoke about the promises of big data for curing cancer. Weinberg and I could not believe our ears. Afterwards, we talked to him, but to no avail. The head of the Society had been persuaded, not wanting to fall behind all the other organizations that fund big data research. That was the end of our project to make young people health literate. All the funding went to the industry.

3

Machines Influence How
We Think of Intelligence

'The most profound technologies are those that disappear. They weave themselves into the fabric of everyday life until they are indistinguishable from it.'

Mark Weiser[1]

'I believe that at the end of the century [i.e., by 2000] the use of words and general educated opinion will have altered so much that one will be able to speak of machines thinking without expecting to be contradicted.'

Alan Turing[2]

It was after Deep Blue and AlphaGo became kings of the gameboard that many felt that humans were no longer the crown of evolution. A flood of popular writers began to talk of a coming superintelligence, a singularity, and the melding of brains with computers into immortal cybercreatures. The most pessimistically inclined announced the end of humanity, with us ending up as pets on the leash of robots, as exhibits in zoos, or as the first species to use its intelligence to extinguish itself. All these stories make the same mistake. Both enthusiasts and pessimists equate computing power with human intelligence.

How did the view come about that intelligence is what computers do? One might expect there to be solid proof, but it's based on analogy, not evidence.[3] New technologies have always inspired new psychological theories. There is nothing wrong with that as long as one recognizes the analogy for what it is and doesn't confuse it with the real thing. Similarly, the human tendency to anthropomorphize may make many especially keen to attribute human intelligence to non-human entities.

Consider the marvels of human memory. People can learn to recite tens of thousands of lines of the Mahabharata of ancient India or conduct entire symphonies by heart. To understand how this is possible, a wide array of analogies has been used, from wax tablets to libraries. The most influential of these were new technologies, which suggested that memory is like a hard disc, a telephone switchboard or a hologram. The same holds for our understanding of the marvels of human intelligence. While we know how a hologram or a computer works, we have only a limited understanding of how intelligence functions. So we take what we know and try to understand what we don't. And there are indeed similarities: both the computer and the human nervous system are electrical; artificial neural networks also have networks of connections, and brains have a neural network of synapses. But every analogy has its limits. If the mind were a computer, we could calculate the square root of the number 1984 in a fraction of a second. If a computer were a mind, it could just as easily pass the CAPTCHA test for proving that you are not an algorithm. Moreover, it could not only win at chess but also have fun while playing.

Although minds are not computers, the creation of this analogy is a fascinating story. Computers themselves have been inspired by human systems; in fact, the computer was originally modelled after a new social system, the division of labour.

THE FIRST COMPUTERS
WERE SOCIAL SYSTEMS

The French Revolution set out to destroy an aristocratic society that lived luxurious lives, spent millions on rich banquets and couldn't have cared less if the heavily taxed peasants perished from hunger. One side effect of the revolution was the attempt to make our measurement systems more rational: to introduce the decimal system for measuring weight, height and almost everything else (up to dividing days into ten hours, with a hundred decimal minutes, each of which had a hundred decimal seconds, but that was going too far). The new system required calculating logarithmic and trigonometric tables, difficult calculations that had previously been the task of mathematical prodigies. Yet the French Revolution also brought about a new vision of calculation. Inspired by Adam Smith's *The Wealth of Nations*, the engineer Gaspard de Prony invented a social hierarchy with a three-tiered division of labour. At the top were a few famous mathematicians who devised the formulas, in the middle seven or eight persons trained in analysis, and at the bottom seventy to eighty unskilled persons who simply added and multiplied millions of numbers.[4] The world had never seen such a project before.

Some years later, the English mathematician Charles Babbage (1791–1871) was amazed that elaborate calculations could be performed by an assembly of workers knowing so little. Going from there, Babbage conceived replacing the workers with machinery and set out to build his first digital computers. These did not really work, but eventually calculators that functioned were built over the following century. My point here is that computers and concepts of intelligence are deeply interwoven. In the beginning there was a new social organization of work, and the computer was created in its image.[5] The first computers were humans.

How Calculation Became Divorced from Intelligence

A computing system with unskilled workers and Babbage's mechanical machines clashed with deeply held beliefs. In the seventeenth and eighteenth centuries, during the age of Enlightenment, the ability for mental calculation was considered the sign of a brilliant intellect. In the psychology of the time, the innovative mind constantly took apart ideas and rearranged them into new ones. Thought was understood as a combinatorial calculus, and great thinkers were proficient calculators. The story of the mathematician Carl Friedrich Gauss (1777–1855, figure 3.1) is probably the best known. Gauss came from a poor family in Brunswick, Germany, and was nine years old when his primary school teacher posed an addition problem to the class.[6]

Schoolmaster Büttner, a whip in hand, told the pupils to write down all numbers from 1 to 100 and add them up. Within a short time, the young Gauss wrote down the answer on his slate, and said, in the town's dialect: 'There it lies!' Disparagingly, but with some compassion, the teacher looked at the little scamp, who apparently had the cheek to claim he had found the result to a problem that cost the entire class bitter sweat. Young Gauss explained to the teacher how he had reasoned. The hundred numbers make 50 pairs (1 + 100, 2 + 99, and so on), each of which adds up to 101. Therefore, the sum is 50 times 101, which is 5,050. To the teacher's credit, he realized Gauss's genius and concluded 'the boy can learn nothing new in my school'. Büttner ensured that Gauss was sent to a better school.

Prodigious mental reckoning was a favourite theme in the eulogies of great mathematicians. But the story of Gauss's brilliance in arithmetic was one of the last. The demonstration that calculation could be done by unskilled workers and by machines slowly put an end to its glorification. No longer was it considered the hallmark of a genius. When calculation shifted from the cohort of great men to that of the

FIGURE 3.1: The German 10 Mark bill featured Carl Friedrich Gauss, including among others the formula for the normal distribution he devised. The bill was issued in 1991 and circulated until the euro was introduced in 2002. The normal distribution is the basis of many models in machine learning, economics, psychology and beyond. Gauss was one of the last mathematicians who were celebrated for their excellent mental reckoning. After it was shown that complicated calculations could be done by a social system of unskilled workers and even by machines, calculation was no longer considered the hallmark of a genius.

unskilled workforce, the psychology shifted as well. What was once considered the crown of human intelligence sunk to something merely mechanical. What became known as 'intelligence' in the nineteenth century had little to do with calculation any more. This change set the stage for the new romanticism of the twentieth century, which declared creativity to be a mystical process and sneered at calculation. Even today, high-level politicians and celebrities can count on getting sympathy votes by boasting about their poor grades in maths. Sir Alec Issigonis, famous for having designed the Mini car, once commented, 'All creative people hate mathematics. It is the most uncreative subject you can study.'[7]

WOMEN COMPUTERS

Throughout history (and sometimes even today) occupations that had lost their prestige were opened up to women. After calculation became looked down upon as a mechanical, mindless task, it was delegated to women. Up to the second half of the twentieth century, social systems continued to perform large-scale computation. The Manhattan Project at Los Alamos, where the atomic bomb was built in the 1940s, relied on 'human computers', despite having all the technology for calculation available. These were mostly low-paid women, who repetitively performed the same calculations such as cubing a number and passing it on to another person who incorporated it into another computation.[8] The fact that women did the calculations reflected a shift in the social status of calculation at that time.

Women ultimately staffed the calculation departments in major statistical projects, from observatories to insurance offices to military research (figure 3.2). When calculating machines became more reliable and even indispensable, instead of the machines being viewed as more intelligent, the human calculators were viewed as more mechanical.[9] Calculating machines added up numbers, just as washing machines cleaned laundry and sewing machines made stiches – most of which were also operated by women. The thought that these machines embodied artificial intelligence occurred to no one.

The low prestige of calculation also explains why computer science

FIGURE 3.2: 'Women computers' processing data from the 16 Foot Wind
Tunnel in NASA's Ames Research Center in 1943.

became a field open to women, as opposed to the rest of engineering. In
the early 1980s, almost 40 per cent of US graduates in computer science
were female. Yet in that decade, when personal computers became available and their ownership widespread, they were marketed to men who
enjoyed playing games, and parents were likely to buy them for boys,
not girls. Since then, the presence of women in computer science departments has drastically declined, down to 18 per cent by 2020.[10]Another
factor that may have driven women out is that computer science evolved
from insignificance to a highly paid profession. Today, the heads of tech
companies are immensely rich and almost all male.

INTELLIGENCE BECOMES
COMPUTATION

The demotion of calculation from an intellectual to a mechanical
activity took a 180 degree turn when electronic computers became
available in research centres. In his last work – the 1956 Silliman

lectures, which he could neither finish nor deliver due to his premature death by cancer – John von Neumann, one of the greatest mathematicians of his time, pointed out similarities between the nervous system and the computer, that is, between neurons and vacuum tubes, but added cautionary notes emphasizing their differences. While von Neumann observed parallels at the level of the hardware, Alan Turing called the observation that both cells and diodes are electrical a 'very superficial similarity'.[11] In his view, the important similarities lie in the function, not the hardware. Turing asked whether machines can think; his famous 'imitation game', popularly known as the Turing test, evaluates whether a machine can imitate a human. Going even further, he considered whether computers could have free will, and contemplated teaching machines by using the same principles used to teach children. Note that Turing asked whether the computer is like a mind, while psychologists, led by Herbert Simon, later asked the opposite question: whether minds are like computers.

In the 1960s and 1970s, Simon, together with computer scientist and psychologist Alan Newell, argued that human intelligence is akin to a computer program. In their view, known as the *physical symbol hypothesis*, intelligence consists of the operation of symbols over time.[12] The symbols are manipulated by rules, generating new symbols as outputs over time. For instance, logic is a system containing symbols such as 'and' and 'or', and its rules are those of logical deduction. Similarly, chess is a system where the symbols are the pieces, and the rules are the legal chess moves. In a digital computer, the symbols are zeros and ones that define memory, and the rules are those of the central processing unit (CPU), which change memory. According to Simon, all these symbol systems resemble the human mind and brain.[13] This view inspired many a movie featuring robots disguised as humans that think just like us, only faster and with less emotion, and, with sufficient computing power, could eventually turn into superhumans.

Simon famously told a graduate class in early 1956 that, over Christmas, he and Newell had invented a thinking machine and 'thereby solved the mind-body problem, explaining how a system composed of matter can have the properties of mind'. As with the first large-scale social computing systems in the French Revolution, the prototype of their first computer program, the Logic Theorist, was made of human components: Simon's wife, children and graduate students.[14] That same year, the term 'artificial intelligence' went public at the now famous Dartmouth Conference. It was coined by the computer scientist John McCarthy, a staunch supporter of free speech who initiated *time-sharing systems*, later to be renamed *servers*, now called *cloud computing*.

Importantly, Simon realized that the computer is more than a calculator; it can manipulate any symbols, from text processing to videos. In hindsight, it is clear how revolutionary the symbol-processing idea was and hard to understand why this potential was not obvious earlier on. For instance, in 1952, Howard Aiken, a pioneer in computing who designed Harvard's Mark I calculator, reminisced, 'Originally one thought that if there were a half dozen large computers in this country, hidden away in research laboratories, this would take care of all requirements we had throughout the country.'[15] We may smile at that anecdote, yet the original idea behind the computer – and the internet later on – was to solve problems in science and engineering, and little more.

How was Simon ever able to convince others that cognition is computation, given that the related idea that intelligence is calculation had been discredited for over a hundred years? When Simon first proposed the idea, no one paid any attention. It was too early. Computers at that stage were large-frame machines that proved difficult to use; getting a program to work could take months. For instance, in an average week in the years 1965 and 1966, the PDP computer at Harvard's Center for Cognitive Studies saw 83 hours of use, 56 of which were spent on debugging and maintenance. Rather than a marvel of intelligence, the computer was a steady source of frustration, as witnessed by the desperate title of one of the Center's technical reports from 1966: 'Programmanship, or how to be one-up on a computer without actually ripping up his wires'.[16]

But in the 1970s and 1980s, electronic computers became fast and cheap and began to populate the desks of psychologists and other researchers. Psychologists finally accepted the view of the mind as a computer only after computers became indispensable tools in their daily routine. With these new desktop tools, the old Enlightenment link between intelligence and calculation – as illustrated by the story of Gauss – was resurrected in a new form. The nature of intelligence came to be seen as computation, that is, what computers do. Ever since, psychologists have spoken about cognition as computation. What else could it be?

The idea that cognition is computation was based not on new evidence but on new tools and inspired by analogy.[17] Thus, computers inspired new theories of human intelligence, just as centuries ago the new social organization of work made mechanical computers thinkable. With today's heavy-duty computing power, this idea morphed into the *AI-beats-humans* argument, the vision of an artificial superintelligence that soon will match human intelligence in all respects, while surpassing the human brain in speed and efficiency. What we see is a new version of the old Enlightenment view that intelligence is calculation.

At the same time, breakthroughs with deep neural networks have revived the belief that AI could encompass all of human intelligence and create a superintelligence capable of doing everything humans can and more. In the next chapters, we will have a closer look at the 'intelligence' of neural networks and see how fundamentally it differs from human intelligence, so that such a fear (or hope) remains science fiction. Let us begin with a practical, mundane dream of automatization.

4

Are Self-driving Cars Just Down the Road?

'I am extremely confident that Level-5 [self-driving cars] or essentially complete autonomy will happen, and I think it will happen very quickly ... I remain confident that we will have the basic functionality for Level-5 autonomy complete this year.'

Tesla CEO *Elon Musk, July 2020*[1]

'Autonomous vehicles are nowhere near as smart as they need to be. Safety features – including manual override – must be top priority.'

US *Senator Richard Blumenthal*[2]

On a dark desert night in March 2018, Elaine Herzberg was pushing her bicycle across a four-lane road in Tempe, Arizona. Herzberg was forty-nine years old and homeless, carrying bags on her bicycle. She had already crossed three lanes when she was struck and killed by an Uber autonomous car.

What should we think about the promise that self-driving cars will soon steer us safely through regular traffic? For one, Uber's cars were not even self-driving; they had human drivers at the wheel as back-ups.[3] The Volvo that struck Herzberg in Arizona was a test car with a back-up driver and had been in autonomous mode for nineteen minutes before the accident. The car was travelling at 43 miles per hour, and its radar detected Herzberg six seconds before impact. Yet the AI's 'perception module' – which builds a model of the environment using cameras and radar – got confused and classified her first as an unknown object, then as a vehicle, and finally as a bicycle. Each of these led to a different predicted path, and for more than four seconds the system did not make the inference that braking was needed. Only one second before impact did it do so – and was unable to come to a halt because the braking technology had been disabled by the Uber engineers.

The reason was previous bad experience, where autonomous cars braked for no good reason and were then rear-ended by human drivers. It was instead the driver's task to hit the brakes. But instead of watching the road, she was apparently looking down at her smartphone and streaming *The Voice*, a popular singing contest.[4] Video footage shows her looking up with a shocked expression immediately before the collision. Who is responsible when a purported self-driving car kills a person? The chief of the Tempe police blamed the homeless victim. Uber avoided a lawsuit by a secret out-of-court settlement with the victim's family within days after she died and later was cleared of criminal wrongdoing. The back-up driver faces manslaughter charges.

Herzberg had been part of a technology experiment without knowing it. Before her tragic end, California regulators had made it difficult for Uber to test their cars in real traffic. Doug Ducey, governor of Arizona, seized the opportunity and tweeted: 'Here in AZ we WELCOME this kind of technology & innovation! #ditchcalifornia #AZmeansBIZ.'[5] The fact that the cars and drivers were unsafe was known. Before the collision with Herzberg, an autonomous car was damaged nearly every other day on the road. Five days before the accident, a manager in Uber's autonomous vehicle unit had sent an email to the company's executives warning that the AI in their prototype robotaxis was dangerous and that back-up drivers were not properly trained.[6] Nevertheless, the state of Arizona and Uber carried on with the experiment. After the deadly accident, Arizona's governor quickly changed his mind and banned Uber's experiments. This time, the governor of Ohio grabbed the chance to lure a big tech company away from Silicon Valley and welcomed it to 'the wild, wild West' of unregulated self-driving car testing.[7] The upshot of this sad story is a race to the bottom of regulation and safety.

THE ADAPT-TO-AI PRINCIPLE

A self-driving car is one that can drive *everywhere* and *under all traffic conditions* without a human as a back-up. The hope is that electronic chauffeurs will dramatically reduce traffic accidents while increasing convenience. Car manufacturers such as Elon Musk (see first epigraph) suggest that this prospect is just around the corner.[8] Yet traffic conditions involve considerable degrees of uncertainty: the erratic behaviour of human drivers who do not always follow rules; cyclists, jaywalkers or animals appearing on the road; driving at night when the headlights of other cars are blinding; and weather conditions such as heavy rain and ice. Given these uncertainties, the stable-world principle questions the widespread commercial fairytales that self-driving cars are just down the road.

The confusion between what technology can actually deliver and what people are made to believe begins with a careless use of the terms 'self-driving', 'driverless' and 'autonomous' cars. This imprecision has fueled unrealistic hopes. Let's clarify the terms. The Society of Automotive Engineers' classification system distinguishes between five levels of automation (figure 4.1). Level 1, long in existence, includes adaptive cruise control and lane-keeping systems as driver-assistance tools. A Mercedes van was one of the first vehicles to demonstrate these skills on public roads, on a German motorway in 1986.[9] Level 2 combines various Level 1 technologies to automate more complex driving tasks, such as automatic parking, and is the state-of-the-art of commercially available cars. It requires drivers to keep their hands near the wheel and *constantly* pay attention in case something unexpected happens. A Level-3 system is a big technological jump and can perform most driving tasks, but still needs a human in the driver's seat who is receptive to alerts from the system and ready to take control if something goes wrong. At all three levels, humans have to be constantly alert in case something unexpected happens.

The next two levels operate without a vigilant human at the wheel. At Level 4, cars are able to drive fully autonomously without human help but only in restricted areas, such as motorways, airports and factories, or in specifically designed cities, but not everywhere

SAE J3016™ LEVELS OF DRIVING AUTOMATION

	SAE LEVEL 0	SAE LEVEL 1	SAE LEVEL 2	SAE LEVEL 3	SAE LEVEL 4	SAE LEVEL 5
What does the human in the driver's seat have to do?	You *are* driving whenever these driver support features are engaged – even if your feet are off the pedals and you are not steering			You *are not* driving when these automated driving features are engaged – even if you are seated in "the driver's seat"		
	You must constantly supervise these support features; you must steer, brake or accelerate as needed to maintain safety			When the feature requests, you must drive	These automated driving features will not require you to take over driving	
	These are driver support features			These are automated driving features		
What do these features do?	These features are limited to providing warnings and momentary assistance	These features provide steering OR brake/ acceleration support to the driver	These features provide steering AND brake/ acceleration support to the driver	These features can drive the vehicle under limited conditions and will not operate unless all required conditions are met		This feature can drive the vehicle under all conditions
Example Features	· automatic emergency braking · blind spot warning · lane departure warning	· lane centering OR · adaptive cruise control	· lane centering AND · adaptive cruise control at the same time	· traffic jam chauffeur	· local driverless taxi · pedals/ steering wheel may or may not be installed	· same as level 4, but feature can drive everywhere in all conditions

FIGURE 4.1: Five levels of automation in cars, as defined by the Society of Automotive Engineers (SAE). The self-driving car is at Level 5. It is defined as a car that requires no human back-up and is able to drive safely everywhere and in all traffic conditions. Current commercial cars operate at Level 2. The stable-world principle suggests that safe driving at Level 5 will be extremely difficult to achieve, while Level 4 is likely by restricting autonomous cars to specific areas and adapting our streets and cities to AI.

and in all conditions. Level 5 refers to self-driving cars, that is, cars able to drive safely under the full range of driving conditions without any human back-up, including all weather, road and traffic conditions.[10] These five levels are often not distinguished, creating the illusion that fully self-driving cars are already zipping along the roads.

Self-driving Cars Require Stable Environments

The uncertainty involved in driving a car can be understood by comparing it with flying a plane. Aviation introduced automation long ago: today, algorithms are what fly planes most of the time. In fact, about half of the costs of a new commercial plane are spent on software validation and debugging. However, the software of a large commercial aeroplane is less complex than that needed for a self-driving car.[11] An autopilot system may have to deal with one or two other aircraft in its vicinity and has time to act because of the large distances between them. The software for a self-driving car needs to deal with dozens of cars, cyclists and pedestrians, and their proximity means that critical decisions about life and death need to be made within fractions of a second.

The stable-world principle has an important implication, the *adapt-to-AI principle*:

To improve the performance of AI, one needs to make the physical environment more stable and people's behaviour more predictable.

If we hand over decisions to algorithms, we have to adapt our environments and our behaviour. This may involve making humans transparent to algorithms, regulating human behaviour or even eliminating humans from the playing field. Applied to autonomous cars, the two principles give us a clue about what is likely to happen:

There will be no self-driving cars (Level 5 automation). Rather, a fundamental change will happen: our cities and roads will be redesigned to create the stable and predictable environment that algorithms need (Level 4 automation), such as wired highways from which human drivers are banned, and cities where human driving is illegal.

In other words, if we want autonomous cars, we have to adapt to their potential. The technology is not just a support system; it requires *us* to adjust our behaviour. Such behavioural shifts have happened before.

When cars were invented by Carl Benz in 1886 and mass-produced by the Ford Motor Company in the early twentieth century, the transition from the horse-drawn age to the motorized age proved to be dangerous. Cars had to share traffic space with horse-drawn vehicles, bicyclists, pedestrians and children playing on the road, without any regulations. For cars to function safely, paved roads and strict traffic rules were needed. Human behaviour in turn became restricted by drivers' licences, licence plates, traffic lights and signs, and rules such as driving on a particular side of the road. That was not the first time. Already in 1831, the Paris police had issued an ordinance that traffic – carriages, horses, mules and pedestrians – should keep to the right to reduce the urban chaos.[12] This rule was followed as grumblingly as an earlier ordinance that people should stop emptying their chamber pots out the window onto the street. Clean streets allow for free-flowing traffic. The modern highway, with its smooth surface made of asphalt or concrete, is the ideal environment for cars. Pedestrians, bicyclists and animals are banned. New technologies don't simply assist us; their effect is deeper. To benefit from their maximum efficiency, we have to be prepared to adapt – to change our behaviour and our environments.

NEURAL NETWORKS IN THE DRIVER'S SEAT

How might engineers build an electronic chauffeur to whom one would entrust one's life? As explained in the previous chapter, there are two visions. Psychological AI would teach computers to drive the way humans drive, that is, replicate the human process of perception, judgement and decision making. This is the spirit of good old-fashioned AI (often abbreviated as GOFAI): to study how humans solve a task, then translate human behaviour into 'production rules' and programme these rules into a computer. An example of such a rule is 'if a child steps onto the street in front of the car, brake immediately'. Yet this idea is doomed in regular traffic because it would bog the AI down with too many rules – including those that tell it how to distinguish a running child from a floating plastic bag. Memorizing thousands of rules is also not the way humans learn to drive. In fact, what we do when seamlessly driving is impossible to describe precisely enough to set down as rules for an algorithm. Research therefore turned to building machine learning systems. This second vision of AI does not attempt to teach machines to drive like humans but uses algorithms to best solve a specific problem, such as recognizing traffic signs and moving objects. The ways machines solve these problems have little or nothing to do with human problem solving and are best known from search engines and recommendation systems.

The big breakthrough in automation – and the big hope for truly self-driving cars – came with a type of algorithm called *deep artificial neural networks*. These are fundamentally different from the algorithms for finding true love or creditworthiness. Computer systems that drive cars are made of three modules. The first, a perception module, consists of cameras, radar and lidar, which is a version of radar that uses invisible pulses of light. Cameras spot traffic signs, traffic lights, lane markings and other features. Radar measures the velocity of objects, and lidar the shapes of the surroundings. This information is used to build a model of the car's environment. Object recognition constitutes a major part of the progress made towards autonomous cars. Second, a prediction module forecasts what the objects 'recognized' are going to do next, such as in what direction nearby cars and pedestrians will move, and how fast. Third, a driving policy module relies on these predictions to decide whether the car should speed up, slow down or veer to the left or right. In the case of Herzberg, the policy module did not decide to slow down because the perception and prediction modules were confused.

Artificial neural networks are sometimes presented as magical machines that only a computer whiz can comprehend. But there is a non-technical way to get a general idea of how they function. Similar to algorithms used for partner matching and credit scoring, they consist of three parts: an input, its transformation and an output. Consider a network that is being trained to recognize a school bus. Pictures of objects form the input, only some of which are school buses. The pictures are digital, that is, an image is divided into thousands or millions of pixels, which is exactly what a digital camera does. Every pixel is analysed in terms of three colour values: red, green and blue. From the perspective of an artificial network, an image is nothing more than a huge table of numbers, each specifying one of the three colours for a pixel. This table is called the 'input layer'. The 'output layer' consists, in the simplest case, of two numbers: '1' for school bus and '0' for all other objects. The big difference to classical AI lies in the way the input is transformed into the output.

Unlike in a love algorithm, the input is not transformed into an output by a (secret) formula. Rather, the input layer is transformed through a series of hidden layers, which make the network deeper – hence the name *deep neural network*. Such a network may have just a few or hundreds of hidden layers. A layer deeper down in the network can contribute to refining the previous layers. This fine-tuning is also called *deep learning*.

Deep neural networks can 'learn' in three kinds of ways: supervised, unsupervised and through reinforcement. Supervised learning is the best known, so called because there is a 'teacher' who provides yes/no feedback but with no rules. It is used for recognizing objects such as a school bus and traffic signs. To learn properly, the network is given thousands or even millions of photos as well as their correct classifications, and then learns a function that matches the input with the output as correctly as possible. In recommendation systems, such as when Amazon suggests books to buy, you are the 'teacher' who clicks or likes certain contents while browsing. Unsupervised learning takes place without feedback. For instance, the network searches for similarities in pictures and generates clusters of similar pictures. This form of learning corresponds to gazing at the stars at night in a quest for patterns without knowing a thing about astronomy. And the third form, reinforcement learning, occurs in tasks such as Go, where the network does not get feedback after each move, but only at the end of the game. In this case, all the network knows are the rules of the game and the goal and has to find its own way to get there. AlphaZero's amazing performance is due to reinforcement learning, yet it may also result in finding unexpected shortcuts. One algorithm that was developed to play Tetris simply learned to pause the game in order to avoid losing.[13]

Although it is relatively easy to understand the general logic of deep neural networks, it's much more difficult to understand what a network exactly 'sees'. Herein lies a major difference between it and psychological AI, where the rule is transparent – at least to the designers if the algorithm is secret. What transpires in the hidden layers of a deep neural network, however, is extremely hard to figure out, even for the engineers who built the network. You may have heard the mortifying story that Google's image classification system identified a dark-skinned couple as 'gorillas'. The engineers immediately reacted, but not in the way you might think. Instead of attacking the heart of the problem, the silent solution was to remove the categories 'gorilla', 'chimpanzee' and 'ape.' Since then, pictures of apes no longer are classified as such.[14] Deep neural networks have grown too complex to be easily understood and corrected.

Traditional computer vision, in contrast, relies on individual features such as edges and colours. For objects such as a school bus, it remains a challenge to write down a rule that defines it exactly. Rules work better for recognizing handwritten numbers, where features may include lower round strokes, as in '5' and '6', and upper round strokes, as in '2' and '3'. In the case of deep neural networks, it is hard to tell whether the individual units in the various layers extract individual features or work together in collective actions.[15] What we do know is that the view that artificial neural networks function akin to traditional computer vision or human vision, only faster, has been proved wrong. We will see this below in the form of the astonishing errors that neural networks make that are alien to human intuition.

Deep neural networks are nothing new. Artificial networks have been known since the 1950s and 1960s. In fact, some statisticians have complained that engineers with little knowledge of statistics have reinvented statistical tools already in existence and clothed these in a misleadingly impressive new jargon, such as *artificial intelligence*.[16] Their complaints are not fully justified; several technical innovations did spark the revival of neural networks. These include the advance in the number-crunching power of digital computers, the development of efficient training methods, the large sets of data now available and the extraordinary power of graphics-processing units that were originally developed for video gaming. Still, the fact that most of supervised and unsupervised learning has been long known helps make it clear that there is ultimately no different quality of 'intelligence' in deep neural networks than in ordinary statistics.[17]

Despite the suggestive term *neural network*, networks do not 'perceive' and 'think' like humans. Their similarity to the neural circuits in the brain is actually quite shallow. Algorithms can solve tasks that are beyond human capacity, but they also have bizarre blind spots and can make mind-boggling errors. The following example brings home what these blind spots can mean for self-driving cars.

Do Neural Networks Know What a School Bus Is?

Autonomous cars need software that can reliably identify what's on the road: traffic signs, but also people and vehicles. On the left-hand side of figure 4.2 is the picture of a typical yellow school bus in the US that a deep neural network has learned to identify correctly. The middle picture shows a multicoloured pattern of pixels. In reality, the pattern is so tiny that it has been magnified here by a factor of ten for the reader to see it. The picture to the right of it was generated by superimposing this pattern upon the first picture. To the human driver, the school bus on the right-hand side is still a school bus, and special attention is required when it is sighted, because kids might be around. For the deep neural network, in contrast, the school bus has disappeared. It now classifies the object as an ostrich.[18]

What constitutes a minute continuous change for humans, almost invisible, such as the difference between the two school buses, is *qualitatively* different for the machine.[19] This kind of error is alien to human intuition. Such qualitative 'leaps' are not limited to image recognition: they also have been discovered in voice, speech, and text recognition.[20]

The reverse phenomenon also exists, where a deep neural network

FIGURE 4.2: Deceiving neural networks. Left: A picture of a school bus that is correctly recognized by a deep neural network. Middle: A pattern of pixels (magnified here by a factor of ten to make it visible). Right: The pattern in the middle is added to the picture of the school bus on the left, resulting in the picture to the right. The neural network no longer recognizes the school bus but classifies it as an ostrich. The colour version can be accessed here: https://arxiv.org/pdf/1312.6199.pdf.

cannot see a difference between two pictures that are strikingly different to human eyes. Consider the picture of the school bus in figure 4.3 on the left. It is the same bus as in figure 4.2 (left) that a trained deep neural network correctly recognized. To the right of the bus is an image of horizontal orange and black stripes, whose colours roughly resemble those of the school bus. After the network learned to identify school buses correctly, it was tested on the picture with the stripes. The network classified the picture as showing a school bus. It was 99 per cent certain of being correct.[21]

These striking errors are not limited to the specific kind of deep neural network tested. Nor are they limited to school buses but crop up for virtually every object tested. One might think that new technology can eliminate these kinds of errors, but that's not the case, and for two reasons. First, new technology may be able to fight individual errors, but not their causes. Second, new technology is constantly being developed to find further ways of fooling deep neural networks. An arms race between protective measures and adversarial algorithms has evolved, including successful one-pixel attacks, that is, low-cost deception by modifying a single pixel in an image.[22]

Why do these errors occur? A first thought is that the neural networks had too small a sample of pictures of school buses to learn from, or only untypical samples in order to deliberately trick them.

FIGURE 4.3: A deep neural network mistakes stripes for a school bus. The picture on the left (same as in figure 4.2, above) is correctly classified as a school bus. But the network is also 99 per cent certain that the picture on the right is another school bus. The stripes and the school bus are similarly coloured.

But neither is the case: the networks were trained on standard image data sets comprising more than one million images; adding more training photos would not have helped. The answer lies in the fundamental difference between human and machine intelligence. Humans have a mental concept of a bus. Children can recognize a bus after seeing just one or a few. A bus has four wheels, headlights, a windshield, is larger than a car, and its function is to carry many people. A deep neural network has no such concept of a bus, nor does it know its function. It does not even know where the bus is in the image.[23] Its intelligence consists of finding statistical associations between pixels and assigning probabilities to pixels. The stronger the association, the more certain the network is. If typical elements of objects are repeated in a picture, the network will therefore likely grow more confident that the object exists in the picture. The striking yellow colour of a school bus framed by black parts appear to be the typical elements it has detected. These colours are amplified by the horizontal stripes.

Similarly, a deep neural network has no concept of a zebra, but searches for typical patterns in images, such as stripes. As a consequence, a picture of a zebra with two additional legs (and thus more stripes) would startle a human but may make a deep neural network more confident that the zebra is indeed a zebra.[24] Why not simply teach a network that zebras cannot have more than four legs? Fixing this specific error will not eliminate the underlying problem: *The network doesn't know that a picture represents something in the real world; it has no concept of things.* Its intelligence is confined to detecting patterns in colours, texture and other features. Human intelligence, in contrast, is about representing the world.

A Colour Patch on a T-shirt

To make a self-driving car safe, a deep neural network needs to recognize objects such as vehicles, pedestrians and traffic signs correctly (the *perception module*), but also to predict where cars or pedestrians are moving next (the *prediction module*). Networks that make these predictions are called *optical flow networks*. Typically, cameras behind the windscreen take many pictures per second and infer from these the location of the vehicles in the next time frame. Predicting where other vehicles or bicycles are heading needs to be impervious to little disturbances; otherwise safety cannot be guaranteed.

However, as in object recognition, deep neural networks can make inferential errors that are totally non-intuitive for humans. A small colour patch, like the example in figure 4.4, can baffle the network when it estimates the flow of traffic.[25] Even a patch that covers less than 1 per cent of the entire picture can completely erase the motion 'seen' in half or all of the picture by the network. The larger the patch, the more disturbing its effects. Such patches can be placed on pedestrians' T-shirts, the bumper of a car or a traffic sign on the street. It takes only a few hours to generate these patterns. If the type of network is known, then it is easier to generate the patterns, although the one shown in figure 4.4 works for different groups of networks, that is, even if the kind of network a self-driving car uses is unknown.

No human would be confused by such a pattern when driving. The

FIGURE 4.4: An example of the colour patches that confuse neural networks' predictions of the flow of traffic when placed on pedestrians' T-shirts or on the rear of a car. These patches are 'universal' in the sense that they confuse not a particular network, but major classes of networks. It is sufficient if a patch covers less than 1 per cent of the entire picture. The colour version of this and other adversarial patches can be accessed here: https://arxiv.org/pdf/1910.10053.pdf.

errors humans make are of a completely different nature. An estimated 90 per cent of crashes are due to human factors such as speeding well above the speed limit, using hand-held electronic devices, ignoring fatigue and driving while drunk.[26] No network would fail because it is tired or distracted by an incoming phone call – although running out of power could have a similar effect. The conspicuous differences in errors here and for object recognition show how machine intelligence differs fundamentally from human intelligence. It is often said that a computer knows only what it has been told. That may be true for psychological AI, but not for networks. A deep neural network can learn to 'know' things we have a hard time understanding.

What does all of that mean? Engineers who build vision systems can be fooled by assuming that when the AI is trained on thousands of pictures of, say, traffic signs and then performs well on a test set, it will also recognize these in new situations in the same way a human would. The blind spots can lead to accidents that are difficult to foresee and comprehend. Moreover, malicious characters can trick deep neural networks to make unexpected mistakes. For instance, a car's computer vision can be trained to mistake a stop sign for a 65 miles per hour speed limit sign and send car and passengers hurtling through an intersection at top speed.[27] Similarly, pedestrians who make unexpected fidgety body movements such as dancing on the street can confuse deep neural networks.[28]

INTUITION AND MORALS

Three-year-old children already understand that people, unlike objects, have intentions and desires and routinely infer intentions from other people's gaze, bodily movement or tone of voice. The ability to attribute intentions to others is also known as *theory of mind*. It is used to foster safe driving. Consider a child standing on the kerb of an urban road. Human drivers can infer in a blink whether the child intends to run out onto the street or not: if the child's gaze is on a ball on the other side of the street, that could well happen; if the child's gaze is instead directed at a woman close by, it is unlikely. Humans have learned to infer intentions using such heuristic rules.

Artificial neural networks have none of these intuitions. Even if the AI could reliably detect a child and an adult woman with its perception module, it would additionally need an intuitive psychology module that can infer what their intentions are, and what they will likely do next. How to program intuitive psychology into a machine remains a riddle. That would require a true breakthrough in software engineering.

If self-driving cars did exist, a huge set of moral dilemmas would arise. Consider three elderly people crossing a road on a red light (figure 4.5). A self-driving car recognizes them too late to brake in time and is about to kill all of them. The car's only other option is to steer into a wall and kill its three occupants instead. How should the engineer program the driving policy module of the AI? Whom should the car kill?

FIGURE 4.5: What moral intuitions should an autonomous car be given? In this hypothetical scenario, a self-driving car cannot avoid an accident and must choose who should live and who should die. The choice is between killing three elderly pedestrians who are crossing the street on a red light or saving the pedestrians' lives by crashing into a wall and killing the car's three occupants (see Awad et al., 2018).

In 2017, the German Ethics Commission on Automated and Connected Driving was the first worldwide to propose ethical rules for this problem.[29] These include that human lives should have priority over animals' and that discrimination by age, gender or any other personal feature should be prohibited. By implication, the car should be indifferent to saving pedestrians or saving passengers. A study with millions of people in over 200 countries found that most disagreed with these ethical rules, apart from sacrificing dogs and cats instead of humans. For the scenario with the three elderly pedestrians, the vast majority voted that the AI should be programed to kill the pedestrians rather than the car occupants. After all, they are old and are disobeying the law by jaywalking. In general, the majority of people worldwide showed rampant discrimination and did not consider their fellow humans equally.[30] People would generally save the life of a human above a dog's but not if the human was a criminal. Similarly, people of lower social status and the homeless were considered less worthy of being spared.

Moral dilemmas, even if hypothetical as in this study, can provide a window into the values of cultures. People in Western countries had the strongest preference for inaction, that is, avoiding the responsibility of actively killing people such as by turning left and crashing into the wall. Eastern countries such as Japan, China and Islamic countries showed the strongest preference for saving the elderly or pedestrians and for sacrificing the unlawful. In contrast, Central and South American countries most strongly preferred saving females, the young and individuals of high social status.

The moral dilemma of the self-driving car is a version of the 'trolley problem' in moral philosophy. This class of thought problems is named after a fictional runaway trolley that will kill five people lying on the tracks unless one takes action, such as by pushing a fat man over the bridge and onto the track so that he stops the trolley, killing him in order to save five lives. These problems can reveal whether someone prefers inaction and letting many lives be taken or actively takes responsibility for the death of a single person to save other lives. But what is most telling is that these moral experiments assume a world of certainty; they shy away from the uncertainty of real life. Their assumption is that the fat man will not defend himself and will fall precisely at the right spot and at the right second on the track. Similarly, even though the AI in the hypothetical scenario has no time to avoid the accident, the assumption remains that the AI has perfect recognition skills, will properly categorize the individuals' ages and behaviour and will be able to determine precisely how many of the pedestrians or car occupants will die. When this hypothetical certainty is replaced by realistic uncertainty, people's firm moral judgements become more permissive and less stringent.[31]

Moral psychology has a long tradition of posing moral dilemmas that ignore uncertainty. As a thought experiment, that is not a problem. But in real traffic, certainty remains an illusion; both human and artificial intelligence are forced to make decisions without knowing exactly what the consequences will be. This key difference may spare engineers from having to worry about how to program a machine to deal with this kind of moral dilemma, and in fact most engineers have discarded the illusory certainty of the trolley problem as a guide to ethics.[32] The hypothetical dilemma of choosing whom to kill may never become reality because it assumes fully self-driving cars with perfect prediction of what will happen after a collision.

THE FUTURE OF DRIVING

As mentioned before, contrary to Elon Musk's suggestive claims in this chapter's first epigraph and to other commercial promises, the stable-word principle suggests that self-driving cars are unlikely to be our future. Safe Level-5 cars would require true breakthroughs in software development. Automatic driving will come, but not in the way we have been made to believe. Instead, it will likely come in two forms, one of which allows humans to drive (Level 3), the other not (Level 4). These two forms are likely to coexist, and, in both instances, humans need to adapt to the potentials of the AI.

When Your Car Reports You to the Police

If self-driving cars are not going to happen, one alternative appears to be training humans to use AI as a support system, but to stay alert and retain control if it fails – which is called *augmented intelligence*. It amounts to partial automation, that is, to sophisticated versions of Level 2 or 3. Yet augmented intelligence entails more than just adding useful features to your car and may well lead us into a different future, where AI is used to both support us and keep us under surveillance. That possible future is driven more by insurance companies and the police than by car manufacturers. Its seeds are in telematics.

Young drivers are reckless, overconfident and an insurance risk, according to the stereotype. Some indeed are, but many are not. Nevertheless, insurers often treat them as one group and charge a high premium. Telematics insurance can change this by offering better rates for safe drivers. The idea is to calculate the premium from a person's actual driving behaviour instead of from that of the average driver. To do so, a black box that connects to the insurer is installed in the car (using a smartphone is possible and cheaper, but less reliable). The black box records the driver's behaviour and calculates a safety score. Figure 4.6 shows the scoring system of one of the first telematics insurers. It observes four features and assigns them different weights.[33]

Rapid acceleration or harsh braking is assigned the greatest weight, followed by driving over the speed limit. For each of the four features, each driver starts with a monthly budget of 100 points. An 'event' results in points being subtracted, such as 20 points for the first rapid acceleration and for driving over the speed limit. At the end of the

Feature (Event)	Weight
Rapid acceleration or harsh braking	40
Driving over the speed limit (more than 20 per cent for more than 30 seconds)	30
Driving at night between 11 p.m. and 5 a.m.	20
Driving in cities	10

FIGURE 4.6: Pay as you drive. A black box in the car reports four features of the driver's behaviour to the telematics insurer. Safe driving is calculated by an algorithm whose features and weights are transparent. The insurer offers better rates if the customer drives safely.

month, the remaining points are weighted as shown and summed up to a total safety score. Although telematics is often called black box insurance, the algorithm is not at all a 'black box' like most love algorithms. It is explained in detail on the insurer's website, and everyone can understand and verify the resulting score.

Personalized tariffs are advertised as promoting fairness. They do so by taking individual driving style into account. But they also create new sources of discrimination when driving at night and in cities is punished. Hospital staff, for instance, may have little choice to avoid working at night and in cities. Thus, some of the features are under the control of the driver, but others not. Interestingly, one feature that is under the driver's control is absent in virtually all personalized tariffs: texting while driving.

And the black box that allows fairness also enables surveillance. Consider a possible future. Why should the black box send a record of speeding only to the insurer? A copy to the police would be extremely handy and save them much effort. It would make all speed traps obsolete. If you speed, the car prints out the ticket or, more conveniently, deducts the fine automatically from your online account. Your relationship with your beloved car may change. There is a slippery slope between fairness and total surveillance.

Would you be in favour of a new generation of cars that send traffic violations directly to the police? In a survey I conducted, one-third of the adults said 'yes', more among those over sixty, and less among those younger than thirty.[34] The technology for this future already exists, as most new cars come with a black box installed. The data it collects do not belong to the owner of the car; they can be used in court against the driver. In Georgia, the police obtained black box data without a warrant after a deadly accident, and the driver was found guilty of reckless driving and speeding.[35]

While the motives for surveillance vary, digital technology supports all of them. One need not even buy telematics insurance. Modern cars have built-in internet connections, and – without it being made transparent in the owner's manual – most send their car manufacturer all data they can collect every couple of minutes, including where the driver currently is, whether harsh braking occurred, how often the position of the driver seat was changed, which petrol or battery-charging stations were visited and how many CDs and DVDs were inserted.[36] Moreover, as soon as you plug in your smartphone, the car may copy your personal information, including contacts' addresses, emails, text messages and even photos. Car manufacturers are remarkably silent about this activity and, when asked with whom they share this data, typically do not reply.[37] That information helps to find out many other things of interest, such as how often drivers visited McDonald's, how healthily they live and whom they occasionally visit at night. Connected cars can support justice and improve safety, but also spy on you. Telematics insurance embodies the double face of digital technology: surveillance in exchange for convenience.

Cities Adapt to Autonomous Cars, and Driving May Become Illegal

In the possible future where cars keep their drivers under surveillance and report traffic violations to the police, drivers will adapt their behaviour. Future Level 2 and Level 3 drivers will be predictable and law-abiding. Speeding, jumping red lights, texting while driving, drunk driving, not wearing seatbelts and other violations of traffic regulations will become the wild west of the past. In this future, humans are still in the driver's seat.

As mentioned before, the adapt-to-AI principle lets us expect a second possible future that may unfold in parallel. It requires rebuilding the current traffic environment to a more predictable one that allows for Level-4 driving – cars without humans at the wheel, but not in all traffic conditions. To begin with, special lanes on highways and areas within a city may be restricted for autonomous cars only. In the long term, adapting to the potential of self-driving cars may require building entirely new cities that provide cars with a stable environment. That may entail outfitting roads with sensors that detect cars and systems that communicate with cars. Human drivers may be banned from the roads, and pedestrians may be given their own secluded pathways. In this future, human driving may become illegal in restricted areas, or entire cities, and humans may eventually lose the ability to drive. Living in this future, you would look back in disbelief to the past when people were allowed to drive themselves and kill others.

One vision is to integrate autonomous cars with public transport. A fleet of robotaxis would circle through a city at low speed for safety reasons. These vehicles would transport people towards bus and streetcar stations, where they can continue travelling faster and for longer distances. That would make privately owned cars obsolete, and cities packed with parked cars history. The space could be used for wide lanes for pedestrians and bicyclists, physically separated by walls or hedges to prevent them from entering car lanes. To encourage this development, use of robotaxis and public transport could be made cheap, private car ownership extremely expensive, and private cars banned from entering cities.

Some countries have already taken steps towards this future and are building new cities around Level 4 technology. For instance, Toyota announced its plan to build a smart city near Tokyo and Mount Fuji that is adapted to autonomous cars and where pedestrians will be consigned to walkways out of reach of the cars.[38] The autonomous cars will drive citizens into the centre of town, Toyota says – although that may also be an obsolete idea, given that there won't be much to do downtown any more. Streaming replaces cinemas, online shopping replaces shopping expeditions, and autonomous cars deliver medication, pizza and everything else you might desire to your doorstep. Similarly, the Chinese government announced its intention to build a city the size of Chicago south of Beijing that can support autonomous traffic. Such radical changes to the public sphere are presently unthinkable in the US and Western European countries, but these may also soon adapt civil rights to reap the benefits of AI by providing it with an environment in which it can flourish.

These two possible futures of autonomous driving illustrate a more general point. The question is how to make AI work in situations of uncertainty. One solution is 24/7 surveillance and behaviour modification through immediate reward and punishment. This method makes humans more predictable. AI can more easily deal with people who follow rules and behave consistently, whether on the road or elsewhere. The second solution is to make the environment more stable and predictable. That means adapting it to the potential of AI, which may require removing pedestrians, cyclists and human drivers entirely from the streets.

Bike-first Cities and Smart Public Transport

A radical alternative to these two visions of autonomous driving is to do away with cars, autonomous and otherwise, as far as possible. One prospect is bike-first cities. Amsterdam, Copenhagen and other cities have already shaken up their infrastructure and redesigned their streets around bikes, not cars. The city of Utrecht in the Netherlands transformed itself from a traditional car-friendly city to one that gives bikes the upper hand over motorized traffic. [39] Ninety-eight per cent of households own bikes. Car lanes have been converted into broad and safe bike roads, and traffic lights are adapted to the speed of cyclists so that they can glide through the city without constant stops. As a result, the city has become much less noisy, the air has become cleaner, and fewer pedestrians and cyclists are killed in traffic. The city invests some $50 million every year in bike infrastructure and saves an estimated $300 million every year thanks to reduced pollution and healthcare costs. 'You really have the idea that people are the boss of the city, not machines,' commented the city's vice-mayor.

Bike-first cities combine well with the second alternative to smart cars, smart public transport. Long-distance bullet trains such as the Shinkansen between Tokyo and Osaka, the Fuxing Hao from Shanghai to Hangzhou, France's TGV, Italy's AGV and the German Inter-City Express operate at 150 to 250 miles per hour. The Shinkansen, for instance, is silent, safe, very comfortable and punctual to the second. The world's fastest short-distance train hits over 260 miles per hour and takes only seven minutes from Shanghai's Pudong International Airport to a metro station in Shanghai. From there, a tight inner-city transport network above and below ground gets you near where you want to be, and the rest can be done by walking, to get some exercise, or taxi. Electric trains are faster and safer than cars and are less harmful to the environment.

The original focus on private, personal cars rather than public transport is probably not an accident. The self-driving car industry is centred in California and other states where well-connected networks of public transport barely exist today after being decimated by car manufacturers in the 1930s and 1940s, unlike in Hong Kong, Seoul, Singapore, London, Paris, Berlin, Madrid or New York. Not only does public transport barely exist, but it is often looked down upon as a system for the poor and underprivileged groups. Fifty-six per cent of US Americans reported that they never use public transport, compared with 2 per cent of Russians, 2 per cent of Chinese, 4 per cent of South Koreans, 12 per cent of the British and 15 per cent of Germans.[40] This cultural bias contributes to the enthusiasm about cars, and may create a blind spot when it comes to alternative solutions.

THE RUSSIAN TANK FALLACY

Much of AI is about prediction, as in the perception and prediction modules of autonomous cars. In Chapter 2, I introduced the Texas sharpshooter fallacy, where an algorithm is fitted to match the data, and its performance is then reported as prediction, without any actual prediction having been made. This makes the algorithm look much better than it is. While this fallacy exists in the social sciences, it is virtually absent in machine learning. When training neural networks to recognize images, it is easy to avoid the sharpshooter fallacy by using cross-validation: by dividing the set of pictures randomly into two subsets, and then training the network on one subset and testing it on the other.

Deep learning, however, can run into a second problem, which stems from the fact that we do not know what a neural network has learned. As seen above, a network has no concept of a school bus or a right-of-way sign. Instead, it learns cues that discriminate between classes of objects in a set of pictures, even when these may be irrelevant and do not generalize to other pictures or the real world. The picture of the horizontal yellow and black stripes illustrates how a network can miss the mark. The problem is this: because the network has no understanding of concepts as humans do, it may focus on irrelevant cues that are present in *both* the training and test set.

I will refer to this second problem as the *Russian tank fallacy*. The name stems from an urban legend that goes like this.[41] The US army trained a neural network to tell Russian tanks from US tanks. As usual, a large data set with photos of tanks was used; the network was trained on one half and tested on the other. Finally, it could master the test with 100 per cent accuracy. But when it was used in the real world, it flunked. Only later was it realized that the US tanks had been photographed on a sunny day and the Russian ones on a cloudy day. The smart network had found the perfect cue: clouds.

Similar stories have been told about neural networks that learned to tell wolves from dogs. In the data set of pictures, the dogs happened to be standing on grass and the wolves on snow. The network found the best differentiating cue: white background. Although these stories may contain more legend than truth, the general point is that although networks are excellent at detecting cues on how pictures labelled as 'Russian tank' or 'wolf' differ, these cues may have little to do with humans' concept of a tank or a dog.

In other words, a researcher in machine learning who avoids the sharpshooter fallacy can still fall into a new trap, ignoring the fact that the network may learn perfect but irrelevant cues. Many studies in machine learning do not make the next move and test the performance of the AI in the real world. In healthcare, for instance, most algorithms are tested on computers, not in hospitals. The assumption that what works in the lab will work in the real world has been called 'the big lie in machine learning'.[42] For instance, one proposed solution has been 'convolutional neural networks' (CNN) that have a built-in bias, such as edges and other structures indispensable to the object in question. But as the following real case illustrates, such networks do not always solve the problem.[43]

At New York's Mount Sinai hospital, one of the oldest teaching hospitals in the US, a deep neural net (CNN) learned to make accurate predictions from chest X-rays as to whether patients were at high risk of pneumonia. At other hospitals, however, it flopped. Eventually, the cause was found by manually inspecting the X-ray images. The AI had learned to detect whether these were taken by the hospital's portable chest X-ray machine or in the radiology department. Portable X-rays were taken of patients too sick to leave their rooms, who had a greater risk of lung infection. In other hospitals, that cue was of little help. Detecting irrelevant cues is one of the reasons why a neural net trained in one hospital typically becomes less accurate if used in another hospital.[44]

The Russian tank fallacy relates to a much deeper issue: the question of external validity. Many machine learning studies proceed by saying, look, here are some real-world data, let's split them into two parts and see how accurately AI predicts the part it has not yet seen. In some quarters, this has become the only method used. While it takes care of the sharpshooter fallacy, it is not the same as predicting the future. In fact, by splitting the data randomly in two, one creates a fairly stable world: the data used to teach the algorithm and the data used for the test are from the same group. Nothing unforeseen can happen, and no future events are predicted. For instance, some lauded studies about computer-based predictions of personality based on Facebook 'likes' and other digital footprints do not actually make any true predictions about the future.[45] In general, machine learning systems that predict well in one setting but not in others have been observed in many instances, such as with patients in different hospitals, images taken by different cameras and biological assays from different cell types.[46] To overcome this limitation, one more step is needed: to test how well an algorithm performs in new situations, such as with new patients in different hospitals. That is true prediction.

The general lesson is: software that displays spectacular results in a computer lab can lose its potency when tested in the real world. If you hear that an algorithm successfully identified children crossing the street or patients at risk of lung disease, check whether the algorithm was tested in the real world. Dividing pictures into two sets, training a network on one set and testing it on the other is important, but not sufficient. What counts is testing it 'in the wild'.

5

Common Sense and AI

> 'The intuitive mind is a sacred gift and the rational mind is a
> faithful servant. We have created a society that honours the
> servant and has forgotten the gift.'
>
> Albert Einstein[1]

> 'Common sense in an uncommon degree is what the world
> calls wisdom.'
>
> Samuel Taylor Coleridge[2]

A human brain is a miracle with its nearly 100 billion neurons and
100 trillion connections, fine-tuned over hundreds of millions of years
of evolution. These are numbers that our conscious mind can scarcely
comprehend. Human brains are also highly energy-efficient compared
with contemporary computer technology. Consider energy, which is
measured in units called watts in honour of James Watt, the British
engineer and inventor of the steam engine. The supercomputer Watson used 85,000 watts when playing *Jeopardy!*, compared with the 20
watts used by each of its two human competitors' brains – as much as
a dim light bulb.[3] The brain's main energy source is glucose. Watson
also needed tons of air-conditioning equipment, while its competitors
could have done with a hand-held fan on the hottest days of the year.
One of the world's most powerful computers, the Blue Waters supercomputer at the University of Illinois, consumes about 15 million
watts and occupies a floor space of 20,000 square feet. It requires a
large cooling system hidden underneath the floor and is not mobile.

The brain needs little space: it is the size of two fists, and easy to carry around. And unlike the supercomputer, it is self-assembled and able to program itself. If all human brains were replaced by supercomputers, the amount of heat generated might well put a swift end to our climate.

THE COGS OF COMMON SENSE

As mentioned before, human intelligence evolved to deal with uncertainty. Among the mental skills humans have evolved to succeed in an uncertain world, four stand out:

- *Causal thinking.* The ability to think in terms of causes develops early. Children persistently ask 'why?' They want to know why the sky is blue, why some people are rich, and why they have to eat their vegetables. Some children pose more why questions than their parents can answer. By doing so, children build causal models of the world. Being curious about causes rather than mere associations is characteristic of human intelligence and is the hallmark of science. Causal thinking is both a strength and a source of superstition, as when believing that crossing your fingers will bring you luck.
- *Intuitive psychology.* Children develop an intuitive psychology in the first years of their lives: they 'know' that other humans have feelings and intentions, and they can take the perspective of another human.[4] Special brain circuits appear to be dedicated to monitoring what other minds know, think, and believe. Lack of intuitive psychology is a sign of autism.
- *Intuitive physics.* Similarly, children develop an intuitive physics and understand the basics of time and space. For instance, they know that a solid object cannot move through another object, that objects persist over time, and that time cannot be reversed.
- *Intuitive sociality.* When children are older than three years of age, they are motivated to follow group norms (cooperation and competition) and develop and defend moral standards.

I refer to the sum of these skills as *common sense*:

Common sense is shared knowledge about people and the physical world enabled by the biological brain, and requires only limited experience.

Common sense arises from a mixture of genetic predispositions and individual and social learning (such as knowing that the world is three-dimensional, or that one should not hurt others' feelings). It can be exercised intuitively or by deliberate judgment. For instance, most people can reliably tell a genuine smile from a merely polite one but cannot explain how they do it. That is called intuition, or a gut feeling.[5] However, when one learns that in a genuine smile, the muscles around both the mouth and the eyebrows move, polite smile only those around the mouth move, that insight enables a conscious judgment. Intuition and judgment are not opposite poles. They rely on the same process: here, the same visual cues.[6]

Common sense is a huge challenge to those in the business of developing artificial intelligence. That holds even for the basic understanding that words and pictures represent objects in the social and physical world. We have not succeeded in programming common sense into computers with the help of rules or by creating deep neural networks that are able to learn it. Sensory motor skills are another big challenge. Although AI can beat a human at chess, the same programme cannot take the chessboard down from the shelf and set up the figures. It is still difficult to build a robot that can move its fingers as flexibly as a violinist can, or a housekeeper robot that can carry out all household chores as well as a human can. In the absence of these skills, one solution is to redesign our living spaces to fit the abilities of AI.

LANGUAGE TRANSLATION

In Douglas Adams's *Hitchhiker's Guide to the Galaxy*, all people need to do to understand a foreign language is insert a small fish into their ear. Down on humble earth, there are no fish that do the job; instead we need translators. When transposing a text from one language into another, a translator needs to understand the source language while having an even better grasp of the target language in order to express idioms and irony. This is why professional translators typically translate into their mother tongue.

What is the best way to build a translation machine? If you followed the psychological AI method, you would assemble professional translators and linguists in a room and try to convert their intuition and judgement into rules that can be programed into software. But that has not worked by itself. A natural language is not a system of well-defined rules: words have not one but many meanings, and the correct one cannot be simply looked up in a dictionary but needs to be inferred from the context and what one knows about the speaker. Similarly, grammatical rules are not absolute but constantly broken. The alternative is to forget about the art of human translation and instead employ software engineers who use massive computer power to analyse the statistical associations between words and sentences in billions of pages of text already translated. Rules and statistics have been the major two ideas about how to build translation machines.

Until the end of the 1980s, not much progress was made in machine translation. The ALPAC Report commissioned by US funding agencies in the mid-1960s described translation research as flawed and useless.[7] Popular stories made fun of this state of affairs. Here is one. A computer program translated a headline from English into another language and then back into English:

Headline: POPE SHOT. WORLD SHAKEN.
Back-translation: EARTHQUAKE IN ITALY. ONE DEAD.

Clearly, the algorithm did 'think' something. More correctly, it made associations. I tried to replicate this result in 2020 with Google Translate, a much better system than in the old days. After translating the headline back and forth into German, and repeating the process, I got this result:

Headline: POPE SHOT. WORLD SHAKEN.
Back-translation: POPE FIRED. WORLD SHAKEN.

The algorithm struggled with an ambiguous word. 'Shot' has two meanings in English: that the Pope *was shot by someone*, or the Pope *shot or fired at someone or something*. Unlike English, German has two different terms for 'shot', one for being shot ('erschossen') and one for having shot ('schoss'). Thus, when translating the headline into German, the algorithm has to choose the proper term. That requires an understanding of the cause: the world is shaken because someone shot the Pope, not because the Pope shot. People with common sense intuitively know what is meant: that the Pope being shot is the reason that the world is shaken. But modern machine translation systems, from Google to Bing, work by making associations in the absence of causal understanding. That the English term 'fired' also has more than one meaning adds to the beauty of the back-translation.

The big advantages of state-of-the-art computerized translation systems are their quantity and speed. Good systems can translate texts from over a hundred languages in a few moments, a breakneck pace and an impressive multilingualism beyond human capacity. Understanding and quality, by contrast, are not their strength.[8] Nor is common sense. A computer would translate the sentence 'My grandfather is pregnant' without a blink; a human translator would be startled. To be startled requires understanding a causal relation – that women can get pregnant, not men. Yet a neural network does not even know that words stand for things. It relates words to words, not to ideas. Therefore, its output ranges from remarkably accurate translations to surprisingly grotesque errors.

Ambiguity and Polysemy Require Common Sense

Lack of common sense is a key problem of all translation systems. For instance, the highly praised system DeepL translated 'Pope shot' into German as 'Papstschuss', which was retranslated into 'papal shot' (with alternatives such as 'shot in the pope' and 'shot in the pope's eye').[9] These systems try to identify entire sequences of words or whole sentences that need to be translated together rather than translating word by word with the help of a dictionary, as in the past.[10] But the quality of the result also depends on the quality of the sources: if many poor translations are on the internet for a particular sentence or topic, then DeepL's suggestions are of poor quality as well. Although translation programs are quite good today, that does not mean that they have common sense. Without understanding, even a good translation system remains an *idiot savant*.

In contrast to logical languages, natural languages have multiple sources of uncertainty. One is polysemy, the fact that one and the same word may have several meanings – like the English word 'shot'. A related kind of uncertainty is a sentence whose meaning cannot be inferred from the individual words, but which requires common sense.[11] Here is a classic example:

Little John was looking for his toy box. Finally, he found it. The box was in the pen. John was very happy.

There is nothing in these sentences that enables the reader to infer the meaning of 'pen'. The most frequent one is a writing utensil, but here it refers to a small enclosure in which a child plays, which is less common. I asked DeepL to translate 'The box was in the pen' into German, which has different words for the two different meanings. DeepL got it right: 'Die Schachtel war im Pferch' – or almost right, since 'Pferch' indicates an enclosure for sheep, not children. When I changed one word, 'The box was in *his* pen', DeepL missed the point, translating it as 'Die Schachtel war in seiner Feder', that is, that the box was in his writing utensil. How to teach a neural network to acquire common sense remains an unsurpassed challenge.

A final source of uncertainty lies in the different grammars of languages. For instance, in German, Italian, Spanish, Polish and French, the words for male and female professionals differ, while in English they are the same. To translate 'nurse' and 'doctor' from English to German, the AI has to make a choice between male and female, which requires understanding the context of the story, an easy task for common sense but difficult for the best programs. Even when translating directly from German to Italian, where gender is marked in both cases, Google Translate makes systematic errors in keeping with gender stereotypes. For instance, the German 'die Präsidentin' (the female president) is translated as 'il presidente' (the male president) in Italian, when it should be 'la presidente'. In an experiment where terms were translated between these five languages, Google Translate changed all female doctors into male doctors, all female historians into male historians and most male nurses into female nurses.[12]

Why does the AI modify the gender to fit the common stereotype? The answer is that Google Translate is English-centric. It does not directly translate from German to Italian, or from Spanish to French, but from each of these languages first to English, and then from English to the target language. In the first step, the gender gets lost in translation, and in the second step Google Translate has to guess it. The best guess is the stereotype.

The Problem Is More General

The fact that AI lacks common sense limits its use not only for translation but for natural language comprehension as well. When people give a reason for a claim, its validity depends not only on the reason but also on 'warrants' that are typically left unspoken. An example is:

> Claim: You should take an umbrella.
> Reason: It's raining.
> Warrant: It is not good to get wet.

Warrants are part of human's intuitive world knowledge. Machines don't have these intuitions. But what if one simplifies the task and provides the warrant explicitly, as above? Can deep neural networks then determine whether a claim is warranted? To test this ability, one can use warrants that support a claim (as above) but also those that do not ('it's good to get wet'). In one study, Google's widely acclaimed neural network BERT (named after the perfectionist character in Sesame Street) correctly concluded whether or not claims are warranted for 77 per cent of similar questions. Given that ordinary people without any preparation did only 3 percentage points better, BERT did a truly impressive job. [13]

Yet we should think twice before concluding that the network has learned to comprehend natural language arguments almost as well as people. To do so, it would need common sense and world knowledge – such as that rain gets us wet and that umbrellas protect us from getting soaked. So what did BERT in fact learn to have been so successful? After digging more deeply, the authors of the study discovered the network's ingenious secret: in the set of data on which it was trained and tested, BERT had discovered that a claim was mostly correct when the warrant contained a 'not', as in the example above. By confirming the claim in such cases, it therefore got the answer right most of the time. Yet this remarkable ability to find correlations has nothing to do with actually grasping an argument. When the warrants were reformulated without any 'nots', the network fared no better than chance at giving the right answers. The research team concluded that the neural network's astonishing appearance of comprehending language can be accounted for by its ability to find spurious cues. BERT's top performance is yet another illustration of the Russian tank fallacy.

The Future of Machine Translation

The statistical approach to translation is dominant in computer translation today, often in combination with a rule-based approach. Semantics (the meaning of a word or sentence) and pragmatics (e.g., what a person intends to do) play little role. To understand how these algorithms work, put yourself in the shoes of a predictive system that suggests the next word or phrase to your sentences as you type them. You are a neural network and don't know what a word means. You also know nothing about spelling and grammar. But you have 'read' millions of articles and books on all kinds of topics, and have a perfect memory that recalls all combinations of words and what word or phrase most likely follows a given word or phrase. You 'see' the words users enter on their smartphones and predict those that might follow based on those millions of articles, without a clue what these phrases mean. It's similar to a human who does not understand Chinese characters, but has learned which one is likely to come after another. The result can be quite impressive, without any understanding of what these words are about.

But when the result is impressive, doesn't that mean that the program understands language? In fact, Ray Kurzweil, who was hired by Larry Page to bring language understanding to Google, argued that statistical analysis is the epitome of understanding: 'If understanding language and other phenomena through statistical analysis does not count as true understanding, then humans have no understanding either.'[14] This statement confuses the outcome with the process. Even if a program translates a sentence correctly, that does not mean that it comprehends its content, just as a parrot squawking 'Ed is a bad boy' doesn't understand what it is saying.

If we could write common sense into a source code, then it would be possible to write it into programs and algorithms. Source codes, however, require a well-defined structure. Language is in a different category – literary texts require understanding of a high level of ambiguity. For that reason, the future of machine translation lies not in the dream of universal automatic translation but in computer-assisted translation systems, including systems that point out inconsistencies in terminology or formatting style within a text. Fast automatic translation will work for well-defined topics that feature logical structures with limited ambiguity, such as news and business texts, and for quick communication where literary quality or creativity is not an issue. It might also work for the needs of the military and intelligence community that funds projects in computer translation to be able to understand the massive amount of foreign language communication they are intercepting. Unlike a competent Arabic translator, a computer can work around the clock and does not need security checks and clearance. Beyond that one will still need expert translators who understand what the text is about.

OBJECT AND FACE RECOGNITION

When a little girl says 'doggie' while pointing to a dog and 'kitty' when pointing to a cat, she recognizes different classes of animals. Object recognition is a fundamental ability; without it, higher-level cognitive abilities such as abstraction, thought and decision making would be impossible. But how do toddlers know that an animal is a dog as opposed to a cat? Do they rely on the shape of the eyes, the contour of the head, or the rest of the body? Studies indicate that three-month-old infants already respond differently to dogs and cats and rely on the features of the face as well as the contour of the head, whereas bodily features do not seem to play much of a role.[15] Precisely what cues are used and how these are integrated is not yet known.

The number of instances children need to learn a category is much smaller than for a deep neural network. The latter needs to see tens of thousands of pictures of dogs and cats in supervised learning. A child may need to see a kitty once or a few times and then will recognize cats under different lighting conditions, in the dark or in sunlight. If a three-year-old watches a bike on a road and is told that this is a bicycle, it is likely that from then on, the child will recognize all varieties of bicycles. The son of a colleague of mine became a car enthusiast at the age of two and could point out all varieties of BMWs on the street, even a model he had not seen before. Children do not appear to be born with this one-shot learning ability but learn it in the first thirty months of life.

Infants Recognize Their Mother's Face

For a computer, recognizing faces is no different a task than recognizing cars. For an infant, these are not the same. Just two days after birth, newborns can already tell their mother's face apart from a stranger's. They also suck more strongly when they see their mother's face in a video.[16] Recognizing their mother's face is apparently tied to recognizing their first source of food. But face recognition does not arrive full-blown at birth. It takes about ten years until children have developed the face recognition ability of adults. On the way, they also lose a remarkable skill. Infants and young children can often recognize faces both right-side-up and upside-down, which few adults are still able to do.

The Brain's Vicarious Functioning

The human perceptual system is designed to recognize objects under changing illuminations, situations and contexts. It is extraordinarily adapted to a constantly changing world. To deal with this uncertainty, the brain uses not one, but multiple routes. If one is blocked, it takes another route. This immense flexibility of the brain to rely on changing cues, according to whatever is available, is known as *vicarious functioning*.[17] It can be found in most biological systems. For instance, migrating birds fly thousands of miles and may rely on the stars to navigate. But if it's a cloudy day, they may instead rely on landmarks or their magnetic sense. Similarly, the brain can recognize a face by the shape of the eyes, nose and mouth. In extreme cases, only a few lines are sufficient, as when we recognize the face of a celebrity in caricatures made with just a few pencil strokes. Face recognition also functions even when parts of a face are covered and internal features such as eyes are hardly visible. In this case, the brain relies on external features such as hair and head shape.

Consider the image of former US president Bill Clinton and his vice president Al Gore (figure 5.1). How do we recognize Gore on the left and Clinton on the right? Is it Clinton's characteristic nose and mouth? Not at all. In the picture, Clinton and Gore have exactly the same nose, mouth and eyes. Their entire faces are identical after digital manipulation.[18] Nevertheless, we perceive them as being different. The only real difference lies in the hair and head shape. This shows that if the internal (facial) features are not conclusive, the brain relies on external features – vicarious functioning.

One might call the fact that we see Clinton and Gore rather than

FIGURE 5.1: Bill Clinton and Al Gore. Really? Their faces have been edited so that they are identical – eyes, nose, mouth and all other internal features. Nevertheless, we recognize Clinton and Gore. Our brains identify the two persons by external features, here the hair and head shape.

two identical faces with different hair and head shapes a visual illusion. Yet dismissing it as such would mean overlooking that the brain, faced with uncertainty, has to try different routes to find out who the people in the picture actually are.

A second general feature in human evolution is that faces need to be recognized from a distance to determine whether they are friends or foes. The brain has to compensate for the human eye, which is unable to see distant objects as clearly as, say, an eagle. This requires successfully dealing with blurred or degraded images. Take the picture in figure 5.2, which was obtained by reducing the photo of a famous person to 19 × 25 pixels ('blocks') of various shades of grey. If you look closely, you will hardly recognize the face. But by stepping back and looking at the picture from a distance, you can. Stepping back can be replaced by squinting, which blurs the picture and fosters recognition. These are humans' adaptations to low resolution, here a few pixels, whereas machine perception generally needs more pixels.

FIGURE 5.2: Faces need to be identified from a distance to decide whether they are friends or foes, which requires recognizing blurred and degraded pictures. If you step back and look at the picture from a distance, a famous face can be recognized. The same effect can be obtained by deliberately blurring the image, such as by squinting.

HUMAN ERRORS DIFFER FROM MACHINE ERRORS

If a system is an improvement on another one, it makes fewer errors – but the errors are typically similar in kind. However, if two systems differ in fundamental properties, like carbon and silicon, these are likely to make qualitatively different errors. Therefore, if artificial neural networks resembled human intelligence, the errors they would make should differ in terms of quantity. In fact, they differ in quality. A qualitative difference is an AI error that is unexpected and non-intuitive for a human, or a human error that an AI would never make. We have seen some examples of such errors in the previous chapter with neural networks that recognize school buses.

Human errors that would be 'baffling' for an AI include calculation errors and those due to social influence. Most of us are slow and not very good at mental arithmetic, while computers can make fast and perfect calculations. Moreover, we are social beings who depend on others, and what we believe is influenced by what our friends and family rightly or wrongly believe. Social influence can even affect total strangers. For instance, in the classic *conformity experiment*, groups of eight students were asked to judge the length of lines drawn on paper.[19] Unknown to the single true participant in each group, the other seven were actors. In some of the trials, the actors gave their best judgements. In a few trials, however, they all gave the same wrong answer. After hearing these, a substantial number of the true participants also gave similar answers. Note that the experiment used a topic as neutral as possible, the length of lines, not political judgements or social issues that lead to group pressure. Even in this situation, a desire for conformity can make many humans err. A computer program couldn't care less what other computers say.

Let's have a closer look at the difference between the errors humans and deep neural networks make.

Counter-intuitive Errors

Consider a network that has learned to recognize handwritten numbers through a sample of tens of thousands of images. To simplify the task, each number is set within the boundaries of a box. Then the network is tested with a sample of new handwritten numbers, 0, 1, 4 and 0, as shown in the first column in the left panel of figure 5.3. It classifies the four new samples correctly. Now comes the interesting part. Take a close look at the second column and you will recognize the same four numbers. But these handwritten numbers are slightly distorted by changes to a small proportion of the pixels, so subtle that the human eye can barely notice any difference. To us, the second column looks like the first; we still see 0, 1, 4 and 0. For a neural network, it's an entirely different matter. It no longer recognizes a single one of the four numbers.[20] The result is the same for the next two pairs of columns.

To us, it is hard to fathom that a well-trained deep neural network doesn't recognize that the numbers in the first two columns are the same. The reason for its confusion is that the pixels have been changed in a tiny but systematic way. When the numbers are distorted by randomly changed pixels (known as 'random noise'), however, the network is not fooled in the same way. The first column in the right panel of figure 5.3 shows the numbers 9, 1, 6 and 9, as does the second column, but with so much noise added that the human eye can

FIGURE 5.3: Deep neural networks and humans make different kinds of errors. Left panel: The first column contains four handwritten numbers, which a trained deep neural network correctly recognized. The second column is obtained from the first by *systematically* changing a small proportion of the pixels. Although this change is barely detectable by a human, the AI could no longer identify any of the four numbers correctly. The same holds for the next two pairs of columns. Right panel: The first column lists four handwritten numbers; the second shows the same numbers but with a large amount of 'random noise'. The deep neural network could still recognize about half of the numbers, while humans can hardly recognize any of them.

barely make out anything. To us, the second column does not look like the first. The network, in contrast, is still able to identify the barely visible numbers correctly in half of the cases. The network can deal better than humans with noise (right panel), but humans can deal better with tiny systematic changes (left panel). Noise is like a picture covered with 'dust'. Slight systematic changes, in contrast, change the picture, but the brain understands that these are irrelevant and barely perceives them. In contrast, the network appears to focus on aspects that are irrelevant for single digits, or is confused by those, reminiscent of the Russian tank fallacy.

The lesson is that the artificial intelligence of neural networks is quite different from human intelligence. Psychological AI would teach the handwriting program to divide the task into subtasks, such as identifying whether there is a horizontal bar or a closed oval shape. That psychological method would not be fooled by systematic changes in irrelevant pixels, as in the second column of figure 5.3 (left). The neural network does not break down that task into such subtasks that are intuitively intelligible to humans.[21] Moreover, when learning novel handwritten digits from 0 to 9, machine learning algorithms may be trained on a standard set of 60,000 images before being able to correctly recognize new handwritten examples as readily as humans would. Humans, in contrast, can learn to recognize a new handwritten character from a few examples only, learn the associated concept and generate new examples themselves.[22] Even for simple objects like handwritten characters, people need fewer examples than the best algorithms and learn in a more general way.

What Do Deep Neural Networks See?

We do not know exactly what a network 'sees' but we can make some educated guesses. Recall the situation from the previous chapter, where networks confused horizontal yellow-black stripes with a school bus. In figure 5.4, these two images are placed above that of an electric guitar. After learning to classify the picture on the left side as a guitar, the network is tested on the right picture with vertical undulating stripes. Here the network is 99.9 per cent confident that this picture is also of a guitar.[23]

Why on earth does the network think that wavy stripes are a guitar? Again, we cannot know for sure, but the juxtaposition of the two errors might give us a clue. In both cases, the misclassified picture has the same dominant colours as the correct object. These are yellow and black for the bus, and brown and white for the guitar. Most guitars are made of wood and therefore brown in colour. The body of a guitar is curved like an S on its left side and like an inverse S on its right side. The wave pattern in the picture on the right captures both forms and repeats them in each vertical wave. At least in these cases, the network appears to identify characteristic colours and shapes while learning from pictures of real buses and guitars. And if these colours and shapes are repeated in another picture, the network is highly confident that this image belongs to the same class of objects.

There is no question that deep neural networks have demonstrated impressive abilities in recognizing objects, often on par with humans.

FIGURE 5.4: Top row: as shown in Figure 4.3, the picture on the left is correctly classified as a school bus by a deep neural network, but the picture on the right is also classified as a school bus with high confidence. Bottom row: the neural network has learned to classify the picture on the left correctly as a guitar but is 99.9 per cent certain that the picture on the right is also a guitar.

A similar level of ability, however, does not mean a similar kind of intelligence. The systematic errors made by neural networks are alien to humans. The networks can be fooled because they appear to rely on recurrent features without comprehending what the object is.

SCENARIO RECOGNITION

Recognizing objects is relatively simple compared with recognizing relations between persons, objects or states. Here, the question is: what is going on in a scenario? Humans infer the answer with the help of their intuitive psychology and physics. How do algorithms compare?

Let's look at how deep neural networks trained to generate image captions fared at recognizing causal relationships (figure 5.5).[24] The image on the left shows a take from a cowboy stunt show at Texas Hollywood. It depicts a violent scene from old Western movies where an outlaw is lassoed and dragged behind the horse. In the background, visitors are watching the performance. What does the network 'see'? The neural network's caption is: 'A woman riding a horse on a dirt road'. The network gets the objects mostly right – the horse and the dirt (the person on the horse is a man, which is hard to see, although that could be inferred from the standard plots of Westerns). What the caption reveals, however, is that the network doesn't have a clue what is going on in the scene. It has no intuitive psychology to infer that the

A woman riding a horse on a dirt road

An airplane is parked on the tarmac at an airport

A group of people standing on top of a beach

FIGURE 5.5: Image captions generated by a deep neural network. The network mostly gets the objects right but fails to understand the relations between the objects, the mental states of the people and the physical forces at work.

person on horseback intends to punish the other person, and that the scene is part of a show. It also has no causal understanding that this kind of punishment may be fatal.

The central image depicts the crash of a passenger plane in Taipei, in February 2015, filmed by a car driver. Shortly after take-off, the right engine had a malfunction, and the pilots mistakenly shut down the still-functioning left engine. In the voice recording, one of the pilots shouted 'Wow, pulled back the wrong side throttle.' The plane rolled sharply, struck a taxi with its left wing and toppled into the river.[25] Forty-three passengers and crew members were killed. The neural network's caption is 'An airplane is parked on the tarmac at an airport'. Once again, it gets some of the objects right, but misses the story.

The third image shows residents in Key West, Florida clinging to each other as they battle the winds of Hurricane Georges along Houseboat Row in 1998. The deep neural network recognizes a group of people on a beach, but cannot make head nor tail of what is happening.

When humans look at these pictures, they rely on their common sense and experience to guess what is going on. Even if we've never seen a Western, a plane crash or a hurricane, our intuition tells us that something is awry. Deep neural networks can be quite good at identifying objects in a picture but, without the ingredient of common sense, struggle to understand how they relate in a scenario.

OF DIFFERENT MINDS

Human intelligence is about representing the world, making causal models and ascribing intentions to other living creatures. To do this, humans distinguish an image from the real thing, such as knowing that the picture of a person is not the person, although similar emotions can sometimes be elicited by both. In contrast, deep neural networks learn to associate images with labels or headlines but do not know that an image refers to some person or object in the real world. AlphaGo and its successors play Go better than human champions without knowing that they are playing a game, and digital assistants like Siri and Alexa don't know what a restaurant is. Does it matter that they don't know?

As long as the assistant is only asked for the best Italian restaurants in your neighbourhood or similar advice, it does not. Yet awareness is extremely important when systems are allowed to automatically make decisions with life-and-death consequences, as with military drones, robot soldiers and other lethal autonomous weapons. A machine may know perfectly how to kill, but it does not know what it is doing and why. What is more, these machines can err in unexpected ways that are alien to our imagination.

The human person that reminds me most of the performance of a deep neural network is Solomon Shereshevsky, the famous Russian mnemonist, with whom readers of my book *Gut Feelings* are already acquainted. His memory appeared to have no limits in its capacity and duration.[26] When asked to read a page of text, Shereshevsky could recall it word for word, both forwards and backwards. But when asked to summarize the gist of what he had read, he was more or less at a loss. He had problems with ambiguity, with words that have several meanings and with different words that have the same meaning, not to speak of metaphors and poetry. Shereshevsky could precisely recall a complex mathematical formula even though he could not understand it (to be sure, it was made up) and also recall it fifteen years later. His mind was very different from that of chess masters who can also perfectly recall complex chess positions but only if they make sense, not random configurations. Shereshevsky struggled with filtering the important from the trivial and reasoning on an abstract level.

Shereshevsky is living proof that evolution could have given all of us perfect memory but at a heavy price. One thing he could not do was forget. Although his vast memory seems enviable, he was distracted by irrelevant details, not unlike deep neural networks that are distracted by irrelevant pixels added to handwritten numbers, as in figure 5.3, or by a patch on people's T-shirts, as in figure 4.4. He may have been the closest humans can get to neural networks, perfect in storing and processing big data but having trouble understanding what it all actually means.

6

One Data Point Can Beat Big Data

'Out with every theory of human behavior, from linguistics to sociology. Forget taxonomy, ontology, and psychology ... With enough data, the numbers speak for themselves. '
Chris Anderson[1]

'There are a lot of small data problems that occur in big data. They don't disappear because you've got lots of stuff. They get worse.'
Sir David J. Spiegelhalter[2]

Astronomy is the science that for centuries has required its researchers to work at night. It is also the science that initiated one of the first big data projects. Launched in 1887 in Paris under the name Carte du Ciel ('sky map'), the project set out to map 2 million stars using 20,000 photographic plates of the night sky, documented in hundreds of volumes of published data.[3] This undertaking fitted the newly created term *big science*, as it gobbled up almost all of the limited resources available to the observatories and the labour and time of generations. Mapping the stars in all hemispheres required international cooperation, using observatories from Helsinki to the Cape of Good Hope to Sydney. The sky map promised to deliver enough images and data to transform astronomy into a day job where astronomers could sit at a well-lit desk rather than out in the dark fields. Most remarkably, it was intended not to promote the fame of individual astronomers but instead to provide a service to future 'astronomers of year 3000 at least'.[4] With the help of the photographic plates, future scientists would be able to detect small changes in the sky that are not noticeable within the lifetime of an astronomer.

The unfinished sky map project was a monument to *positivism*. The term refers to an attitude that what counts are facts, that is, everything that can be observed and measured, as opposed to imperceptible ideas and speculation. Today, positivism has made a comeback with big data analytics.

Astronomers deal with a stable system – the movement of heavenly bodies. The system is stable relative to the short duration of astronomers' lives. Unlike the typical machine learning application, astronomy has theories about stars and planets. In this context, big data is highly useful. In today's world, however, big data is used for fickle phenomena that are dynamic and may change in unexpected ways. Here, the three Vs – volume, velocity and variety – are of limited help, and 'less can be more': using fewer data and less complex algorithms can often lead to better predictions. Even adding a fourth V – veracity, that is, the reliability of the data – can be of little avail. In its place, psychological AI can be more useful. Let me illustrate this less-is-more principle with Google's celebrated showcase of big data analytics.

PREDICTING THE FLU

If you are experiencing high fever, a sore throat, a runny nose and tiredness, you might have influenza, commonly known as the flu. The symptoms appear typically two days after being exposed to the influenza virus and disappear within five to six days. Influenza is estimated to cause a quarter to half a million deaths around the world every year. To indicate where the flu is spreading, the US Centers for Disease Control (CDC) informs the public about the number of flu-related doctor visits in all regions of the country. The problem is that it takes a week or two for the CDC to collect the data.

In 2008, media across the world announced with a fanfare that Google engineers had found a much quicker method to predict the spread of the flu early on. The idea appeared sound. Users infected with the flu are likely to use Google's search engine to diagnose their symptoms and look for remedies. These queries could instantly tell where the flu is spreading. To find the apt queries, engineers analysed some 50 million search terms and calculated which of these were associated with the flu.[5] Then they tested 450 million different models to find the one that best matched with the data and came up with a secret algorithm that used forty-five search terms (also kept secret). The algorithm was then used to predict flu-related doctor visits in each region on a daily and weekly basis.

At first, all went splendidly. Google Flu Trends forecasted the flu faster than the reports of the Centers for Disease Control. Google even coined a new term: to 'nowcast' the spread of flu and influenza-related diseases in each region of the US, with a reporting lag of about one day.

Months later, in the spring of 2009, something unexpected happened. The swine flu broke out. It barrelled in out of season, with the first cases in March and a peak in October. Google Flu Trend missed the outbreak (see figure 6.1); it had learned from the years before that flu infections were high in the winter and low in the summer.[6] Predictions crumbled.

Faith in Complexity

After this setback, the engineers embarked on improving the algorithm. To do so, there are two possible approaches. One is to fight complexity with complexity. The idea is: complex problems need complex solutions, and if a complex algorithm fails, it needs to be made more complex. The second approach follows the stable-world principle. The idea behind it is that a complex algorithm using big data from the past may not predict the future well in uncertain conditions and it therefore should be simplified. Google's engineers went for more complexity. Instead of paring down the 45 search terms (features), they jacked these up to about 160 (the exact number has not been made public) and continued to bet on big data.

The revised algorithm first did a good job of predicting new cases, but not for long. Between August 2011 and September 2013, it overestimated the proportion of expected flu-related doctor visits in 100 out of 108 weeks (see figure 6.1).[7] One major reason was the instability of the flu itself. Influenza viruses are like chameleons, constantly

FIGURE 6.1: A simple heuristic using a single data point can predict the flu better than Google's big data analytics. Shown here is the actual percentage of flu-related doctor visits from 18 March 2007 to 9 August 2015, and its predictions by the recency heuristic and by Google Flu Trends (including three updates). Top: Predictions and observed values in absolute terms. The predictions by the recency heuristic and the observed values are virtually identical. Bottom: Prediction errors. The years signify the beginning of the year, that is, '2008' indicates 1 January 2008. For instance, in the summer of 2009, Google Flu Trends underestimated the spread of the flu thanks to the unexpected breakout of the swine flu, after which it received its first update.

changing, making it extremely difficult to predict their spread. The symptoms of swine flu, such as diarrhoea, differed from those in past years, and the infection rate was higher for younger people than with other strains of the flu. A second reason was the instability of human behaviour. Many users entered flu-related search terms out of sheer curiosity about swine flu, not because they felt sick. But the algorithm could not distinguish between the motivations for search. The engineers asked 'Is our model too simple?' and continued to tinker with the revised algorithm, to no avail.[8] In 2015, Google Flu Trends was quietly shut down.[9]

Some may shrug their shoulders and say, yes, we've heard this all before, but that was 2015; today's algorithms are infinitely bigger and better. But my point is not the success or failure of a particular algorithm developed by the company Google. The crux is that the stable-world principle applies to *all* algorithms that use the past to predict an indeterminable future. Before Google's big data analytics flopped, its claim to fame was taken as proof that scientific method and theory were on the brink of becoming obsolete. Blind and rapid search through terabytes of data would be sufficient to predict epidemics. Similar claims were made by others for unravelling the secrets of the human genome, of cancer and of diabetes. Forget science; just increase volume, velocity and variety and measure what correlates with what. Chris Anderson, editor-in-chief of *Wired*, announced: 'Correlation supersedes causation, and science can advance even without coherent models . . . It's time to ask: What can science learn from Google?'[10]

Let me pose a different question. What can Google learn from science?

Under Uncertainty, Keep It Simple and Don't Bet on the Past

The Google engineers never seem to have considered a simple algorithm in place of their big data analytics. In my research group at the Max Planck Institute for Human Development, we've studied simple algorithms ('heuristics') that perform well under volatile conditions. One way to derive these rules is to rely on psychological AI: to investigate how the human brain deals with situations of disruption and change. Back in the early nineteenth century, for instance, Thomas Brown formulated the *law of recency*, which states that recent experiences come to mind faster than those in the distant past and are often the sole information that guides human decisions.[11] Contemporary research indicates that people do not automatically rely on what they recently experienced, but only do so in unstable situations where the distant past is not a reliable guide for the future. In this spirit, my colleagues and I developed and tested the following 'brain algorithm':[12]

Recency heuristic for predicting the flu: Predict that this week's proportion of flu-related doctor visits will equal those of the most recent data,
from one week ago.

Unlike Google's secret Flu Trends algorithm, this rule is transparent
and can be easily applied by everyone. Its logic can be understood. It
relies on a single data point only, which can be looked up on the website of the Centers for Disease Control. And it dispenses with combing
through 50 million search terms and trial-and-error testing of millions of models. But how well does it actually predict the flu?

Three fellow researchers and I tested the recency rule using the same
eight years of data on which the Google Flu Trends algorithm was tested,
that is, weekly observations between March 2007 and August 2015.
During that time, the proportion of flu-related visits among all doctor
visits ranged between 1 per cent and 8 per cent, with an average of
1.8 per cent visits per week (figure 6.1). This means that if every week
you were to make the simple but false prediction that there are zero flu-
related doctor visits, you would have a mean absolute error of 1.8
percentage points over four years. Google Flu Trends predicted much
better than that, with a mean error of 0.38 percentage points (figure 6.2).
The recency heuristic had a mean error of only 0.20 percentage points,
which is even better.[13] If we exclude the period where the swine flu

FIGURE 6.2: Less can be more. Using a single data point, one can predict
the spread of the flu better than Google Flu Trends, a big data algorithm.
The mean absolute error (from figure 6.1) in predicting the proportion of
flu-related doctor visits is 0.38 for Google Flu Trends, but only 0.20 when
using one single data point, that is, recency. Both algorithms were tested on
the same weekly data between 18 March 2007 and 9 August 2015 (see text).

happened, that is before the first update of Google Flu Trends, the result remains essentially the same (0.38 and 0.19, respectively).

'Fast-and-frugal' Psychological AI

The case of Google Flu Trends demonstrates that in an unstable world, reducing the amount of data and complexity can lead to more accurate predictions. In some cases, it might be advisable to ignore everything that happened in the past and instead rely on the most recent data point alone. It also shows that psychological AI – here, the recency heuristic – can match or beat complex machine learning algorithms in prediction. In general, my point is that 'fast-and-frugal' heuristics that need little data are a good candidate for implementing psychological AI.

The flu example is neither a fluke nor an exception. Under uncertainty, simple rules such as recency have also been shown to be highly effective in comparison with complex algorithms, be it in predicting consumer purchases, repeat offenders, heart attacks, sport results or election outcomes.[14] A group of economists, including Nobel laureate Joseph Stiglitz, showed for instance that the recency heuristic can predict consumer demand in evolving economies better than traditional 'sophisticated' models.[15] The great advantage of simple rules is that they are understandable and are easy to use.

Nevertheless, it's difficult for many of us to get our heads around the idea of deliberately leaving out data when we're trying to make an informed decision. Why is having more information often a hindrance rather than a help?

As mentioned in Chapter 2, in order to successfully predict the future, one needs a good theory, reliable data and a stable world. The usefulness of big data depends on these three conditions. Let's first take a look at situations where one has lots of correlations but no theory.

CORRELATIONS AND THE TEXAS SHARPSHOOTER

Although not as popular as the Oscars, the Nobel Prize is one of the most prestigious international awards, and its winners make the headlines each year. The US has about ten Nobel Prize winners per 10 million inhabitants, the UK almost twice as many. China and Brazil are at the low end, with less than 0.1 winner per 10 million, while Switzerland and Sweden are at the top, with over thirty Nobel laureates per 10 million. What causes these differences? And what should scientists and writers from other countries do to match the level of Switzerland?

The answer of big data is to find out what individual behaviours or organizational structures are associated with the proportion of Nobel laureates. It could be the quality of the preschool system, or that of the universities, or the motivation to succeed. If one indiscriminately combs the data in search of an association, an astonishing answer pops up.

It's chocolate! The rate of Nobel laureates in a country can be 'predicted' by its chocolate consumption. The more chocolate eaten, the more Nobel Prizes (figure 6.3). And the relationship is extremely strong.

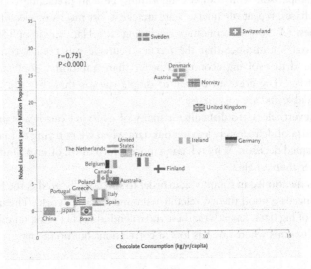

FIGURE 6.3: An impressive but useless correlation. The chocolate consumption is strongly correlated (r = 0.79) with the number of Nobel laureates per 10 million population across countries. The value p < 0.0001 means that if there were no correlation in reality, a correlation at least as strong as this one would be expected to occur only once in 10,000 cases, or even less frequently.

The Chinese and Japanese consume very little chocolate and have very few Nobel laureates per capita. The Swiss consume on average over 26 pounds of chocolate per year and are at the top of the Nobel laureate scale. The US is somewhere in the middle in both respects. (One exception to the rule is Germany, whose citizens consume as much chocolate as the Swiss yet have fewer Nobel Prizes per capita; another exception is Sweden, whose citizens get their high share of Nobel Prizes despite eating only an average dose of chocolate.)

The recommendation seems to be to modify the Chinese, Japanese and US diet to one that contains substantially more chocolate, preferably Swiss chocolate. That may provide chocoholics an alibi for upping their chocolate intake but will not likely bring them any nearer to winning a Nobel Prize.

Impressive but Useless Correlations

The 'r' that measures the association in figure 6.3 is called a *Pearson correlation*. Karl Pearson, born in 1857 into a Quaker family of stern, industrious Yorkshire barristers, was a man whose profound curiosity about the world led him to study as much as he could: mathematics, physics, physiology, history, Roman law and German literature in Cambridge, Berlin, Heidelberg and Vienna. He also was a man of profound self-doubt, worrying that his name would survive merely as that of a correlation coefficient. At a time when women were not allowed to vote, he argued for the equality of men and women and a strong independent women's party. More relevant to the present topic, Pearson worshipped quantification and argued that our perceptions are the basis of all knowledge: we can perceive correlations but not causation.[16] He was not the first to claim this. The Scottish philosopher David Hume famously argued the same 150 years earlier. As the first epigraph to this chapter shows, big data enthusiasts have pushed Pearson's and Hume's argument to the extreme, arguing that causes are not even needed; rather, with petabytes in our hands, 'correlation is enough'.[17]

The strong association between chocolate consumption and Nobel laureates shows that correlation is not enough. Data mining may even lead us on the wrong trail. Big data can unearth any number of similar useless correlations. When developing Google Flu Trends, for instance, the engineers found a strong correlation between searches for *high school basketball* and flu-related doctor visits. No causal connection exists, only the coincidence that both the flu and the high school basketball season last from November to March.[18] Applying their common sense, the engineers eliminated this irrelevant feature by hand.

Blind searching through millions of variables can reveal many other surprising correlations (figure 6.4).[19] Every year, around a hundred Americans fall into swimming pools and drown. Why? Data mining shows that this number is strongly associated with the number of movies in which the actor Nicolas Cage appears. As you can see in the figure, these numbers closely follow each other over a period of ten years. The correlation between drowning and the number of Nicolas Cage films is 0.67, which amounts to an unusually high correlation in the social sciences (a value of 1 is a perfect correlation, a value of 0 means no correlation). Do more people really drown because the actor has appeared in more films? Likely not. If you search the gigantic amount of data available on all actors and all causes of death, you'll likely find more of these associations, at least within some time interval, even if they make no sense.

Similarly, a correlation of 0.79, as strong as between chocolate and Nobel laureates, has been reported between the number of non-commercial space launches and the sociology doctorates awarded in the US (figure 6.4). Granting more PhDs in sociology then promises to be a thrifty way to launch more space shuttles.

Even more impressive is the correlation of 0.87 between the age of Miss America and the number of people murdered by steam, hot vapours and hot objects. A correlation of 0.87 is a rare event. When Miss America is twenty years old or younger, fewer murders occur. The older Miss America is, the more people are murdered. Following that logic, the beauty pageant committee makes life-and-death decisions every time it chooses a winner.

None of these findings, however, can compete with the virtually perfect correlation of 0.99 between the divorce rate in Maine and the per capita consumption of margarine in the US. Recall the attempts of psychologists to predict divorce rates, reported in Chapter 2, using

FIGURE 6.4: If you collect enough data, you can find whatever you want. A mixed bag of nonsensical correlations obtained from a blind search.

the Texas sharpshooter's method. They were studying the verbal and non-verbal interaction between husband and wife. What this near-perfect correlation suggests is that the true cause of divorce appears to have escaped the psychologists, namely eating too much margarine. That in turn suggests we can predict divorce rates perfectly. And it also suggests a solution: by striking margarine from their grocery lists, couples would stay together until death do them part. Once again, by indiscriminately searching through *all* food sources and *all* states in the US, you might also strike it lucky in digging up another perfect correlation. If the divorce rates in other states or within other time intervals were chosen, this perfect correlation would dissolve into hot air.

In all of these cases, common sense tells us that the correlations are meaningless. Although the examples here are comical, the problem becomes serious when it comes to areas such as nutrition and health, where so many possibilities exist that something is sure to correlate with something else. Much of the nutritional advice we've received over the past years stems from spurious correlations found in studies: eat blueberries to prevent memory loss; eat bananas to get a higher verbal SAT score; eat kiwis late at night to sleep better.[20] The common feature is that next year you may well read the opposite advice.

Another serious problem emerges when an agency relies on blind search to make decisions on people's creditworthiness. As the founder of a credit agency proclaimed, 'we observed that people who did not repay their loan had a very particular font on their computer'.[21]

Millions of Bullet Holes

By now, you may have recognized the method behind these correlations. Big data analytics provides a whole new ballgame for the Texas sharpshooter method. Only here the sharpshooter no longer needs to shoot at the barn first and then paint the target around the bullet holes so that the bull's-eye is in the middle. Instead, millions of bullet holes are already out there, and the sharpshooter can use a fast search algorithm to find a pattern where the holes appear to be aligned before painting a target around it, as in the four cases in figure 6.4. Once again, the blame is not on big data, but on how it is being used.

You might stumble over an unexpected correlation but, before proclaiming it to be a fact, would need to independently test whether it holds up at other points in time or with other groups of people. By skipping this step and presenting the coincidental pattern that happened to be found as a scientific result, you would be promoting the sharpshooter fallacy. There are strong incentives to commit this fallacy, including the media's and public's insatiable hunger for breaking news and the desperate hope of those who suffer from an incurable disease of finding a cure.

The incentives to report a finding before it is independently confirmed are particularly strong in healthcare. Every couple of weeks, a headline appears about a new tumour marker that promises personalized diagnosis or even a cure for cancer. After raising excited hopes, these breakthroughs often prove to be false, again due to spurious correlations. When another study is done, at a different point in time or in a different part of the world, the correlation vanishes into thin air. A team of scientists at the biotech company Amgen tried to replicate the findings of fifty-three 'landmark' medical articles. In forty-seven cases they failed. Likewise, the pharmaceutical company Bayer examined sixty-seven findings in oncology, cardiovascular medicine and women's health and were able to replicate the results in only fourteen cases.[22] Ian Chalmers, one of the founders of Cochrane, and Paul Glasziou, chair of the International Society for Evidence-based Health Care, estimated that 85 per cent of all health research is 'wasted' by not being reproducible, resulting in $170 billion in losses worldwide per year.[23] This dismal situation has been dubbed the *replication crisis*. Results cannot be replicated because they were nothing more than spurious correlations.

Mere correlations without theory are one factor that limits the success of big data analytics; unreliable data are another.

BAD BIG DATA

A *Forbes* journalist received an ad to join an association for retired people. He was puzzled; not only did he not feel like sixty-five, but he was in fact in his mid-thirties.[24] After more ads arrived, he began to realize that a profile of him had been made and sold by data brokers to the association. Data brokers tend to act in the shadow of better-known companies, and many of their products – that is, people like the journalist, you and me – haven't even heard of Acxiom, Oracle Data Cloud and the other companies that construct profiles of hundreds of millions of people. These profiles are based on cookies, browsing behaviour and other sources. They have been bought, for instance, by Facebook to learn more about its users.

The journalist contacted both Acxiom and Oracle and, eventually, got his hands on the profiles. At first glance, they were absurdly off base. He was listed as over sixty-five, married, a frequent shopper at Victoria's Secret and a consumer of huge amounts of nappies, baby food and imported beer – none of which was the case. Three-quarters of the information was utterly wrong, and each broker provided different misinformation. When he asked Acxiom where it got these data, the company insisted that this was a trade secret and continually reiterated how accurate their data are. This case may be an anomaly, and the data on the other millions of people may be correct. But when a Reuters journalist also asked Acxiom for his profile, he found it inaccurate in similar ways.[25] When he too asked why so much was plain wrong, the company explained that most of what was on his profile was inferred by making guesses from other data, such as from his postcode and household history. Further reporters who checked their profiles similarly found an alarming level of false information.[26]

These are individual anecdotes, so what does research show? One field study investigated how accurate the services of data brokers are for delivering ads to the right audience.[27] The ads were for a charity campaign, whose targets were males between the age of twenty-five and fifty-four (who comprised 27 per cent of the male population). To identify this age group shouldn't be that difficult. Emulating a typical advertising campaign, the researchers used the combined services of data brokers and ad-buying platforms (which 'optimize' campaigns and help select the websites on which the ads are placed). Nineteen leading data brokers and six ad-buying platforms were examined. Surprisingly, the average accuracy was a disappointing 59 per cent, meaning that 41 per cent of the ads were off-target. The best provider showed the ads to the right targets 72 per cent of the time, the worst provider only 40 per cent. A second study looked at the ability of data brokers to identify the same target group alone, that is, without the help of any ad-buying platforms. This time, their accuracy dropped below chance level. Similarly, simply guessing did a better job than data brokers of identifying gender. The best results were obtained when data brokers identified audience interest, such as interest in sports and fitness (an increase of 20 and 34 percentage points, respectively, over guessing). Interests appear to be more easily inferred from browsing behaviour. All in all, the quality of the data provided by brokers does not look like the promised 'new oil' or 'new gold'.

Moreover, advertisers have to pay good money for the oil. The authors of the studies concluded that, for standard display banner ads, the additional costs of targeting are often so high that these may outweigh the additional gains.

BIG DATA AND UNSTABLE WORLDS

Beyond mere correlations and unreliable data, lack of a stable situation is the third factor that makes big data analytics of limited use. Consider children at risk of failing school and families at risk of losing their jobs and homes. If an algorithm could identify those at risk, authorities could anticipate the problems before they arise and send social workers to work with these families. A team around researchers from Princeton University challenged the scientific community to predict the future of over 4,000 'fragile families', which were mostly single parents or families of unmarried couples.[28] For each family, the life outcomes to be predicted included the child's expected GPA at age fifteen; the child's grit, that is, the ability to work hard and persevere; whether the primary care giver will lose his or her job; and whether the family will be evicted from its home for not paying the rent or mortgage. The researchers provided big data collected over fifteen years, including personality tests, biometric data, interviews and in-home assessments. There were over 12,000 measures per family, resulting in a total of millions of data points.

One hundred and sixty science teams participated in the challenge, many of them using complex state-of-the-art machine learning methods to make their predictions. The result was discouraging. Most of the algorithms predicted worse than a simple rule that used four data points only, such as the mother's marital status and the child's performance when it was tested the last time, six years ago. The team in charge of the challenge concluded that even the best algorithms predicted poorly and only slightly better than the simple rule.

In the UK, a similar study was conducted.[29] Thirty-two different machine learning algorithms were tested on whether they could predict which child or young adult was at risk. Not a single one of the complex algorithms predicted well: on average, they missed four out of five children at risk. And, when an algorithm did conclude that a child was at risk, it was wrong for six out of ten children. That means if family services were to trust these algorithms and send social workers to solve the problem before it arises, they would miss most of the children at risk and spend their time working with the wrong families in the wrong places. Last but not least, families might be stigmatized in the process.

You may be surprised by these findings. Didn't machine learning beat the best chess player years before these studies were made? Perhaps, one might suspect, the scientists did not collect enough data. But there was in fact more than enough information. The answer is instead a very different one. Life is not like chess; it contains plenty of uncertainty. Too many factors determine what happens to a child, adult or family, and in fragile families the interplay between these factors may even be amplified. Computational power and big data are of limited help when uncertainty reigns.

We hear about highly accurate data and powerful predictions not always because they actually exist, but because these stories need to be told to sell products and stay in business. In many countries, the use of automated decision making – such as for identification of vulnerable children, predictive policing, face recognition mass screening – increases despite mounting evidence of its inaccuracy.[30] Its spread is driven instead by economic and psychological factors. The main psychological drivers include a belief in the objectivity of algorithms and the fear of missing out and falling behind other countries or companies. This combination of beliefs and fears pushes us into ever more commercial and governmental surveillance, even if it is riddled with errors.

DO NUMBERS SPEAK FOR THEMSELVES?

Numbers, big or small, cannot speak. Numbers are like children, requiring attention and guidance. They need to be understood. The Covid-19 crisis brought this message home. When, in mid-February 2020, the number of new infections suddenly sky-rocketed in China from one day to the next, the world panicked. But the numbers had changed their meaning. China had lowered the criteria for diagnosing people as infected, no longer on the basis of lab test results, but of symptoms and CT scans only. That made the number of new infections soar. It also made the numbers before and after no longer comparable. When one Sunday in mid-March 2020 the number of new infections dropped for the first time, people hoped that the downward spiral had begun. But the numbers were collected on a daily basis from the local health authorities, which were only partially staffed on weekends and unable to report all numbers. On Monday and Tuesday, numbers rose again and the hopes sank. Slowly, the public learned that the lower infection numbers that began to appear every weekend were due to the delay in reporting, not to less viral activity. The number of new infections reported on one day was not the actual number of new infections that day.

The most frightening numbers publicized in 2020 were the coronavirus death counts. The Covid-19 dashboard maintained by Johns Hopkins University reported the numbers by country. Yet these numbers were hardly comparable either. Countries and even regions counted deaths in different ways. Italy, which was hit first in the Western world, counted people who had died *and* had a positive Covid-19 test result. That means the person may have died *from* the virus, or may have died *with* the virus but from another cause. Moreover, the cause of death is notoriously difficult to determine if the deceased had several serious diseases. During the pandemic, the dimensions of this problem became clear when the Italian Health Organization published the data for the first 45,500 coronavirus-related deaths.[31] Ninety-seven per cent of those had one or more pre-existing severe diseases, including 11 per cent stroke, 17 per cent invasive cancer, 22 per cent dementia and 28 per cent ischemic heart disease. Only 3 per cent had no co-morbidities. In addition, half of those who died were between 82 and 109 years old. In many of these cases, it is not clear what the cause of death was – possibly even several causes that worked together.

If all countries used the same definition – death *and* positive test – then it would at least be possible to compare the numbers. Consider Belgium, where the total number of coronavirus-associated deaths was higher than in Germany, despite its much smaller population. It turned out that the Belgian authorities reported Covid-19 deaths for people who had not even been tested, such as people who died in care facilities for the elderly in which another resident tested positive. The general lesson is: numbers need to be understood before they are added and compared. This is true for all data, whether big or small.

So where is big data useful? As mentioned earlier, it is most useful in situations that are stable, where data are reliable and where theory can guide the search. Examples of these situations are astronomy and the analysis of past data, as in health records – unless the algorithms are gamed. Big data is less promising in situations that may change unexpectedly and where one is looking for the needle in a huge haystack of data. Examples of these situations are predicting spread of the flu, currency exchange rates, children at risk or human behaviour in general.[32] In statistics, the *law of large numbers* describes a situation where having more data is better for making predictions. According to it, the more often an experiment is conducted, the closer the average of the results can be expected to match the true state of the world. For instance, on your first encounter with roulette, you may have beginner's luck after betting on 7. But the more often you repeat this bet, the closer the relative frequency of wins and losses is expected to approach the true chance of winning, meaning that your luck will at some point fizzle out. Similarly, car insurers collect large amounts of data to figure out the chances that drivers will cause accidents, dependent on their age, region or car brand. Both casinos and insurance industries rely on the law of large numbers to balance individual losses. Yet that works only as long as the situation in which they are operating remains stable.

PART TWO

High Stakes

'The first principle is that you must not fool yourself, and you are the easiest person to fool.'

Richard P. Feynman[1]

PART TWO

High Stakes

7

Transparency

'Personal data shall be processed lawfully, fairly and in a transparent manner in relation to the data subject.'
Article 5 (1a), EU General Data Protection Regulation[1]

'Everything should be made as simple as possible, but not simpler.

Attributed to Albert Einstein[2]

Eric Loomis, a Wisconsin man, was arrested after being caught driving a car that had been used in a shooting. Loomis denied having been part of the shooting but pleaded guilty to less severe charges: attempting to flee a traffic officer and driving a car without the owner's consent.[3] To determine his sentence, the judge consulted his criminal history, as usual, but also a risk assessment algorithm, which classified Loomis as at high risk of reoffending. Loomis was sentenced to six years. Neither the defendant nor the judge knew how the algorithm calculated this risk: the algorithm, known as COMPAS (Correctional Offender Managing Profile for Alternative Sanctions), is a business secret. Loomis appealed on the grounds that the judge violated due process by relying on an opaque algorithm that may discriminate against black men. However, the Wisconsin Supreme Court ruled against Loomis, arguing that it would have imposed the same sentence regardless of the algorithm and that secret algorithms do not violate due process, while also recommending sceptical caution in their use. According to a *New York Times* headline, Loomis was 'Sent to Prison by a Software

Program's Secret Algorithms'.[4] That headline may have overstated the case, but it put a general problem on the table.

A *black box algorithm* is an algorithm that is not transparent, either because it is secret or too complicated for users to understand. Varying by country, secret algorithms influence the lives of many citizens by determining decisions among others about parole, bail, sentencing, social assistance, loans and creditworthiness in general. Given that they lack transparency, which violates our intuitive understanding of justice and can conflict with due process, wouldn't it be better to ban them entirely from the courtroom? After all, risk scores can be equally obtained from more transparent algorithms, where it is easier to determine whether these are trustworthy and whether they discriminate against certain groups of people, meaning that it is also much easier to improve or correct them if they fail. Defendants and judges alike should not be left in the dark about how a risk score is calculated.

BLACK-BOX JUSTICE

Forecasting criminal behaviour is difficult, surprisingly difficult. Psychiatrists and health professionals are regularly asked by courts to predict the probability that a defendant will commit a violent act in the long-term future. According to the American Psychiatric Association in a communication to the US Supreme Court, its 'best estimate is that two out of three predictions of long-term future violence made by psychiatrists are wrong'.[5] When they predict no violence, they are still wrong in one out of ten cases. Despite these sobering numbers, the US Supreme Court ruled that such testimony is legally admissible as evidence, noting that the experts 'were not always wrong . . . only most of the time'.[6] Alongside psychiatrists, judges have also been blamed for being unreliable. An infamous study in Israel made the headlines by concluding that judges are literally influenced by their guts. At the beginning of the day, judges granted parole to about two-thirds of the prisoners, a proportion that declined steadily over time to nearly zero. After the judges had a meal or snack break, the next prisoners in line once more had a two-thirds chance of being granted parole, and this chance steadily declined a second time towards zero as the judges grew hungry again.[7] After the next food break, the pattern repeated itself. Yet the authors had overlooked an important point: that the order of prisoners was not random. The court tried to complete all cases from one prison before a break, and unrepresented ones, who are less likely to be granted parole than those with attorneys, tended to be last in line. Thus, the story of the irrational judges guided by their appetite is a case of a correlation being all too quickly interpreted as a causation, without carefully analysing other factors. Even so, experts are humans and can indeed make judgement errors for a variety of reasons. For nearly a century, criminologists have reported that many poor people, people of colour and other vulnerable groups have been unfairly jailed.[8]

Here is where AI is called upon. Warning about the failures of human judgement, commercial companies urge shifting one's trust in humans to trust in software. The justification appears quite clear. In a first step, the algorithms could assist in improving judges' decisions. After all, we are told that an algorithm is impartial, has no prejudices and would never alter its evaluations on an empty stomach. In the next step, with more computing power, black boxes could populate the benches and automatically output guilty/not guilty decisions in a blink, with the years of sentence attached. In the final step, this program could extend to other challenges such as litigation, solve the problems of severe case backloads and send millions of judges, defence lawyers and prosecution lawyers into early retirement.

Black-box justice would finally resolve an old and enduring problem that even legal professionals have complained about: a surfeit of lawyers. A raft of bad lawyer jokes testifies to this sentiment:[9]

Q: *Why didn't the shark eat the lawyer?* A: *Professional courtesy.*
Q: *What are five lawyers at the bottom of the sea?* A: *A good start.*

Jokes aside, we are already moving towards black-box justice. In the US, the police arrest over 10 million people every year. After arrest, a judge first needs to decide whether the defendant is released until trial or retained in custody. Increasingly, judges and police rely on black-box risk-assessment tools to predict whether a defendant is likely to fail to appear at a court hearing, to reoffend at some point in the future or to commit a violent crime. The COMPAS algorithm alone has been used in US courts for over 1 million defendants to inform judges on bail recommendations and prison sentencing.[10] It is difficult to know how many sentences have actually been influenced, but it is my guess that not every judge would dare to contradict the precise risk scores delivered by an algorithm. Is that trust in a black box warranted? Can recidivism algorithms actually predict better than experienced judges?

The stable-world principle indicates that the answer is 'no'. Judges typically face decisions under considerable uncertainty. In these situations, complex algorithms are unlikely to succeed, and simple algorithms may be as good while also being transparent. But that is a hypothesis. Let us look at the evidence.

Ordinary People Can Be Just as Accurate

The COMPAS algorithm uses up to 137 features of a defendant and their past criminal record to predict whether they will commit a misdemeanour or felony within the next two years. How accurate is the algorithm? To find out, one could compare its predictions with those made by legal professionals, if such a study existed. Or one could use a lower bar, comparing the algorithm with ordinary people who have absolutely no experience in sentencing. One such study does exist.[11] The researchers behind it recruited 400 people via Amazon Mechanical Turk, an online crowdsourcing service. On this platform, anyone can earn a little cash by participating in scientific studies. Each participant was given short profiles of fifty real defendants (containing only seven features such as sex and age from the more than 130 features that COMPAS uses) and was asked to predict whether each defendant would reoffend within two years. We can assume that few of the participants were highly motivated to spend much time on each case: for making all fifty predictions they were paid as little as a dollar, with a small bonus if their predictions were accurate. As a consequence, most of these low-paid workers no doubt rushed through the task as hastily as possible. The results bowled over both legal scholars and the authors of the study.[12] COMPAS had predicted the behaviour of 65 per cent of the defendants correctly and erred on 35 per cent of the defendants (counting both false alarms and misses); the ordinary people, who knew next to nothing about recidivism, got it right just about as often.[13] And, if you take the majority vote of twenty ordinary people, they predicted 67 per cent correctly. The result is not limited to COMPAS alone. A review of it and eight other risk-assessment algorithms concluded that the accuracy of all nine of them has been found wanting.[14]

Let's stop a second and consider what that means. Say that you are standing trial. A black-box algorithm advises the judge that you are at high risk of committing another offence. Will your judge listen? The chances appear to be high. Now imagine that your judge is instead told that the greater part of twenty random people on Amazon Mechanical Turk believe that you are at high risk. What judge would trust judgements made in a few seconds by unqualified people online? Although, as we have seen, the expensive risk assessment tool fared no better than the general public, the nature of its being a black box imbues it with a mystical aura of power. It also impedes authorities from questioning how accurate such an algorithm actually is.

TRANSPARENT JUSTICE

Black-box algorithms have set off an emotional debate about being unfair to certain groups, such as the poor or people of colour. Yet there is an even more fundamental issue: transparency. Without transparency, it is hard to determine in the first place whether an algorithm is fair or not. For instance, ProPublica tried to reconstruct the COMPAS algorithm and concluded it is racially biased, while other researchers arrived at the opposite conclusion.[15] Lack of transparency also conflicts with many people's understanding of justice and dignity. Most of these problems could be avoided by using a transparent algorithm.

Decision lists are one type of transparent risk assessment tool that already exists. The CORELS algorithm is a machine learning tool that generates such lists from data on previous cases with crystal-clear logic.[16] Take the case of having to predict whether a defendant will be arrested within two years. The decision list is this: if the defendant is between eighteen and twenty years old and male, then predict arrest. If the defendant is between twenty-one and twenty-three and has two to three prior offences (whatever sex), then predict arrest too. If not, then check whether the defendant has more than three prior offences. If that's the case, predict arrest. In all other cases, predict no arrest (figure 7.1).

Note that only age, sex and prior offences enter the decision list. There is nothing mystical about it, no crystal ball hidden in a black box. What the machine-learning tool does is extract the most important features and determine the exact rule. Despite its simplicity, the decision list with only three features predicts arrest as accurately as COMPAS with its up to 137 features. This finding that black-box algorithms for predicting future arrest are no more accurate than transparent and simple algorithms is the rule rather than the exception.[17]

The decision list illustrates what I mean by *transparency*. The algorithm is not kept secret *and* it is also understandable:

> *An algorithm is transparent to a group of users if they can understand, memorize, teach and execute it.*

Looking at the decision list, you know exactly how the prediction is made. Decision lists increase transparency, make it easier to test for potential discrimination, save the costs of paying for secret algorithms and demystify the procedure. In the present case, the simple list is as good or bad as the complex secret algorithm. But a judge who likes to use algorithms as decision aids can at least readily use and understand these lists.

Another transparent tool that is more widely known is the *Public Safety Assessment* (PSA). Its purpose is to help judges decide whether a defendant should be released before trial. For instance, in order to

IF	age between 18–20 and sex is male	THEN predict arrest (within 2 years)
ELSE IF	age between 21–23 and 2–3 prior offences	THEN predict arrest
ELSE IF	more than three priors	THEN predict arrest
ELSE	predict no arrest	

FIGURE 7.1: A transparent algorithm for predicting whether a defendant will be arrested within the next two years (created by CORELS). The combination of these four rules is called a *decision list*.

predict the risk that a defendant will fail to appear at a court date, it uses only four features (figure 7.2). For the first three features, a 'yes' results in one risk point each; the last feature, 'prior failure to appear in the past two years', leads to two risk points; and if the defendant failed to appear twice or even more within that time frame, this makes four points. Defendants and judges can easily see what the features are and how these are weighted and look up on the internet how the final risk score is calculated.[18] Using different sets of features, the PSA also predicts new criminal activity, such as a violent offence prior to the defendant's case. Like the decision list (but unlike COMPAS), it is not commercial.

The logic of the PSA is similar to that of the pay-as-you-drive algorithm (figure 4.6): a point system with a small number of features scored by simple numbers. Just as in the case of telematic car insurance, transparent risk assessment allows defendants to adjust their behaviour, such as to avoid missing a court hearing. Changing their behaviour for the better is impossible if the algorithm is secret. Business secrets are one reason to prevent customers from understanding an algorithm, but it is not the only one. Another reason is complexity. Even when an algorithm is made public, it can be so complex that laypeople and professionals can barely figure out how a decision is made or a score is calculated. Transparent algorithms are not confined to decision lists or point systems; other possibilities are presented throughout this book.[19]

Transparency has many virtues. In emergency situations, it is

Feature	Risk points for 'yes'
Pending charge at the time of the arrest?	1
Prior conviction?	1
Prior failure to appear older than two years?	1
Prior failure to appear in the past two years?	once: 2 more: 4

FIGURE 7.2: A transparent risk assessment tool known as the Public Safety Assessment (PSA). Shown are the four features used to predict the risk of failure to appear at a court date. If the answer to any of the four questions is 'yes', then a number of risk points is assigned.

important that professionals have easy-to-memorize triage rules in order to execute these quickly and effectively. Transparency also helps determine whether an algorithm contains bias, such as racism. We can see that neither PSA nor the decision list above includes race as a feature. Still, we can't entirely rule out the possibility that the other features they look at are correlated with race. But again, their transparency makes it easier to check whether this might be the case, such as if one of the four questions was whether you live above 125th Street in Manhattan. When there are more than a hundred features, by contrast, race can be correlated with many of them, making it a huge task to identify the hidden biases.

Transparency alone, however, cannot guarantee that the resulting scores are any more accurate than those of black-box algorithms; in both cases the actual outcomes are fundamentally uncertain. In the case of the PSA, studies mostly report that it is moderate to good in its predictions.[20] A more important question is whether a risk assessment tool actually improves judges' decisions that would be made on their own, without any algorithms, and how it compares with other tools. When I searched for answers, the most striking result was the lack of studies that posed these questions.[21]

PREDICTIVE POLICING

Predictive policing has been marketed as a magic bullet. *Time* magazine named it one of the best fifty inventions of the year 2011.[22] Big data companies promise that their algorithms can predict the location of future crime scenes and identify persons at high risk of becoming an offender. That would make policing more objective and efficient. Police officers would no longer need to walk the streets to observe first-hand what's going on but could conveniently stay at their office desk and see what the program says. Chicago and Los Angeles were among the first to buy in and announce their predictive policing as prestige projects.[23]

In 2012, the Chicago Police Department introduced predictive policing software to determine which citizens are likely perpetrators or victims of crimes. The software scored people by analysing myriad factors, such as their criminal histories. The motto was, 'We know who they are'.[24] Within a few years, about 400,000 individuals ended up on a list, their risk scores included. This list did not undergo an independent check, nor was its impact measured. Eight years later, the Chicago Police Department quietly buried the programme after researchers from the RAND Corporation published a report with a devastating conclusion: there was no evidence that the programme had reduced violence. Instead, the obscure inner workings of the software created a high level of public fear and mistrust.

A year earlier, in 2011, the Los Angeles Police Department had launched Operation LASER to target violent repeat offenders and gang members with 'laser-like precision'. The image was of police officers functioning like trained surgeons who use laser technology to remove tumours.[25] Once again, people were put on a list, and it somehow happened that 89 per cent were not white, indicating that the software reflected the racial biases among white Americans. Eight years after LASER was introduced, the LAPD issued its own devastating report on the unreliability of the 'laser-like' risk scores and improperly trained personnel. It shut the programme down.

Nevertheless, companies have been aggressively moving into the rest of the world, claiming to make policing objective, transparent and effective. Not everyone buys into these promises. The Oakland Police Department cancelled the programme, worrying about discrimination against certain neighbourhoods and eroding community trust.[26] The Hamburg Police Department refused to purchase predictive policing software on the basis of marketing claims but did their own homework and studied its potential. The Police Department concluded that predictive policing cannot fulfil the hyped expectations and decided against acquiring the software.[27]

Why does predictive policing fail to meet the promises made? A typical answer is that more data are needed. In fact, just as much information is available for predicting crime as for predicting recidivism or the flu. The answer instead lies in the uncertainty surrounding human criminal behaviour. Too many factors determine who commits a crime and where, and it is not possible to identify these factors on the basis of past cases and predict future behaviour. The data may be 'dirty' and contaminated by racial or other prejudices, which leads to faulty risk scores and a negative impact on individuals. The positive lesson in the cases of

Chicago and Los Angeles is that journalists, civil society organizations and, finally, public commissions worked together to abolish a commercial pseudo-scientific project. In the case of Oakland and Hamburg, it was even stopped before it started.

An alternative to complex black-box algorithms in these or similar situations would be psychological AI. Consider geographic profiling and the case of a serial offender who has committed six armed robberies in a city within the last weeks. Where should the police begin searching for the criminal? Psychological AI analyses the intuitions of experts and turns their heuristics into algorithms. For instance, experts know that most offenders live in the area where the crimes happen. This intuition translates into the *circle heuristic*, which predicts that the offender lives within a circle whose diameter is defined by the distance between the two furthermost crime locations. Taking that strategy, the police might start searching at the centre of the circle, and work from there. When researchers tested the circle heuristic, they found that it predicted as well as or even better than commercial black-box algorithms, particularly when the number of offences was smaller than ten, which is usually the case.[28] In addition, when police officers were subsequently trained to use the circle heuristic systematically, they out-performed complex algorithms at locating offenders.[29]

As with predicting recidivism, psychological AI in the form of simple rules such as the circle heuristic can provide transparent alternatives to over-complicated and opaque geographic profiling algorithms. In my research, I have found that simple heuristics often match or out-perform complex algorithms in making predictions about healthcare outcomes, financial outcomes and other uncertain situations.[30] These heuristics can be used to augment expert decisions while enabling experts to understand their logic.

WHY ALGORITHMS CAN PERPETUATE DISCRIMINATION

Even its most enthusiastic fans largely concede that AI has a bias problem. Discrimination by gender or race has been reported for AI systems used by police, courts, employers, credit-scoring agencies and beyond. Personalized algorithms have offered the better-paid jobs to white males, and, as mentioned before, Google's image classification system notoriously identified a dark-skinned couple as 'gorillas'. AI is supposed to be neutral, objective and data driven, so how can it be unfair to women, people of colour or other marginalized groups?

It is important to understand what discrimination is and what it is not. Consider the Vienna Philharmonic, one of the best orchestras in the world. A music aficionado can identify the orchestra from the very first chord by its lustrous sound. Yet someone who is tone deaf might also do so with the help of their eyes rather than ears, by spotting the small number of female musicians. It took until 1997 and enormous public pressure before the first woman, a harpist, became a full member (she had already played in the orchestra for decades at low pay and was retired soon after). The fact that more men than women have been hired by orchestras worldwide is, by itself, not proof of discrimination. It could be that, among the best available players, more are male. However, if men are found to be preferred over women *who play equally good or better*, that is proof of discrimination. When blind auditions behind curtains were introduced with jurors who could not see the gender of the candidate, it became clear to everyone that orchestras had indeed discriminated against women. By 2020, the proportion of women in world-class symphony orchestras had reached about 40 to 45 per cent, up from 5 to 10 per cent in the 1970s.[31]

Like human jurors, algorithms may discriminate against women, people of colour or other marginalized groups. This can be relatively easily found out if the algorithm is transparent. Consider the pay-as-you-drive algorithm (figure 4.6). Neither gender nor race is part of the features it considers; thus, there is no evidence that it discriminates. The absence of gender or race information corresponds to a blind audition where this information is not available. However, if there are other features that correlate with gender or race, such as income or neighbourhood, bias might enter through the back door – although that can also be easily checked as long as the algorithm is transparent. If, by contrast, algorithms are secret and use many features, as COMPAS does, it can be quite difficult to detect. Discrimination is one strong reason why all sensitive algorithms should be made transparent.

Algorithms that are non-transparent by design, such as deep artificial neural networks, pose a greater problem. Here, the reason for discrimination is not that gender or race is used as a feature. The programmer does not even determine the features; the neural net finds its own. Instead, the data may be a source of discrimination. Consider philharmonic orchestras again. Assume a tech company trains a deep neural network to find the best players. It is fed the profiles of a hundred thousand applicants to top orchestras worldwide from the past fifty years, including information about whether or not they were hired. The network will soon find out that being male is a strong predictor and will reproduce the bias of the past.

This phenomenon occurs in other fields where women have been rare. For instance, Amazon's machine learning specialists built an algorithm that rates applicants for software development positions and other technical jobs based on their profiles.[32] The idea was to give the machine a hundred profiles, and it would spit out the top five candidates to be hired. To their surprise, the machine did not 'like' women. Once again, the bias was located in the data, which contained the profiles of applicants from the last ten years, the far majority of those who were hired were male. Removing applicants' first names did not help much; the AI found ways around this, such as inferring gender from the names of all-women colleges.

Discrimination also exists in facial recognition systems that are trained to tell whether a face is male or female. These systems are used, among others, to identify perpetrators from security video footage; errors can lead to wrong accusations of crime. In a study, three commercial gender classification systems from Microsoft, IBM and Face++ were shown portrait photos of males and females with lighter or darker skin.[33] When the systems classified a face as 'male', they made only 0 to 1 per cent errors if the men had lighter skin. But if the men had darker skin, the error increased to 1 to 12 per cent, depending on the system. When the systems classified a face as 'female', they were incorrect in 2 to 7 per cent of the cases if the woman had lighter skin, but in 21 to 35 per cent if she had darker skin. Every system made more errors with female faces than with male faces, and faces with darker skin than with lighter skin.

Where does the bias come from? It can be found in the pictures used to train the systems. About half of the photos were of white males, the rest mostly white females, while individuals with darker skin, particularly females, were few.

After the study was published, the three corporations whose commercial systems were tested quickly updated their systems and reduced the bias. Even after revision, however, the IBM system still had an error rate of 17 per cent for females with darker skin. IBM solved its discrimination problem in an ingenious way. It did not count all errors but only those where the system was more than 99 per cent confident that it was right, which allowed the company to report an error rate of only 3.5 per cent.[34] Most interestingly, the study did not appear to have an impact on corporations that were not named in it, such as Amazon and Kairos, who continued to have large error rates for darker females, confusing them with males. Naming may be shaming, but only for the named.

Neural Networks Can Increase Bias

Biased data are at the heart of discrimination, but deep neural networks may intensify the problem. Consider a case in point. A neural network was fed tens of thousands of pictures of human activities and taught to identify the activities and the genders of those portrayed.[35] These pictures had a typical gender bias, showing more men involved in outdoor activities such as driving and shooting, and more women microwaving and shopping. When the network then had to identify gender and activities in a new large set of pictures, the bias increased. For instance, when the activity was cooking, 67 per cent of the pictures were of women. The network, however, concluded that 84 per cent were women, misidentifying about half of the male cooks.

Why would a network intensify discrimination? One reason is that researchers evaluate a network's performance by the number of correct answers, not by the degree to which it discriminates. The network can actually increase performance by increasing discrimination. Say a network knows nothing except that two-thirds of the cooks are female. To attain the best results, it would guess that every cook is female, which means that two-thirds of the answers would be correct. This, of course, increases the bias to a maximum. To avoid amplifying the bias, the network could randomly guess that the cook is a woman for two-thirds of the pictures, and for one-third that it is a man. In that case, however, it would get only about 56 per cent of the answers right.[36] In general, if there is a bias in the data, amplifying it can lead to better performance than by trying to be 'fair'.

AI is not alone with its bias problem. The people at tech corporations who want to transform every aspect of our lives are predominantly male. *Wired* magazine reported that at leading machine learning conferences, only 12 per cent of the contributors were women, and that among Google's machine learning researchers, only 10 per cent were women.[37] This is a move backwards. Recall that in the early 1980s, almost 40 per cent of graduates in computer science were female. Dr Timnit Gebru, a staff research scientist at Google and one of the authors of the gender classification study, was one of the 1.6 per cent of Google's workforce who are women of colour. A new study that she co-authored found that Google's large language models – which try to produce what looks like meaningful new text and conversation – run the risk of reproducing the racist and sexist language embodied in the huge amounts of text from the internet on which they are trained.[38] Moreover, this training consumes enormous amounts of computing power and, thus, electricity, thereby producing substantial rises in carbon dioxide emissions. All of this business tends to benefit wealthy organizations, whereas climate change hits the poor communities first. When Google's leadership saw the paper, it decided to censor it and fired Gebru. Thousands of Google employees and supporters from academic and civil organizations signed a letter of protest in which they did not mince words: 'Dr Gebru is one of the few people exerting pressure from the inside against the unethical and undemocratic incursion of powerful and biased technologies into our daily lives.'[39]

AGAINST UNINFORMED CONSENT

In healthcare, *informed consent* refers to an ideal of how doctors and patients interact. Patients are informed in an understandable way about the treatment options, including their benefits and harms, and then permit the doctor to go ahead with their preferred option. Informed consent involves more than signing a form or clicking 'I accept'. It is *shared decision making*. The second half of the twentieth century has saw the spread of this ideal, overthrowing an earlier paternalism where doctors decided and patients had to agree – if they were even told what treatments would be performed on them.[40] Informed consent goes hand and hand with human dignity and an educated citizenship.

The informed consent forms in hospitals are a version of terms-and-conditions contracts, also known as terms-of-service contracts. Similar to when you lease a car, you get a contract that defines each side's benefits and obligations. To enable informed consent, the language needs to be understandable, clear and brief. The Harding Center for Risk Literacy, which I direct, is one of the organizations dedicated to making information about risks understandable and evidence-based, and the information communicated by health authorities and institutions is indeed improving from decade to decade.[41]

However, the twenty-first century has seen powerful attempts to reverse this positive development in online contracts such as terms-of-service agreements and privacy policies. Have you ever tried to read what you agree to online? We are constantly reminded to read the terms of service, but that is easier said than done. Consider *sign-in-wrap* agreements, which websites require you to accept. Unlike *clickwrap* contracts, where users have to click 'I agree', sign-in-wraps simply say that by signing in, the user agrees to the contract. Even if readers took the time to read these contracts, which are legally binding, could they understand what they are signing?

Study Privacy Policies for Thirty Days a Year

In healthcare, a rule of thumb is that consent forms should be written at the level of eighth grade at most. An analysis of the 500 most frequently visited US websites in 2018, such as Amazon, Airbnb and Uber, showed that the average sign-in-wrap was written at the level of 'fifteenth grade', which corresponds to the language in academic journals. In 70 per cent of these contracts, the *average* sentence length was longer than twenty-five words.[42] The authors of the study estimated that virtually all contracts, more precisely 498 out of 500, were unlikely to be understood by consumers. These contracts appear to be deliberately written in a way that dissuades the few who try to read them from continuing. In addition, privacy policies – which are required by law if users' data are collected – are much too long and abundant. To read the average privacy policy may take about ten minutes. To read all privacy polices one encounters in a year would require on average about thirty full workdays, according to the estimates of two Carnegie Mellon professors.[43] What is more, on some websites, you may be offered the choice to opt out of targeted ads, yet some services have been reported to override your intention, that is, to simply ignore your Do Not Track setting and continue tracking you without your knowledge.[44]

When we log in online, we enter the age of uninformed consent. At the same time, courts hold us responsible, whether or not we have read the terms and conditions. That is, the law expects consumers to read contracts, but suppliers have no obligation to make these comprehensible.

In healthcare, patients can say 'no' to a treatment; on the internet, users may be excluded from services if they do not accept the terms. If you do not agree to your smart bed sharing minute-by-minute data – your movements, position, heart rate, noises and other audio signals – with third parties whose identity is not revealed, then you are told that the company cannot guarantee your safety or provide desired features and services to you. You may ask, why can't you own a smart bed, thermostat, fridge and TV that do not send personal information to unidentified third parties?

To endow users with informed consent would be detrimental to many sources of profit in the digital world. That by itself explains why tech companies have little incentive to state in clear terms what they are doing. And it is not only tech companies: almost everyone in business on the internet is cashing in on personal information.

The One-Pager

Legislation has been slow to protect citizens from feeling helplessly adrift in this ever-changing business fashioned to be opaque, deceptive and confusing. This hesitancy is surprising given that proper regulation can work. Consider the practice of overly lengthy and opaque privacy policies. In 1999, it took only about two minutes to read Google's privacy policy. By 2018, reading time increased to thirty minutes. Yet that year, the European Union's General Data Protection Regulation went into effect, and Google reacted with a new policy that not only took half the time to read but was also more concise and comprehensible.

During my term on the Advisory Council at the German Ministry of Justice and Consumer Protection, we went even further and proposed making the one-pager the rule.[45] The terms of service should be written on a single page, maximum 500 words (to avoid small print), and the language used must be understandable to the average person. The terms need to lay open what personal information is extracted and to which third parties it is sent, as well as who owns your data, pictures and videos. So far, a few companies have followed suit and produced one-pagers. But more legal courage is needed to end the age of uninformed consent. To enforce transparent one-pagers, contracts that do not stand up to these requirements should be considered invalid by courts, and those who drafted them should be fined.

WHY DO WE USE BLACK-BOX ALGORITHMS WHEN WE DON'T NEED TO?

On the Advisory Council, we discussed many critical questions. Should consumers have the right to know why they are denied a loan or not invited for a job interview? Should credit scorers be obliged to reveal the features and weights of their algorithms to the public rather than only to data protection agents? Should business secrets be valued above the rights of citizens to understand their scores? Although such ethical issues were at the forefront, I soon noticed that one issue was taken for granted: that complex black-box algorithms are accurate. The idea that transparent rules might do just as well did not even remotely occur to most governmental officials.

Faith in Complexity and Opacity

In 2018, the analytics company FICO, Google and various universities organized a prestigious competition, the Explainable Machine

Learning Challenge. With the help of FICO, which provided data from thousands of individuals, including their credit history, the task was to create a complicated black-box model for predicting loan default and to explain the black box.[46] Competitions between algorithms are nothing new, but this was one of the first landmark events that acknowledged the need to make sense of complex black-box models. Even so, underlying the Challenge was the assumption that predicting loan default actually requires complex models. Only one of the teams that entered the contest, a group of researchers from Duke University, took a radically different approach. They developed and tested software that is understandable and includes visualizations that allow people to play with credit factors to see how these influence loan application decisions. Not only was the AI they developed transparent, but it was just as accurate at predicting loan default as deep neural networks and other complex black-box models. The team won the FICO Recognition Award for 'going above and beyond expectations with a fully transparent global model and a user-friendly dashboard'.[47]

The Challenge illustrates a deep faith in two propositions:

Faith in Complexity: Complex problems always need complex solutions.
Faith in Opacity: The most accurate algorithms must be inherently incomprehensible.

Put these two faiths together, and you get the belief in the *accuracy–transparency dilemma*: The more accurate the algorithm, the less transparent it will be. This dilemma is widely – and wrongly – believed to be generally true.[48] It holds in well-defined games and other stable situations, but not under uncertain conditions. As the one team participating in the Challenge showed, when predicting loan default, understandable AI can be as accurate as black-box AI. Here is the general insight:[49]

Transparency-meets-accuracy principle: Under uncertainty, transparent algorithms are often as accurate as black-box algorithms.

Nevertheless, black-box algorithms populate courts and other locations where high-stakes decisions are made, because of unconditional faith in complexity and in opacity. A second reason is that firms exploit this faith. Their salespeople knock on the doors of courts and police departments, just as pharmaceutical sales representatives persuade doctors to recommend their products to patients. Organizations that develop freely available and transparent risk-assessment products usually do not have the same number of resources to pay for extensive promotion. For instance, the decision list for predicting recidivism shown in figure 7.1 is free and little known, while the software licence of COMPAS is expensive and widely purchased. There is also another reason for favouring black boxes: defensive decision making. As a judge, if you are inclined to grant a defendant bail but the risk calculator establishes high risk, then you may change your mind to be on the safe side: if the defendant does commit another crime or threatens a witness, you would otherwise have some explaining to do.

'Less-Is-More' Is the Key to Explainable AI

Faith in complexity and opacity remains deeply ingrained and has misled leading scientists, bank and other business executives, the military and many others. In the US, for instance, the DARPA (Defense Advanced Research Projects Agency) project on explainable AI (XAI) assumes that understandability comes at the cost of accuracy.[50] As a consequence of this misunderstanding, it still features complex blackbox algorithms and tries to explain their workings in simple ways that are not necessarily correct. For instance, an explanation of how a deep neural network predicts loan default or classifies an object as a tank may have little to do with how the neural network actually works. These explanations are rough guesses at best, and incorrect at worst.

The true alternative is to replace complex algorithms with transparent ones whenever appropriate. This solution is based on the empirical finding that simple, transparent rules can match or beat black-box algorithms at making predictions under uncertainty. I've often seen this happen.[51] If you work for a retailer, you know how important it is to predict which previous customers are likely to return again in a given time frame. Many retailers have databases containing tens of thousands of customers, making it expensive to send all of them flyers or catalogues, especially when some are not likely to purchase anything again. A study with thirty-five retailers found that a simple rule used by experienced managers, known as the *hiatus heuristic*, predicted customers' new purchases even better than complex machine learning methods and sophisticated marketing models.[52] The hiatus heuristic is a version of the recency heuristic described above and relies on a single powerful cue, the most recent purchase: *if a customer has made a purchase within the last nine months, the customer is likely to purchase in the future, otherwise not.* (The hiatus – the number of months – can vary from business to business.) This rule is transparent and can be easily explained, dispensing with the need to try to explain more complicated methods in simple terms that are not necessarily correct.

Herein lies the key to a new understanding of explainable AI: to routinely test whether transparent algorithms work as well as complex ones in a particular situation, and, if so, to work with the simpler tools. That is the real future of explainable AI.

COUNTING KEYS

Transparent algorithms can be broken down into several families. The 'one-good-reason' family, as the name indicates, is made up of algorithms that base their prediction on a single but powerful reason.[53] As we have seen in the case of predicting the flu, one of these, the recency heuristic, can outperform big data analytics. A second family consists of algorithms using only a few reasons that are given different but simple weights, such as the pay-as-you-drive algorithm in figure 4.6 and the PSA. A third family is made up of short decision lists, such as the one for predicting recidivism. In machine learning, decision lists have also been around for a long time.[54] In what follows, I describe another family, known as *tallying*, that simply counts the reasons for and against a potential event.[55] All of these rules correspond to psychological AI, which, like human psychology, is particularly fit to deal with predictions under uncertainty.

The Keys to the White House

On 8 November 2016, more than a few people around the world could not believe their eyes. The polls, the election markets and big data analytics had predicted Hillary Clinton's victory by a large margin. 'If you believe in Big Data analytics, it's time to begin planning for a Hillary Clinton presidency,' announced columnist Jon Markman in *Forbes*.[56]

It the end, big data nose-dived. Admittedly, predicting who gets the keys to the White House is easier said than done. It is less like a lottery, where we know the probabilities of winning or losing, than like predicting the course of the flu or another viral infection. Statistician Nate Silver and his media business team FiveThirtyEight had correctly predicted the Obama victories but missed Trump's win in the primaries and, on election day, predicted a 71.4 per cent probability for Clinton. Two weeks before the election, when his estimate was 85 per cent in favour of Clinton, Silver discussed in detail how the probability depends on the assumptions made. If his model considered only data since 2000, as opposed to 1972, Clinton's chances would rise to 95 per cent. If it assumed a normal distribution of votes (a concept introduced by the mathematician Carl Friedrich Gauss; see figure 3.1), instead of fat tails (a concept featured in Nassim Taleb's book *Black Swan*), that would get Clinton 87 per cent, and if it assumed that state outcomes are not correlated with each other, that would boost her chance of winning up to 98.2 per cent.[57] Silver's valuable reflections bring an important insight home that is too often forgotten: *big data does not speak by itself.* Instead, the outcome depends on the assumptions made. More data and more computing power do not guarantee the truth. That's why statistical thinking matters.

Silver's discussion also reveals something equally interesting: it focuses on reasons for or against statistical models, not on the actual reasons why people might vote against Clinton and for Trump. It dispenses with psychological, political or economic theory. The alternative is to begin with the psychology of voters' reasons. That is precisely what Allan Lichtman, a distinguished professor of history, did.

Lichtman's was one of the rare dissenting voices among the mass of experts who predicted a clear win for Clinton. He predicted that Trump would win. It was not the first time he was right; he had predicted all elections correctly since 1984.[58] His method does not rely on number crunching with big data, nor does it deliver ostensibly precise probabilities of winning. It simply predicts who will win. The system is called 'Keys to the White House' and is based on a historical analysis of the reasons why Americans vote the way they do.

A key is a reason that matters for voters. There are thirteen of these, each stated as a proposition that can be answered by 'yes' or 'no'. A 'yes' favours election or re-election of the candidate from the incumbent party, and a 'no' does not.

Key 1: *Incumbent-party mandate*. After the midterm elections, the incumbent party holds more seats in the US House of Representatives than it did after the previous midterm elections.

Key 2: *Nomination contest*. There is no serious contest for the incumbent-party nomination.

Key 3: *Incumbency*. The incumbent-party candidate is the sitting president.

Key 4: *Third party*. There is no significant third-party or independent campaign.

Key 5: *Short-term economy*. The economy is not in recession during the election campaign.

Key 6: *Long-term economy*. Real annual per capita economic growth during the term equals or exceeds mean growth during the two previous terms.

Key 7: *Policy change*. The incumbent administration effects major changes in national policy.

Key 8: *Social unrest*. There is no sustained social unrest during the term.

Key 9: *Scandal*. The incumbent administration is untainted by major scandal.

Key 10: *Foreign or military failure*. The incumbent administration suffers no major failure in foreign or military affairs.

Key 11: *Foreign or military success*. The incumbent administration achieves a major success in foreign or military affairs.

Key 12: *Incumbent charisma*. The incumbent-party candidate is charismatic or a national hero.

Key 13: *Challenger charisma*. The challenging-party candidate is not charismatic or a national hero.

You may note something peculiar. Almost all the keys concern the incumbent party and their candidate, only a single one (the last key) concerns the challenger. Some of the keys require no judgement, such as whether the incumbent-party candidate is the sitting president, while others, including charisma, do. Lichtman dealt with this problem by defining the rare charismatic leaders such as Dwight Eisenhower and John F. Kennedy, and settling 'yes' or 'no' before the election. In the case of Clinton versus Trump, neither was classified as charismatic.

The question is, how should the keys be combined into a prediction? The knee-jerk reflex of many data scientists would be to develop a scoring system like those in online dating or credit scoring, where each key is given an 'optimal' weight. Yet there haven't been many presidential elections to base the scores on, and irregular voting behaviour makes the task even more difficult. Instead, Lichtman developed a transparent algorithm that simply counts the nos:

If six or more keys are negative ('no'), the challenger will win.

This tallying rule is radically simple. In late September of 2016, weeks before the election, Lichtman considered the keys to be 'settled' and made a count.[59] Six keys turned against Hillary Clinton, the incumbent-party candidate.

Key 1: The Democrats were crushed in the midterm elections.
Key 3: The sitting president was not running.
Key 4: There was a significant third-party campaign by libertarian Gary Johnson, anticipated to acquire 5 per cent or more of the votes.
Key 7: There was no major policy change in Obama's second term.
Key 11: Obama did not have any smashing foreign policy successes.
Key 12: Hillary Clinton is not charismatic in comparison to, say, Franklin Roosevelt.

Six negative cues meant that Trump was predicted to win. Six is the minimum required, which reflects that the outcome of the election was close and certainly not easy to predict. It is worth pointing out a caveat. The rule is intended to predict who will win the majority vote, which Trump did not. But no prediction system is perfect, and Lichtman's tallying rule came closer to the end result than the polls, prediction markets and big data analytics.[60]

The Keys to the White House is transparent. Its transparency enables us to see the theory behind the predictions. And there is indeed a theory behind them, unlike in the typical machine learning exercise, which is about getting the best prediction, no matter how. As mentioned, almost all keys concern the incumbent party and its candidate. They relate to the economy, social unrest, foreign policy successes, scandal and policy innovation. That means if people perceived that the country fared well in the previous term, the candidate of the incumbent party will be elected. If a challenger like Trump wins, the victory has little to do with him personally, but solely with how people perceived the incumbent party's performance in the previous term and with their expectations regarding the party's candidate.

Many were flabbergasted on election day, asking what in the world had driven Americans to vote for a man who had insulted women, Muslims and the Pope, among many others. The radical logic underlying the tallying rule suggests that this is the wrong question. US voters did not vote for Trump; they voted against Obama and Clinton. Forget TV debates, raising large amounts of money and investing in advertising. Do not believe that campaign managers and consultants had a large impact on the outcome. If the theory underlying the keys is right, there is a positive message to political parties: focus on governance, not on costly advertising and campaign tactics.

WANTED: THE RIGHT TO TRANSPARENCY IN SCORING

In a black-box society, people in power use software to better predict and modify the behaviour of the others, without disclosing their algorithms. Why are particular people denied bail or credit and others not? Why does YouTube's recommender system steer us towards less fact-based and more extreme videos?[61] The characteristic feature of black-box societies is not the absence of transparency, but its asymmetry, like a one-way mirror.[62] Black box societies have existed since time immemorial. For centuries, ordinary Europeans were unable to read. For them, the Bible and other sources were black boxes written in Latin or Greek, which only the educated from wealthier circles understood. With the help of the printing press, invented by Johannes Gutenberg, translators such as Martin Luther opened the black box. Thanks to this technological breakthrough, books and translations could gradually be made accessible to everyone. Now people could find out what the Bible actually said. Gutenberg's invention levelled the disparity between priest and layperson, between initiated and follower. When the internet spread in the 1990s, physicians envisioned a similar revolution: 'The internet can help us to level the disparity between doctor and the patient, the infallible and the uninformed.'[63] We may need another Gutenberg to open the black boxes that predict and modify people's behaviour.

One of our proposals at the Advisory Council for Consumer Affairs was that *all black boxes used to score people and have serious consequences for their lives should be made transparent to the general public and subject to quality control.*[64] Serious consequences can occur in health scoring, credit scoring, recidivism risk assessment and predictive policing, among others. The proposal concerns algorithms that are imposed on people, not those chosen deliberately for entertainment or personal growth, such as video games or love algorithms. Disclosure should include all features of an algorithm as well as its logic (such as a decision list or a point system, as in figures 7.1 and 7.2).

When we discussed the proposal with international scoring companies, they raised legitimate objections. One was that their algorithms are business secrets. But that was exactly the point of the proposal: to change the law and rank people's rights above commercial profit. Moreover, telematic and health insurers already make their scoring algorithms fully transparent, and it does not seem to hurt them. The next objection was that people would not understand the source code (the program of the algorithm), so making it transparent would keep it in the black box. But we were not asking them to disclose the source code, which would indeed be of little help for most consumers, but rather to disclose the features and the logic of the algorithm. Knowing the features would allow consumers to find out why, for instance, they pay high interest for a loan. It might simply be because they live in an apartment house in which some tenants didn't pay back their loan in time. That's called geo scoring.

The companies' next objection was that there is no way to make deep neural networks transparent. Although that is true, we found that commercial scoring systems for credit, health, telematics and recidivism rarely, if ever, rely on neural networks. A final objection was that if users knew the features, they could change their behaviour and game the algorithm. Yet that is exactly one of the stated purposes of credit scoring, health scoring or telematic scoring: to lead people towards healthier or more financially sound behaviour. For instance, if people find out that owning too many credit cards is one reason for their low credit score, they can act on this. Gaming is only a problem when algorithms use proxies instead of the real features, such as when a health insurer gives customers bonus points for joining a gym rather than for actually exercising there.

In the European Union, the General Data Protection Regulation (GDPR) marks the start of a new era in privacy law. It requires that 'meaningful information about the logic involved' in automated decision making be provided and that people 'have the right not to be subject to a decision based solely on automated processing' that affects them 'legally' or 'similarly significantly'.[65] Yet the moment a human decision-maker appears at the end of the chain, as with judges and police, these regulations no longer apply. In general, the GDPR remains highly abstract, showing that it has identified a regulation problem but not yet resolved it. Meanwhile, hundreds of mathematicians have called to stop all work on predictive policing, demanding that the algorithms undergo a public audit to prevent abuses of power.[66] People have protested against the secrecy of credit-scoring companies, demanding the legal right for all of us to look at the logic behind the algorithms that predict and modify our behaviour. Governmental authorities are called upon to become more aware of the motivation behind these algorithms, and of the persistent lack of quality control.

Secrecy and mystique are one aspect of the 'black box'. Yet the term has a double meaning; it also refers to a recording device. In the next chapter, we deal with this other side of the black box.

8

Sleepwalking into Surveillance

'It's time to start paying for privacy, to support services we love, and to abandon those that are free, but sell us – the users and our attention – as their product.'

Ethan Zuckerman, inventor of the pop-up ad.[1]

'I imagined the future SmartFridge stationed in my kitchen, monitoring my conduct and habits, and using my tendency to drink straight from the carton or not wash my hands to evaluate the probability of my being a felon.'

Edward Snowden[2]

One popular episode of the British TV series *Black Mirror*, called 'Nosedive', plays in a future world where each person wears smart contact lenses that zoom in on every other person in sight, be it at a party or on the underground train. The lenses immediately display the others' names and their social scores. Similar to Amazon products, everyone has a score, from 1 to 5. No matter what you do, your behaviour is rated by others: in a restaurant, the waiter scores you and you score the waiter; at work, your boss scores you and you score your boss; in a taxi, the driver scores you and you score the driver. Scoring is made easy: all you need to do is type a score into your smartphone and point it at the person in question. Living in this future, Lacy, an attractive young woman, wants to move to a better part of the city. Her score is 4.2, too low for an affordable apartment in that neighbourhood, for which she needs at least 4.5. Lacy dutifully practises smiling in her mirror. She does everything to please other people and behave in a way that will win her more points. Increasingly, Lacy's life revolves around her score. She has become remote-controlled by others' ratings in order to move to a location that others have rated as desirable. In the episode, as its title indicates, her efforts did not end well.

Many who have seen 'Nosedive' are appalled by this vision of a world in which only one thing counts: one's score. But the same people who react so adversely engage in various forms of scoring themselves without much thought. They rate the Uber driver, restaurants, doctors, hospitals, hotels and tax accountants, and distribute 'likes' to posts and 'hearts' to pictures. Scores are becoming the hard currency for trustworthiness, not unlike for Lacy. Eyeglass computers that record what wearers are seeing and hearing already exist and, similar to security cameras, alter how people comport themselves in public so that socially accepted behaviour increases.[3] They could easily be adapted to display the names and scores of everyone around. Wouldn't it be handy to see immediately how trustworthy a person is, instead of finding out the hard way?

SOCIAL CREDIT SYSTEMS

Credit scores such as the FICO score try to measure your credit worthiness, that is, the likelihood that you will pay your debts in time. The engineer Bill Fair and mathematician Earl Isaac introduced these scores in the 1950s, when they created Fair, Isaac and Company – thus the name FICO. The score is a number between 300 and 850, determined by payment history, debt burden, length of credit history and recent credit enquiries, among others. Your neighbours' credit scores also matter; if the person next door defaulted on a credit, your score may go down. Almost everyone has a score, even those who are not aware of it. Banks, telephone companies and employers use your score to determine whether you will be considered worthy of a loan, a phone contract, a job or an apartment. When you order a pair of shoes from an online shop, you may not notice that your credit score is being checked while you make a few clicks to finalize the purchase.

Online shoppers are subject to these credit checks all around the world. The result may determine the payment options you are given. You won't even see the options you are denied.

Social credit scores try to measure your trustworthiness in all respects, not just financial honesty. They are like FICO scores but integrate whatever data can be gathered about you. These may include previous speeding tickets, your criminal record, your commitment at work, your engagement in voluntary social services, the degree to which you fulfil your family duties, your political statements on social media, the websites you watch and your entire digital footprint. Crossing the street at a red light means losing points; visiting your elderly parents brings points. Playing video games for too long may cost you points; watching parenting lessons or learning foreign languages will add points. If you have online friends with low scores, that may also lower your own score. This system influences your behaviour best if your social credit score is made public, just as people's scores in 'Nosedive' are and the count of 'likes' or 'hearts' on social media that everyone can see. People with a low score may feel ashamed and worry about what others will think of them. The moment you begin to worry, you have swallowed the bait.

'Nosedive' is science fiction, but social credit scores are not. Led by China, various governments in Asia, South America and Africa, including Thailand, Myanmar, Vietnam, Venezuela and Tanzania, have introduced social credit systems for individuals and businesses, or announced intentions to do so.[4] In addition to public shaming, incentives and penalties are added. Those with high scores are rewarded perks, such as access to cheaper credits and free healthcare checks, while thousands of people with low scores have been denied access to aeroplanes and fast bullet trains, and their children denied access to the best schools. People have begun to unfriend others on their social media on the basis of their scores. In lonely hearts ads, young men and woman advertise their social credit score next to their age, weight and interests. Nobody is forced to do so, but an ad without a score may raise suspicion. In an online survey of participants of social credit systems in China, 94 per cent said that they have changed their behaviour to positively influence their social credit score – they adhered to traffic regulations, reduced time playing online games, volunteered for community service, shared different content online and used mobile payment apps, among others. Fifty per cent said they had already shared their score with family and friends.[5] What counts as proper behaviour is determined by governments and big technology companies, unlike in the world of 'Nosedive', where everyone can up or down everyone else's score.

Chinese society is rooted in a Confucian version of collectivism, where the 'greater good' dominates individual rights. It has a long history of social control, best known from Mao's Cultural Revolution. Digital technology for mass surveillance took off with the Beijing Olympics 2008, for fear of terrorist attacks on participants and the public, and became amplified in response to the 2009 Xinjiang conflict with separatist groups. China is also striving to control the problems emerging from large parts of the population relocating from rural to urban areas. With digital technology, surveillance is now 24/7. Its goal is to improve people's moral behaviour, eliminate corruption and create a culture of 'sincerity' and 'harmony'. Surveys indicate that the vast majority of Chinese citizens are in favour of this system, even more those with higher education.[6] Many believe that it provides a true alternative to democracy, fostering sincerity, harmony and economic growth for all.

Like credit scoring, social credit systems have a double function: to protect people and influence their behaviour. Credit scorers offer their services to protect businesses from fraudulent customers who don't pay their bills; otherwise, honest customers would have to pay higher prices to compensate for fraud. As a consequence, more people pay their bills on time, avoid owning too many credit cards and do not overspend. Similarly, governments justify social credit systems because these protect citizens from selfish free riders, criminals and terrorists. To avoid punishment, such as being barred from purchasing a plane ticket or seeing one's face and address on a downtown billboard for having jumped a red light, more citizens respect laws and social norms, which in turn increases social stability. In the Western press, these systems are often called 'Orwellian' projects, which misses the point. Social credit systems are more in the spirit of B. F. Skinner's *Beyond Freedom and Dignity*. The Harvard psychologist Skinner declared freedom to be our greatest problem: it allows people to exploit others and their environment. His proposed solution to the problem was a system of strict behaviour control that rewards fair and responsible social behaviour. If Skinner had lived to see social credit systems, he might have been delighted to see his methods of behaviour modification applied to more than a billion people in the world. The difference is that in Skinner's view positive reinforcement alone, not punishment, is effective in encouraging social behaviour. Apart from that, the digital age offers the technology to turn his vision into reality.

The Slippery Slope into Social Scoring

Social credit scores with carrots and sticks attached often make the headlines in Western countries, largely because they are seen as incompatible with the Western ideal of a democracy that values freedom and privacy. Yet Western attitudes towards privacy appear to be shifting towards Chinese ones, adapting to what digital technology offers. And it seems to be happening faster than we are willing to recognize. Take Germany, the land of data protection and privacy. In their history, Germans learned the hard way about the value of privacy during the Third Reich and the German Democratic Republic, regimes that surveilled, controlled and suppressed their citizens. In these eras, shrugging one's shoulders and saying 'I have nothing to hide' would have meant conforming to the injustices of either system. As a reaction to this history, the first article in the German Constitution addresses human dignity.

Given their past, one might think that Germans are united in rejecting surveillance, and particularly a social credit system for behaviour modification. Yet they appear to be shifting their stance. In 2018, only 9 per cent of Germans thought that a social credit system was a good idea for their future.[7] By 2019, the figure had already risen to 20 per cent.[8] Similar enthusiasm was recorded in Austria, particularly among the political right.[9] Even Germans appear to be getting used to the fact that their smartphones, smart TVs and smart cars are already recording their steps – why not get an additional few bonuses from the government for behaving properly?

Credit companies, health insurers, car insurers, Payback, Google, Amazon, Microsoft, Facebook, IBM, Apple and everyone who asks you to accept cookies collect data about you. These companies build their own secret profiles of you. This may seem no big deal, because the data are not added up into a single credit score. Now imagine a data broker who collects data from thousands of these sources and creates a profile for every person, which can be used to calculate a social credit score. This is no fantasy; the companies already exist. Data brokers such as Acxiom and Oracle Data Cloud advertise these services, and work on constructing a comprehensive profile for every citizen. In the US, Acxiom has gathered health data on 250 million consumers, including prescriptions, medical history and data from hospitals, labs and health insurers.[10] It also includes criminal records, voter records, item-level purchase data across hundreds of thousands of stores and pharmacies and real-time location data from mobile apps and from tens of thousands of sensors physically placed in malls, airports, cinemas and college campuses. Even homebodies are not free on surveillance: Acxiom collects second-by-second TV viewership data and everything else your smart TV records about you. Personal profiles are sold to banks, insurers, credit card issuers, healthcare providers and governments, including your email address, phone number, IP address and postal address. Acxiom claims to have collected data on more than 700 million people worldwide, and up to 3,000 data points for each individual. Not all of what they collect is accurate. Nevertheless, Facebook has purchased data about their users from brokers, containing all these errors.

In popular culture, Facebook has been branded the villain in profiling its users, yet data brokers track us much more intrusively. We need to talk about the entire data broker industry, not just Facebook and the apps it owns, such as Messenger, WhatsApp and Instagram. And we are silently profiled by other organizations we would never think of. Graduates from major US universities discovered to their surprise that their alma mater collects dossiers about them, more than one hundred pages in length and compiling everything from marriage and divorce to financial status broken down into liquid and illiquid assets, in order to find out how to target them to donate.[11]

Companies such as Acxiom use the same technology that enables China's social credit system. Yet they collect the data as surreptitiously as possible, while China is at least upfront about doing so. Openly or secretly, commercial companies and governments alike build a world of surveillance. Being watched will be our future – unless people, legislators and courts intervene to stop the scoring of the public.

PRIVACY ISN'T WORTH A DAMN

Privacy refers to the right not be subjected to invasions of one's private sphere by government, corporations and individuals. It includes the right to be left alone, to prevent intrusions to one's physical space and to maintain a sphere of intimacy. Privacy is not a central value in every culture, nor has it been one throughout Western history. It is primarily a product of the nineteenth and twentieth centuries. When postal services introduced the postcard in the 1870s, the reaction was moral outrage because people believed the motivation was to spy on their private correspondence. In the 1980s, hundreds of thousands of angry Germans went on the streets and protested against a governmental census that asked for private data, such as date of birth, gender, personal status and education. Americans have been taught to guard their social security number carefully; otherwise, someone might open a bank account or apply for a loan in their name.

Most Westerners react with horror and repugnance when hearing about the erosion of privacy by social credit systems in other countries. The media disparagingly note how useful these systems would have been for the Spanish Inquisition, the KGB and the East German secret police. As often occurs with such outbursts of aversion, however, there is a paradox. The same people who complain about social credit systems are willing to hand over their personal data to commercial companies without a blink: what they buy, where they are all day and with whom, what websites they visit, whether they pay their bills on time, and when they visit a doctor and for what purpose. The discrepancy between privacy declarations and actual behaviour has a name:

Privacy paradox: The same person who claims to be worried about privacy is not willing to pay a penny for it. Rather, they give their private information away on social media and other platforms without much thought.

The term *privacy paradox* was originally used in a study that reported that US undergraduate students said they wanted to keep personal information private but nevertheless posted it on Facebook.[12] The students did not seem to realize that Facebook is a public space where parents and future employers can read the entries. Yet the privacy paradox is more general; it even exists when people are aware that they are being surveilled and their data collected. More people in Germany than in any other European country are aware that free internet services take their data and analyse it.[13] More than three-quarters say they are concerned about privacy in the digital age.[14] If they are concerned about privacy in the social media and also well informed about what happens with one's data, then they should be willing to pay a fee for the service, as they do for Netflix, radio, TV and other services, instead of paying with their data. How much is privacy worth?

In 2019, I conducted a survey together with an insurance company, where we asked a representative sample of 3,200 people in Germany: what do you think is the greatest danger of digitalization? Half of the respondents (51 per cent) said loss of privacy, namely that their personal data are collected and made accessible to companies and governments.[15] Then we asked: if you could pay for social media – Facebook, WhatsApp, Instagram and all others – in exchange for keeping your personal data, how much would you be willing to pay per month?

Here is the sobering truth:

Nothing	75 per cent
Up to 5 euros	18 per cent
6 to 10 euros	5 per cent
More than 10 euros	2 per cent

I was taken aback by the answers. Three-quarters were not willing to pay a penny! If privacy is truly the greatest concern for half of these people, why is it not worth anything? After all, the social platform companies need some source of revenue. One might speculate that young people are probably those least willing to pay. That was not the case. The unwillingness to pay with a fee instead of with one's personal data was similar for all age groups, from eighteen-year-olds to those over sixty-five. Only 7 per cent were willing to pay six euros or more. At first I thought that the privacy paradox may be specific to Germans, for whatever reason. But it is not.

In another study by Norton LifeLock, participants from sixteen countries or regions were asked whether they are concerned about their privacy. On average, 83 per cent of participants said they are somewhat or strongly concerned. The lowest concern was in the Netherlands, with 66 per cent, but that's still a majority. The highest was in China, Mexico and Taiwan, where over 90 per cent were concerned. Then the same people were asked whether they would be willing to pay at least a dollar a month to ensure protection of their personal information on all social media. On average, less than a third were willing to pay a single dollar. For instance, in the US, 85 per cent of participants said they were concerned about privacy but only 28 per cent were willing to pay a dollar for privacy. The willingness to pay varied strongly between countries and regions (figure 8.1). People in the United Arab Emirates, Brazil, Mexico and China were most willing to pay a dollar, compared with very few in Germany, Australia, Canada, New Zealand and the Netherlands. All in all, the privacy paradox appears particularly pronounced in Europe, the US and the Commonwealth countries.

Why would so many people say they are very concerned about privacy and at the same time be reluctant to pay even the smallest amount?

FIGURE 8.1: The privacy paradox by country/region. Percentage of people aged 18+ who are willing to pay $1 per month for social media in return for keeping their personal data. The study included 16,000 adults (aged 18+), 2019.

When asked why, a typical answer is 'I have nothing to hide.' But then why would one be concerned about privacy in the first place? And how readily would any of us hand over our smartphone to a stranger on the street so that they can download its contents? That's essentially what Google, Facebook and others do without asking us – that's the deal we make with them by paying with our data rather than a fee. You may think that you are just one of the millions of users and that what you do is of no interest to the rest of the world. Yet companies may try to infer whether you are inclined to depression and an easy target for persuasion, or pregnant so that you buy their pregnancy products, if you are an undecided voter who can be swayed, if you are having an affair and with whom, what your boss and colleagues think of you and whether you have a severe medical condition. Those data can be of great interest to advertisers, health insurers, political parties, private detectives, employers and quite a few others. Similarly, your smartphone and your smart car send minute-by-minute information about where you are, even if you aren't actively using them. Access to that information may attract other groups of people, including burglars who want to know whether you are at home or stalkers who want to know where to find you. The business of stalkers – following, watching or harassing others, often former partners, to create fear and do harm – has become much easier. In fact, social media and surveillance apps on phones have created a stalker's paradise. As one female victim reported, 'my abuser magically knows where I am'.[16] These are just a few of the multitude of reasons why it's in our best interest to maintain some degree of privacy.

The two features digital technology offers, convenience and surveillance, conflict with privacy. Many people feel helpless and cannot see any other options. Others prefer immediate convenience over long-term loss of privacy. Still, it is remarkable that most people are not willing to pay even a dollar a month to regain their privacy. Some of them might not trust social media corporations to honour such a deal, or believe that other agencies will collect their data anyhow. Whatever the reasons, the privacy paradox may well soon become a strange blip in history. Perhaps surveillance will one day be seen as nothing more than a natural byproduct of convenience – nothing worth worrying about.

Newspeak: Privacy Is Theft

In Orwell's *Nineteen Eighty-Four*, the ultimate art of thought control is called 'Newspeak'. Newspeak is a new language that determines what you can think and what you cannot. Its purpose is to express the world view of an ideology and to make thinking differently unthinkable. Newspeak does so by altering the meaning of concepts and even inverting them to stand for the contrary. In Newspeak, war is peace, freedom is slavery, and ignorance is strength. It could well be that the privacy paradox will be resolved in a similar way. Privacy is theft. Surveillance is sharing and caring.[17]

When users pay with their data as opposed to their money, withholding personal information might well be considered theft. This business model requires eroding users' privacy to make money from their data. Facebook is a prime example. It originated in an act of privacy violation.

Hot or Not was a website founded in 2000, where users could score women's and men's attractiveness on a scale from 1 to 10. Voicing opinions about the looks of women passing by or whistling at them is a tired old game, but now at least both sides could rate each other. Soon, Hot or Not morphed into various dating services and inspired the creation of the first social media sites.[18] It also stimulated the invention of YouTube, which was originally intended as a video version of Hot or Not where people uploaded videos of themselves, but failed at drumming up sufficient video material (if TikTok had then existed, which makes it easy to create selfie videos, YouTube might have ended up as the largest dating platform).

Hot or Not also provided the inspiration for the first version of Facebook, conceived by Mark Zuckerberg in 2003, then an undergraduate at Harvard. It was called FaceMash and used pictures of female Harvard undergraduates. Zuckerberg had hacked into the websites of Harvard's dormitories to gather pictures from the 'face books', which originally were paper-based directories containing photos of the women in Harvard's dormitories. Without asking the women or the houses for permission, he then posted their photos in pairs next to each other and asked users to rate which woman was 'hotter'. Harvard University quickly shut down the site for violating individual privacy and copyright. A year later, the first version of what was now called Facebook was launched for Harvard students and rapidly spread across the globe.

Since this initial breach, Facebook has attempted numerous attacks on users' privacy in order to monetize their data. For instance, in 2007, Facebook introduced Beacon, a program that allowed advertisers to track users through the internet and disclosed users' purchases to their personal network of friends. To illustrate, in a violation of the Video Privacy Protection Act, Beacon showed on the news feed the titles of the videos users had rented from Blockbuster Video. After a massive protest, Zuckerberg apologized, and Facebook paid $9.5 million as part of a settlement. Two years later, Facebook changed their users' privacy settings without warning or asking permission, a practice that made personal posts public, and which the federal government called 'unfair and deceptive'. In response to the protest, Zuckerberg declared that the rise of social media means that people can no longer expect privacy.[19] He may in fact be right, but note that he was talking about a select group of people. Facebook managers tend to use all means to shield their private lives, and their employees typically have to sign non-disclosure contracts that bind them to silence, unless they want to risk legal prosecution. The surveillance business model requires that users alone, not the managers and actual customers of tech companies, relinquish their privacy. That's the deal, plain and simple.

Since then, privacy violations have continued and been tolerated by many users for whom Facebook is the main platform for conducting their social lives. In 2018, the British *Observer* and the *New York Times* revealed that Cambridge Analytica, a political consultancy, had extracted personal data from millions of Facebook accounts and secretly used it to craft political ads targeted at unknowing users. Facebook knew about this problem since 2015 but did little to remedy it. Instead, the technology company threatened to sue the Guardian Media Group, which owns the *Observer*, if they publicized the scandal.[20] Only after another wave of public outcry did Facebook promise to reduce the amount of data shared with third parties and make it easier for users to control privacy settings. Following that scandal, hashtags to delete Facebook went viral. But these had next to no impact: a month later, Facebook announced that its membership had actually grown.

Facebook collects heart-rate data and ovulation data, among others, from apps and tries to infer from posts whether young people are feeling stressed, defeated, overwhelmed, anxious, useless or a failure.[21] All that information is supposed to enable its customers to target users with the right ads at the perfect moment. That reminds me of earlier eras, such as in sixteenth-century France, when neighbours would have known everything about you and listened to every creak of the stairs. Under those conditions, little room for privacy existed, and the iota that was left was easily filled by gossip. In such a culture, everyone was watching and policing everyone else 24/7. At that time, people like you and me were owned and reigned over by sovereigns, the sole inhabitants who were not constantly subject to public scrutiny (at least they were walled away from the masses). These sovereigns dictated the terms of ordinary people's lives in exchange for protection and other services. Today, tech companies are the new nobility that dictate the terms, written at such length and in barely comprehensible language so that the modern subordinate simply clicks and accepts. These terms may include the rights to your personal data, photos, videos and other products. As Wikipedia illustrates, there is an alternative to this autocratic vision of the internet.

PAY WITH YOUR MONEY, NOT PRIVACY

For some, the dawn of the digital age felt like the French Revolution of 1789, without the blood. For others, it felt like 1989, when the people of East Germany toppled a regime that had controlled the media and kept their citizens under surveillance. Twenty years later, during a wave of demonstrations in the Middle East and North Africa known as the Arab Spring in 2010 and 2012, social media began indeed to play a substantial role in coordinating public protests. The Arab Spring was the proof that fuelled a new excitement about the liberating force of the internet. Everyone can know everything. Secrets are a word of the past. Open access to knowledge for all humans is possible. The world will be like science in its ideal form, not politics and marketing, free of censorship and profit interests – or even more liberated than science, where a handful of publishing companies charge prohibitive fees for open access to articles. The internet once was the big dream of liberty, equality and fraternity.

When in their mid-twenties, Sergey Brin and Larry Page, the young founders of Google, had a similar vision. In 1998, as mentioned in the first chapter, they criticized other search engines that relied on advertisement for income, arguing that advertising money distorts what is listed at the top. In their own words, 'advertising funded search engines will be inherently biased towards the advertisers and away from the needs of the consumers' and that it is 'crucial to have a competitive search engine that is transparent and in the academic realm'.[22] After the dot-com crisis hit Silicon Valley in 2000, startups were forced to shut, traffic to Google's website was surging, and its top venture capitalists pressured Google's founders.[23] Finally, Brin and Page caved in, did a volte-face and built an advertising-based business model whose algorithms are now among the best-kept secrets in the world. Borrowing from Christian terminology, one might call this turn to an ad-based business model the 'original sin' of the internet.[24] Users were driven out of the paradise of knowledge to become the object of surveillance. After Page and Brin made personalized advertisement their business model, a spot in paradise was reserved for Google's new customers, the companies who paid them for placing targeted ads.

Surveillance Capitalism

To deliver a service in exchange for personal data rather than cash is a new form of economy, known as *surveillance capitalism*.[25] It was perfected by Google and imitated by Facebook and others. Data about users are collected and profiles are constructed that allow advertisers to target those who are most likely to click on the ad and, eventually, make a purchase. The advertiser pays the platform for every click, impression or purchase a user makes. To function, this business model requires secretly invading people's privacy, and more invasion promises better personalized targeting. Unlike industrial capitalism, which manufactures and trades physical goods, surveillance capitalism collects and analyses personal data. It is extremely important to understand that surveillance capitalism is not an inevitable consequence of a smart world. It is a new business model invented by human beings to make profit. A smart world enables unforeseen possibilities for surveillance, but would function more healthily without it.

How did we get there? Consider the icon of surveillance capitalism, 'cookies', the bits of code that pass information between your computer and servers of tech companies. So-called third-party cookies are used by companies to track and compile a user's long-term record of browsing, such as which websites the person has looked up and when. When cookies were developed in the 1990s, there was serious concern about privacy. For instance, in 2000, the US government banned cookies from all federal websites, and in April 2001, Congress was debating bills that included regulating cookies.[26]

Yet something unexpected happened. With the trauma of 9/11, everything changed. Fear of terrorism pushed privacy concerns back in favour of security. Surveillance technology suddenly became of great interest to governments. The US government launched the Patriot Act, limiting laws that protected civil liberties. The UK, France and Germany followed, implementing similar acts. The Total Information Awareness (TIA) programme and subsequent programsme allowed US tech companies to collect data with few restrictions and in turn obliged them to deliver the data to the government if requested. Its official goal was to detect and identify foreign terrorists before they attempt an assault. The TIA programme was abruptly cancelled after the public learned about it. Fear of terrorism also instigated an unprecedented collaboration between Google and the US intelligence community, particularly the NSA. Google later collaborated with the Obama presidential campaign to identify wavering voters who could be persuaded to vote for Obama in the 2008 and 2012 elections, which further cemented the link between the tech industry and government.[27] Revolving doors tightened the link once more. By 2016, twenty-two former White House officials had left the administration to work for Google, and thirty-one Google executives had joined the White House or federal advisory boards. Another twenty-five former intelligence or Pentagon officials moved to Google, and three Google executives took up positions at the Department of Defense.[28] The iconic nightmare of 9/11 enabled and boosted the rise of surveillance capitalism.

Fear of terrorism also led to quite a few citizens' willingness to accept government and commercial surveillance above privacy and freedom. Surveillance cameras began to populate buildings and streets. When we hear about governmental surveillance, most in the West automatically think of China. But the US has about fifteen CCTV surveillance cameras installed per 100 people, which is slightly more than in China, and European countries such as UK and Germany have put up about half as many, with numbers growing.[29] When it was finally revealed that the NSA secretly collected phone records of millions of Americans and their personal data from Facebook, Google and other top tech companies, government officials justified this intrusion into citizens' lives as a means to protect them from terrorists.

There is a deep irony to this. There is little evidence that mass surveillance technology has prevented more terrorist attacks than traditional anti-terrorist expertise previously did. For instance, the claim by the US government that fifty-four terrorist plots had been thwarted thanks to surveillance turned out to be fake news.[30] An in-depth analysis of 225 individuals recruited by al-Qaeda and other terrorist groups who were charged in the US with having committed an act of terrorism revealed that virtually all of them had been caught by traditional investigative methods, such as tips from local communities. Mass surveillance appears to have played a role in at most 1 to 2 per cent of all cases.[31] Similarly, as we saw a chapter earlier, the predictive policing algorithms developed since have not lived up to the promises made. These results are consistent with the stable-world principle: combating terrorism is not a well-defined problem that you can easily solve with big data. Despite lack of evidence that mass surveillance works, governments around the world, joined by private companies, nonetheless seized the opportunity to do so, politely called 'bulk collection'.

This brief account of how we got into both governmental and commercial surveillance makes one thing clear:[32] neither form of surveillance needed to happen.

Pay a Fee for Service

It's not only privacy that is at stake in surveillance capitalism. It's also your time. A tech company can ask more money from advertisers if more people spend more time on its site. Therefore, its engineers enlist a bag of tricks to keep users, young and old, as long as possible on their sites (see next chapter). The result is that you waste hours of your life in a state of perpetual distraction and disruption by advertisements and notifications. As one study jokingly reported, the attention span of the average user is rapidly declining and already on average shorter than that of a goldfish.[33] The increasing number of people who report having difficulties concentrating for more than a few minutes is a dangerous development – think of teachers and judges not being able to focus their attention, not to speak of surgeons and pilots. For instance, 78 per cent of 439 US perfusionists, who operate heart-lung machines during open-heart surgery, said that using mobile phones for texting, surfing, posting and the like while working is a safety risk for the patient. At the same time, one-third of them also reported having witnessed other perfusionists get distracted by using mobile phones during bypass surgery.[34] Moreover, the psychological tricks used to glue users to the phone and compete for 'likes' appear to have disturbing psychological consequences for some teenagers. Since smartphones became available in 2007, depressive symptoms, self-harm and seriously considered suicide have gone up, and feelings of liking oneself and self-competence have gone down. Yet these observations are correlations, not necessarily causes. Whatever the reasons, digital natives appear to be more anxious than previous generations, and less comfortable with face-to-face conversations.[35]

What can we do about all of this? One popular proposal, known as 'data dignity', calls for social media companies to pay users for their data.[36] That amounts to a minimal solution that would reduce neither surveillance nor the loss of privacy, time and attention span. On the other hand, it would at least introduce some degree of fairness. How much compensation would this proposal realistically earn each user? I have met people who believe that their data are worth at least a hundred dollars a year, and that's what Facebook should pay them. Let's do a rough calculation to check.[37] Facebook has about 2.7 billion monthly active users.[38] In 2019, its revenue was about $70 billion, and profit (net income) was $18.48 billion.[39] If Facebook were to pass on half of the profit to its users, how much would everyone get? The answer is $9.24 billion divided by 2.7 billion users, which is about $3.40 per year, or 28 cents per month. In other words, users would get about a cent a day, making them the worst-paid workers on the globe. This is a very rough calculation, but even if you refine it, there won't be much more in the bank. In other words, getting paid for our data promises to be a lousy deal.

What is the alternative? In my opinion, we need to make a radical move. To stop the surveillance business model, tech companies need to adopt the business model of charging a fee for their services. This would be the key to rescuing privacy and preventing a future of commercial surveillance that can easily flow over into governmental surveillance. Consider an analogy with the postal system. If the post office changed its business model to surveillance capitalism, you would no longer have to pay any rates to send your mail; delivery would be free. In exchange, in order to earn money, the postal system would openly or secretly read all of your mails and sell the content to interested third parties. To preserve privacy, you have to pay with money instead of personal data. In exchange, social media platforms would need to provide verifiable assurance that our usage is not tracked. This solution would take care of the entire chain of damage, from surveillance to loss of time and attention to psychological problems that hurt our children.

To get there requires strict legislation that curbs surveillance capitalism, and also citizens who are willing to pay a small fee. How much would that be? For a very rough estimate, we can make another back-of-the-envelope calculation. How much would users have to pay Facebook to compensate it for lost revenue? Facebook earns most of its money from advertising. Let's be generous and reimburse Facebook for its entire revenue. $70 billion divided by 2.7 billion users would make about $26 a year, or about $2 a month. If one takes account of the $47 billion expenses Facebook had in 2019 and the fact that part of these expenses would vanish if there were no need for collecting, storing and analysing users' personal data any more, then Facebook would make a larger profit, or the fee could be reduced. Although some users might quit, most would likely stay attached to the platform. This rough calculation indicates that a fee-for-service model could be a viable alternative.[40]

A flat fee is not the only alternative. Micropayments can also eliminate the intrusive and privacy-compromising ads that reign on the internet. Mozilla and other companies have announced a $100 million grant programme to bring the dream of an internet without ads to fruition. This would also resolve the ongoing arms race between ad-blocking software and counter-measures by advertisers, such as ads dressed up as news.[41]

To enact this change, we need governments who are willing to resist social media lobbyists along with their customers, and aggressively regulate corporate privacy practices and business models. This extends beyond social media to all companies who try to get their hands on our data. Acquiring the right to say 'no' to cookies is not enough; quite a few companies then deliberately make it a time-consuming chore, annoying users by asking them to go through a series of clicks and scrolls at every step until many eventually give up and say 'yes' with a single click. At the same time, we ourselves need to care about the increasing degree of surveillance and its psychological consequences, and understand that paying with data is at the heart of the problem. Taking that step will be equally challenging, given that most of us are now accustomed to free services and reluctant to pay for privacy. It's time to wake up and make this move. We can enjoy social media without such negative consequences.

Mass marketing of our attention began with the business model of Google and was intensified by many competing social media platforms. Pay-for-service would stop that. Yet that measure by itself would not stop a related surveillance business that has moved from online into our offline world. Our behaviour is now monitored by almost every product prefixed with the term 'smart'. Have you ever wondered why your new mattress or TV came with a privacy policy?

SLEEPWALKING INTO SURVEILLANCE

Sleepwalking, or somnambulism, is a mixture of sleep and wakefulness. Sleepwalkers walk with their eyes open. When they wake up far away from their bed, they tend to be surprised and disoriented: how did they get there? Sleepwalking into surveillance means walking away from freedom and privacy with one's eyes open and, when waking up, being bewildered about how one got there. For some, it began in their playroom.

Smart Dolls

Mattel's Barbie was based on the comic-strip character Lilli in the German tabloid *Bild*, a sassy and exhibitionist ponytailed blonde bombshell, designed to satisfy the taste of *Bild*'s adult male readers. Like Lilli, the first version of Barbie had unrealistically long thin legs and a chiselled waist; the 1963 version even came with a book entitled *How to Lose Weight*, recommending 'don't eat'.[42] Barbie contributed to teenage girls' feeling that their own body was inferior and too fat. Then came the second version of Barbie in 1992, which could speak phrases such as 'Maths is hard. Let's go shopping.'[43] Those words of wisdom reinforced girls' feelings of not being up to boys in maths and relegated them to consumers. The third version entered the US market in 2015, named Hello Barbie but soon to be dubbed 'eavesdropping Barbie'. This interactive Barbie can respond to the worries, hopes and feelings that children entrust to their doll. Unknown to them, however, the doll records their intimate conversations and sends them over the Web to a server for analysis. These conversations are sold to third parties, including parents who can choose to receive the audio recordings daily or weekly.[44] Hello Barbie got the Big Brother Award for enabling parents to spy on their children.[45] One can imagine how a child may feel after eventually finding out that the beloved doll – and parents – eavesdropped on them and betrayed them.

But perhaps something more fundamental will change in a developing mind. Children may not even feel betrayed because they take constant monitoring for granted and develop no concept of private space and time. In this possible future, children adapt their feelings to the potential of technology. Play is surveillance. Surveillance is security.

Eavesdropping is one intrusion; changing the nature of a child's conversation is another. Children have always talked to their dolls and stuffed animals, attributed to them a personality, built a close relationship and engaged in role play and conversation. Now the algorithms in Hello Barbie drive the conversation and talk to children about products they want to market: pop culture, other Barbie products, the latest movies, and music artists. Without being able to freely practise their own imagination and creativity, children are likely to lose whatever they have developed so far. They have to adapt to the limited possibilities of the technology, and to the values of the corporation behind it: fashion, the desire to be thin and an obsolete view of women's purpose in life.

Smart Homes

In one session of the German Ministry of Law and Consumer Protection, we had a closed meeting with two men clad in hoodies, whose CVs sported an intriguing combination of professions: each of them was both a hacker and a professor of internet technology. They came to testify on questions of internet security and what the law can do about it. At the end of the meeting, I asked them what they thought was the greatest danger in the commercial digital world. Their answer came without a blink: smart homes.

A smart home contains devices and appliances such as refrigerators and coffee machines that are networked and linked to the internet. Thanks to this technology, you can switch on the coffee machine with your smartphone before getting out of bed, ask your digital assistant what time it is or access the internet with your TV. When you are away on vacation, smart alarm systems allow you to check day and night whether some suspicious-looking person is hanging around the house. Being connected with the internet also allows your TV or fridge to transmit data minute by minute about your actions to its home company, such as Samsung. In the near future, you might well get targeted ads on the surface of your fridge or your walls.

Smart homes have been advertised as security systems, so the hackers' answer was surprising. Why did they believe these pose such a great safety risk? Their concern was that smart homes invite security disasters. Even apparently benign smart devices, such as smart light bulbs, electricity meters and alarm systems, can provide entry points for hackers. If you have programed your light bulb to turn on and your alarm system to switch off when you are at home, then a hacker who can access your light bulb and set it 'at home' can disable the alarm system. Smart light bulbs, fridges, TVs, security cameras and other appliances have little protection from hackers; otherwise they would be prohibitively expensive. Because they are mass manufactured, a hacker only needs to buy a single device and figure out its weaknesses and can then apply that knowledge against all those who own that product.[46]

In a study, 50 experts in security, cyber-security, antiterrorism and the social sciences worked together and developed twenty-four scenarios of security breaches enabled by smart home technology.[47] The scenario judged to be most likely is smart home blackmailing. Hackers can use ransomware to tap into smart home applications, including webcams to record and blackmail the victims. For instance, researchers from the University of Michigan hacked into Samsung's Smart Things platform, allowing them to control the light bulbs and program their own PIN code in the front door lock to open it.[48] The researchers concluded that there are too many vulnerabilities in smart homes to be able to fix all of them readily. Another scenario judged as highly likely is sex crimes, such as a prospective sexual assaulter gathering information from smart home appliances about the intended victim's habits and whereabouts in order to know when to strike. That scenario also includes hacking into appliances such as webcams or smart TVs to watch and record the inhabitants' sexual activities. In a final scenario, which made it into the novel *Blackout*, smart electricity meters are hacked to cause a power outage.[49] As a result, food supply grows scarce, people fight over gas, riots start, smartphones run out of energy and nuclear plants run on emergency electricity until they begin to melt down and radioactive clouds emerge. *Blackout* is science fiction, but smart homes with smart electricity meters are reality. The Fukushima Daiichi disaster has shown what a breakdown of emergency cooling systems in nuclear power plants means.

To provide their services, smart homes have to surveil their owners. Smart home technology allows a degree of surveillance unprecedented in history, which is attractive because it is often useful, from parents monitoring the breath of their sleeping infant on their smartphone to later tracing the whereabouts of their teenagers. But there is a slippery slope from useful monitoring to less desirable forms. The same kind of apps that allow parents to oversee where their teenage children are at any point in time can be adapted to apps that allow people to check where their ex-partners are right now. When everything becomes connected, the world becomes much more convenient and much more vulnerable.

Yet few smart home owners are aware that together with convenience they bought surveillance. In a survey I conducted, only one out of every seven people were aware that a smart TV records whatever they say. It is not so hard to find out. 'Please be aware that if your spoken words include personal or other sensitive information, that information will be among the data captured and transmitted to a third party,' Samsung's privacy policy reads.[50] And if you are a person of interest for secret services, they can observe you using your smart TV even when it is switched off, as former CIA director Michael Hayden confirmed: 'You want us to have the ability to actually turn on that listening device inside the TV to learn that person's intentions. This is a wonderful capability.'[51]

Yet the smart home was not initially conceived for spying on its inhabitants. In 1991, the US computer scientist Mark Weiser dreamed of the smart home, comprising an entire smart world, where tiny computers are in everything, from clothing to kitchen devices.[52] All these would be built into the environment as invisible servants. In his dream of 'ubiquitous computing', the internet would weave itself into the fabric of everyday life, being freed from specific devices such as personal computers and smartphones. People, in turn, would be freed from an unhealthy life sitting all day in front of computer screens in windowless offices. Weiser took into account the possibility that overzealous government officials and marketing firms could make unpleasant use of this technology, but believed that cryptographic techniques would safeguard private information. Weiser had a clear view into the future of smart technology, but could foresee neither its exploitation by surveillance capitalism, invented a decade after his dream, nor its alliance with governments. Such surveillance also comes in other, more or less subtle forms.

BIG NUDGING

Social credit systems influence people using carrots and sticks: if rewards do not work, undesirable behaviour is punished. Yet there is a subtler way to influence people. *Nudging* is a system of control that needs neither carrots nor sticks, but instead takes advantage of people's psychology to steer them into some desired behaviour.[53] Big nudging is the combination of big data (or digital technology in general) with nudging. The idea is to identify people's weak points and exploit these to influence behaviour on a large scale.

Assume that the top management of a tech company is worried about a political candidate who has announced her intention to regulate the company and make it pay taxes like everyone else. The management would of course prefer that people elect another candidate who opposes regulation. But they can't use carrots and sticks, nor can they buy all the votes. What else could they do? Big nudging is the answer: to find something in people's behaviour that could be used to make them want to vote for the management's favourite candidate themselves. Here is an example:[54]

> *Urge to click*: Many people lack click restraint, that is, they cannot resist the urge to click immediately. As a consequence, about 90 per cent of all clicks are on the first page of a search result, and half of these on the first two entries.

The next question is, how to exploit the urge to click? The company can modify the page rank algorithm of its search machine so that the positive reports about their favoured candidate more likely appear on the first page, and the negative reports on the pages further down – and vice versa for the candidate they want to eliminate. The vast majority of users, who rarely get past the first page, will consequently more likely land on the positive reports of the favoured candidate and not read the negative ones. This will shift their opinion, which in turn will make them more likely to vote for that candidate. There is no need to persuade, bribe or coerce a single voter.

But will it work? It won't work with voters who have already made up their minds, but it might well influence those who are undecided.

With many elections won by small margins, these are the ones who can make the difference.

Psychologist Robert Epstein (as you recall, the man who went for a date with the woman who'd posted a picture of another woman – he also happened to be Skinner's last graduate student) put this idea to the test.[55] He showed that search engine manipulation worked in lab experiments. But can it also work in real life?

Elections in India are the largest democratic elections in the world, with more than 800 million potential voters. In 2014, there were three candidates for prime minister: Narendra Modi, Arvind Kejriwal and Rahul Gandhi. Modi is best known as a Hindi nationalist, Kejriwal for his campaign against corruption, and Gandhi as the uniter of the country, reducing caste and religious tensions. Epstein recruited 2,150 undecided voters throughout India right before the election. He seated them in front of computers where they could search for information about the candidates using an internet search engine. The web pages had been manipulated: for one group of voters, more positive texts about Modi popped up on the first page and more negative ones on later pages. For the other groups, the same was done for the other candidates.

The manipulation went virtually unnoticed; 99.5 per cent of participants showed no awareness of it. Sadly, it worked. Epstein reported that the biased search engines could shift the voting preferences of undecided voters by about 20 per cent. How much is that in absolute terms? Think of one hundred voters, ten of whom are undecided. Without search engine manipulation, half of these ten would eventually vote for your favourite candidate.[56] After the manipulation, this number would increase from five to six, that is, an absolute increase of one percentage point. If more voters are undecided, the effect will be larger. One percentage point is not much, but could be enough to flip a close election.

Given this possibility, it is hard to believe that the executives behind search engines would not be tempted to use their power in critical elections. After all, it would be difficult to detect when it happens because the page-ranking algorithms are top secret. In most countries, where the majority of people rely on a one-and-the-same search engine, a single company can tip the ballots.

Big Nudging, Small Effects

How can people be influenced to vote in the first place? To use big nudging, one again needs to identify a psychological bias and exploit it. Let's take the 2010 US congressional elections. On the day of the election, 61 million Facebook users were sent a message encouraging them to vote, including a link to the local polling places. The reminder had no effect at all.[57] Only when users were also shown up to six pictures of close Facebook friends who said they had already voted was turnout increased by 0.39 percentage points. Again, that is not much, but for these millions of users, the authors estimate that the social message increased turnout by about 60,000 people. And if these in turn motivate their best friends, that snowball effect may add up to many more. Once again, a psychological predisposition was exploited:

Imitate your peers: Do what your closest friends do.

In fact, showing the familiar faces of friends who said they had voted made all the difference. This study nicely illustrates how understanding psychology is necessary for technology to work successfully. That can be done for the greater good of everyone, such as increasing participation in political decision making. But big nudging can also be used by someone who wants to influence the outcome of elections towards a particular candidate. If Facebook prompted only users who are likely to vote for a specific candidate or party, they could increase voter turnout in favour of that party.

This study led to much concern about Facebook's and other tech companies' allegedly unprecedented power to influence and manufacture votes.[58] At the same time, the study documented once again that big nudging, like campaign advertisements, tends to have little effect on manipulating voters both for or against political candidates.[59] Yet in close elections in winner-take-all systems, such as in the US presidential elections of 2016 and 2020, even small effects can change the winner. When small effects are scaled up by big numbers, they gain force.

Can Facebook Manipulate Your Emotions?

You may have read about a study run by researchers at Facebook and Cornell University demonstrating that the company has the ability to make you feel good or bad simply by tweaking what shows up in your news feed.[60] Over 689,000 Facebook users unknowingly participated in this mass-scale 'emotional contagion' experiment. For some of them, the researchers filtered out a number of posts in their news feed containing positive emotions; for others they omitted posts containing negative emotions. Then they read the users' subsequent posts and counted the number of words with positive and negative emotional content. Users who saw fewer positive words subsequently posted messages with fewer positive words, and those with reduced negative words posted messages with fewer negative words. The *Guardian* and many other reputable newspapers reported how Facebook has discovered the means of making us feel happier or sadder, and both awe and horror of this power over our emotions fuelled a heated debate.[61] Many were angry that Facebook had manipulated their news feed and treated them like lab rats, unaware that they had in fact consented to such experiments when signing Facebook's Data Use Policy. After all, it is in Facebook's interest to find ways of manipulating their users' emotions in order to allow advertisers to target users when they are in the right mood: some products are more likely to be sold to those who are sad and vulnerable or to those in a state of bliss.

What the debate mostly overlooked was an important question: how big is the effect in the first place? When positive posts were reduced in the news feed, the percentage of positive words in people's status updates decreased by 0.1 percentage points, from about an average of 5.2 per cent to 5.1 per cent positive words, and the percentage of negative words increased even less, by only 0.04 points. That is all the study actually showed. In addition, it is unclear whether that minuscule change is really due to emotional contagion, as claimed. If Facebook filters out the positive post I receive from Joe, this by itself can lead me to not responding with any positive words to Joe. And if the same happens to all other users, this adds up to fewer positive words across the board.

What do these experiments tell us about the ability of the British company Cambridge Analytica to influence elections? These experiments suggest that the effect was smaller than Alexander Nix, its former CEO boasted, such as when US senator Ted Cruz paid over $5 million to Cambridge Analytica to influence voters, or when Russian hackers

tried to help Trump win in 2016. Despite the promises made by companies advertising the power of their predictive analytics and persuasive
advertising to sway voters, there is a general reason to doubt that these
effects are big. The stable-world principle suggests that in an uncertain
world where voters are subject to many kinds of influences, predictive
analytics will be of limited success, and subsequent attempts at voter
manipulation will have only a small effect. The experimental evidence
reported above confirms this theoretical statement. However, it remains
worrying because even small returns of big nudging can provide the
tipping point in close elections.

My conclusion is that big nudging can indeed manipulate the public without being noticed, but its effect has also been oversold by tech
companies to make political parties and others buy their services.
*The more powerful instrument to control people's behaviour are the
sticks and carrots of social credit systems, combined with 24/7 surveillance and justified by governments to protect their citizens.* The
hidden attempts to manipulate our behaviour and feelings by big
nudging and the overt attempts to do so by social credit systems once
more illustrate the importance of staying in control of technology.

INTO THE FUTURE

In the early days of the internet, a *New Yorker* cartoon showed a dog
sitting at a computer: 'On the Internet, nobody knows you're a dog.'
At the time, that was a joke. Twenty years later, Edward Snowden sat
at a computer while working for an NSA contractor and was able to
read a stranger's emails, listen to his phone conversations and watch
him sitting in front of his computer, a toddler on his lap.[62] The spy
software is known as XKeyscore, which allows almost unlimited surveillance of anyone anywhere. Remember the photo Facebook's CEO
Zuckerberg posted to celebrate Instagram's growth to 500 million
users? In the background it showed his laptop with its camera taped
over. The times when dogs were free to go undercover in the internet
are long gone.

In *Beyond Freedom and Dignity*, Skinner argued that freedom is not the solution, but the problem. People are free to exploit their employees, destroy the environment and wage wars. Instead of revering freedom, we should reward fair, environmentally friendly and peaceful behaviour so that harmful behaviour is not even learned. Skinner truly believed that strict control of behaviour is the way to change the world into a better one. As we will see in the next chapter, social media companies have adopted his techniques but with a different motivation. Skinner's techniques are employed to keep people on the app, and to create an urge to return quickly. Protecting the environment plays little role. On the contrary, the internet and the vast servers and data centres that support it account for about 3 to 4 per cent of global greenhouse emissions, similar to the amount produced by the airline industry, contributing to climbing temperatures, increased wind speeds and more wildfires.

Where does the invasion of privacy lead us? We can start with two peculiar features that may shape the future. First, there is the flawed ideology of *technological solutionism*, whereby every social problem is a bug that needs to be fixed by technology. For instance, in response to the problems of fake news and hate speech, tech leaders have proposed building more AI tools.[63] Second, tech companies and governments work much more closely together than most of us think. Take these two features together, and we get a glimpse at what might happen (figure 8.2).

When I interviewed experts on social scoring on behalf of the German Ministry of Law and Consumer Protection, a possible scenario emerged – while keeping in mind that all predictions about the future are notoriously uncertain. The scenario consists of three phases.

FIGURE 8.2: An artistic rendering of the evolution from Homo sapiens to Homo digitalis, sleepwalking into digital surveillance.

Phase 1: China Is Overt about Surveillance, the West Is Secretive

Let's begin with the world's largest data projects run jointly by governments and tech companies, the social credit system in China and Aadhaar in India. Aadhaar builds a database of India's 1.3 billion citizens, including demographic and biometric information, such as iris scans.[64] Both programmes collect data in order to protect their citizens and control their behaviour. In a first phase, which is happening at present, China, India and other governments, helped by their tech companies, are developing and experimenting with the software and hardware, and with remarkable public acceptance. The awareness that one is scrutinized by the 'digital eye' changes behaviour, reduces violence and boosts moral behaviour and economic output. The successful tracking of infected people during the coronavirus pandemic in China demonstrated the benefits of close surveillance and gave the government an opportunity to scale and speed up the technology. Trust in government and the educating effect of surveillance is high. For instance, in an anonymous online survey, 80 per cent of Chinese approved of social credit systems, while only 1 per cent disapproved (the remainder were indifferent).[65]

In the first phase, most people in the West pay little attention to what happens and consider this development a 'Chinese problem'. Few seem or desire to notice that similar developments are happening in the West, despite Edward Snowden's revelations that the US government was secretly working with Apple, Facebook, Google, Microsoft and other tech companies to run national and global surveillance programmes. Surveillance does not mean that someone personally reads your messages or listens in on your phone calls, although that may occur. It means that your metadata are recorded, that is, minute-by-minute data of which websites you looked at, where you are, where you spent your night, with whom and for how long – your entire digital footprint. When Snowden revealed the scale of government surveillance unknown in the US to them, the majority of Americans shut their eyes and were instead in favour of criminally prosecuting him for treason.[66] In Britain, the Government Communications Headquarters (GCHQ) created a similar mass surveillance programme, code-named KARMA Police, that tracks their citizens' instant messages, emails, Skype calls, phone calls, visits to porn sites, social media, chat forums and everything else people do online.[67] GCHQ also hacked European companies' computer networks and the largest SIM card manufacturer in the world, Gemalto, by secretly stealing encryption keys that protect the privacy of mobile phone communications.

All in all, the exchange of information between governments and tech companies goes in one of two ways: direct orders kept secret from the public, and upstream collection of data kept secret from the companies surveilled.[68] The PRISM programme enabled the NSA to ask Google, Facebook, Microsoft, Skype and others to hand over user data, including email, photos and video and audio chats. Upstream collection is even more invasive and managed by NSA's Special Sources Operations unit, which embedded secret wiretapping equipment in corporate facilities around the world. How does that work? Imagine you open a web browser, type in search terms and hit enter. No longer does your request go straight to that server: on its way, it has to pass through secret servers installed at major telecommunication corporations throughout countries allied with the US. The programs installed on these servers make a copy of the data coming through and check it for suspicious key terms. For instance, if you are curious about XKeyscore (the spy software) and type the term into your search engine, you are likely to be singled out, and an algorithm decides which of the agency's malware programs to use against you. The malware can access all your data, not only metadata, and is delivered to you along with the website you requested.[69] All that takes less than a second, without you noticing a thing.

These actions have been conducted in absolute secrecy. In no case has the public had a chance to voice its opinion in the process. Mass surveillance was given the harmless name 'bulk collection', reminiscent of Newspeak. The Chinese government, in contrast, has been open about constructing its surveillance system. Western governments also tend to tolerate Western surveillance capitalism and may even take advantage of it by accessing the data collected by a select group of immensely rich companies that reign over the internet and buy up competitors rather than creating a competitive market. Democracies have failed to prevent the concentration of too much power and data in too few hands. When Twitter closed President Trump's account, many considered it long overdue, while others were alarmed and called it undue censorship. The real issue is that Twitter and similar companies virtually alone have the power – once confined to absolute monarchies – to decide who has the right to speak and who must remain silent.

During this first phase, Westerners grow accustomed to surveillance by tech corporations thanks to the pay-with-your-data business model. It's *personalized* advertisement, not advertisement per se, that buries the original dream of the internet connecting all people to expand their horizons. Instead, the algorithms nudge us into filter bubbles where we see more of the same, not different viewpoints. If you live in Israel and are rooting for existing Israeli policies, you are likely to see videos on Instagram of rocket launches by Hamas adjacent to hospitals. If you are pro-Palestinian, you might instead see reports on an Israeli sniper who murdered Gazan children.[70] For each side, it is difficult to be aware of what they don't see. Personalized advertisement increases political polarization. And it's not only social media; virtually every organization, from academic institutions to charities to online shops, now uses cookies to collect data about visitors on the internet.

At the same time, surveillance changes behaviour. The technologically sophisticated can bypass surveillance and withdraw into the darknet. But ordinary people notice that everything they do is being recorded and begin to think twice about what websites they watch and what they post and say. As Google's former CEO Eric Schmidt reminded us: 'If you have something that you don't want anyone to know, maybe you shouldn't be doing it in the first place.'[71] That moral advice could have come from many an authoritarian government as well.

Phase Two: Social Credit Systems Boost Autocratic Systems Worldwide

In a second phase, the social credit system has been fully implemented in China. Commercial systems such as Sesame Credit and governmental systems have morphed into a single unified system. China will export hardware and software to other governments with similar regulatory interests, which have by now realized that there is an efficient alternative to democracy, namely an autocratic system well managed by AI. For instance, together with strict environmental laws for individuals and businesses, the social credit system enables governments to rapidly build renewable energy capacity, reduce greenhouse gas emissions and build cities in which all taxis and buses are electric.[72] It promises to do away with the economic inefficiency of earlier autocratic governments, such as communist systems and dictatorships. Consider Africa, where the Chinese Communist Party has supported revolutionary and anti-colonialist movements since the 1960s. The West may blame China for propping up African leaders, yet Western companies and governments themselves have also paid millions in exchange for mining rights or political allegiance. Eventually, countries in Africa and also in Asia and South America will likely take loans and advice from China to install a social credit system, which will in turn permit China to set the rules and secure access to their data.[73] Some countries in Europe may also seize the opportunity, such as Hungary and Poland.

China will also export its Great Firewall, the software that isolates a country's internet from that of other countries and determines what the people within the country can see and share. Tech companies will compete over getting their share of contracts to build Great Firewalls around the world, as they already did before when Cisco helped build China's Great Firewall from American 'bricks'.[74] Similarly, Yahoo, once the hottest tech company, launched a Chinese subsidiary that Reporters Without Borders dubbed a 'Chinese police auxiliary'.[75] When Google launched its Chinese search engine, it complied by preventing Chinese citizens from accessing forbidden information. For instance, searches for 'Tiananmen Square' on Google.cn resulted in lots of tourist photos and no tanks.[76] Facebook reportedly developed censorship tools that prevent posts from appearing in users' news feeds in specific countries, in order to help the company regain entry to the Chinese market.[77] In the second phase, tech companies will continue to comply with governmental surveillance. They cannot be trusted to protect users from censorship.

During this second phase, the public may learn to appreciate that the Firewall protects them from terrorists, scammers, child-molesters and other dangers from the outside world. People will still be freely able to discuss political problems, political leaders and corruption, insofar as they know about these. The primary aim of the Firewall, combined with the social credit system, is not to keep information out but to prevent the emergence of group solidarity against the government. The spread of the internet recruitment policies of the Islamic State and other terrorist organizations – alongside international solidarity movements such as Occupy or Fridays for Future – will become history.

People will enjoy new levels of convenience, including a single app, a superior form of WeChat, that allows a wholly mobile lifestyle. All payments, utility bills, business transactions, doctors' appointments, entertainment, selfies and one's entire social life can be conducted using a single tool. This app also provides data for individual social credit scores. Those with high scores are granted easy access to loans, upgrades on flights, fast-track visa application and preferential treatment at hospitals. The social credit score has also become the currency of social life. People post their score on their dating profiles and reduce time spent reading blogs on political opinions that diverge from the mainstream, playing video games, watching porn sites and on other distractions because this behaviour lowers their score. Those who don't adapt will be isolated and denied services; their friends on social media will unfriend them because contact with low scorers brings down their own score. In contrast, the highest scorers are the new celebrities, admired by all. Everyone can see their friends' social score online, and even perfect strangers' scores can be checked out by pointing one's phone towards them on the street. It has become easy and convenient to know whom to trust.

Smart homes and cities provide further convenience. All monetary transactions are by mobile payments, resulting in a reduction of corruption and crime, and an increase in trust. Mass surveillance will create substantial amounts of erroneous data and false accusations, but, once the system is in place, people will learn to live with these problems and work around them. Newspeak will assist by changing minds. Surveillance Is Safety. Freedom Is Danger. Eventually, most citizens will think of their new autocratic world as just and convenient, as economic progress and security, not as a loss of freedom.

Phase Three: Will Democracy Survive?

In the third phase, the remaining democratic governments face competition with their all over the world whose social credit systems closely watch, reward and punish its citizens. Many of these democracies will find themselves surrounded by countries whose citizens trust their governments considerably more than citizens in democracies do. Countries once considered backward now implement decisions more quickly, be it for environmental protection or dealing with a pandemic, and circumvent the endless debates and compromises characteristic of a democracy. Checks and balances, such as the separation of powers and free media, are considered 'passé'. No energy is wasted by fights and rivalries between political parties, no endless debates with committees and interest groups. No longer are election outcomes influenced by big nudging, fake news or bots. After all, as a Chinese friend noted, a well-managed government that has its citizens willingly under control would not have to clean up the mess created by voters who favoured Donald Trump, Brexit or other belligerent leaders and populist issues. AI provides the fuel for new autocratic systems that dispense with privacy and freedom and, at the same time, make their citizens efficient and happy. B. F. Skinner's dream of a society where the behaviour of each member is strictly controlled by reward has become reality.

Eventually, the dream of the internet upholding freedom will morph into a marriage of social credit systems and surveillance capitalism, a powerful blow to the ideals of privacy, dignity and democracy. The new ideals are fast access, high credit scores and faith in government. In this new world of technological paternalism, laws are automatically enforced by computers. People can't cheat on taxes any more, corruption is immediately detected, drivers won't speed and be rude to pedestrians. Surveillance brings justice, law and order. Many people will like it.

Democracies will have to make a choice if they are to survive. One option is to abandon the original ideal of the internet as a place for free information and adopt the social credit system and Great Firewall established in other countries, until democracy becomes a thing of the past. Another option is to stick with the ideal while facing the fact that democracies have tolerated the growth of tech monopolies that have abused and jeopardized the ideal to make huge profit. Doing so requires governments with enough courage to bare their teeth at tech companies and with a vision of how to build an internet from scratch that defends rather than dilutes democratic ideals. In other words, to go back to the original concept of the internet that is based on free exchange of knowledge rather than on surveillance capitalism.

9

The Psychology of Getting Users Hooked

'We can no longer afford freedom.'

B. F. Skinner[1]

'We call these people users and even if we don't say it aloud, we secretly wish every one of them would become fiendishly hooked to whatever we're making . . .'

Nir Eyal, Hooked[2]

When I was a student of psychology, one of our professors held a lecture on Skinner's theory of operant conditioning. After class, we huddled together and designed an experiment to test whether we could use the theory to control his behaviour. The professor had a habit of wandering back and forth across the front of the classroom while speaking. During the next lecture, when he walked to the right side of the room, the students sitting there nodded approvingly at what he was saying. When he walked over to the left side, the students sitting there showed no reaction at all. Shortly afterwards, the professor spent more time on the right side of the room. Then we reversed the positive reinforcement so that the students on the left began to nod their heads and the ones on the right remained expressionless. After a while, the professor now began to spend more time on the left side. Honouring experimental ethics, we disclosed the purpose of the experiment to him afterwards, and it turned out that he had not been aware of our manipulations. Yet we had managed to control his strolling simply through our nodding and smiles.

The logic of operant conditioning – also called instrumental conditioning – is simple and powerful:

behaviour → positive reinforcement → increased frequency
of behaviour.

It looks trivial, but its world view is profound. Your behaviour is controlled from the outside, by the positive reinforcement you receive from a human or a machine. The professor didn't stroll to the right because he wanted to; his students modified his behaviour by nodding.

All this clashes with our feeling of being in control, and with most theories about human nature. These assume that behaviour is caused by an inner state, called desire:

desire → behaviour.

Desires are also called preferences and needs in psychology. In the 1940s, the American psychologist Abraham Maslow arranged needs into a pyramid-like hierarchy, with the more fundamental ones at the bottom. The pyramid includes physiological needs such as food, sleep and sex in the bottom layer, moving up a layer to safety needs such as health and financial security and then to needs for social belonging, such as to family; at the top of the pyramid are self-esteem and self-actualization, such as becoming the ideal parent, artist, athlete or scientist. The view that desire causes behaviour also underlies Western ideas about free will. I do what I do because I want to do it and no one can stop me, unless they put a gun to my forehead. It is the morale underlying most legal systems: people are responsible for what they do and can be sentenced to jail, unless they were drunk or underage.

According to the psychologist B. F. Skinner, all that is an illusion. Skinner, who spent much of his career at Harvard, is one of the most famous psychologists ever, and one of the most controversial to boot. Although we love to believe that we're sitting in the driver's seat, he argued that our behaviour and desires are determined from the outside. Worse yet, we do not even notice that we are only in the back seat of our life, or at least do not want to know this.

Skinner Boxes and Pigeon Warriors

Long after this experiment, when I was a visiting scholar at Harvard, my office happened to be next door to Skinner's. It was a few years before his death, a time when, thanks to an army of critics, his star had lost some of its lustre. He had given up his floor of experimental rooms in William James Hall, once filled with blinking apparatus, tons of pigeon food stacked in the corners, and pigeons confined in 'Skinner boxes' with slide projectors and videos for stimulus presentation. In each box, a lonely pigeon was housed, and its behaviour – such as the frequency of pecking at a key to get food pellets – was shaped by a fully automatized programme of reinforcement.

Skinner also appeared a bit lonely, and we ended up having tea and cookies together several times. He told me that evolution and operant conditioning shape humans' and other animals' behaviour, and that the only difference between humans and animals is the speech muscle; our behaviour is shaped by the same rules. And he proudly described how he had taught pigeons during the Second World War to guide air-launched missiles to their targets, enemy warships. The pigeons were positioned inside the nose of a missile, where they could see through a glass, and had been conditioned to peck at pictures of ships, thereby guiding the missile towards the target. Before the pigeons could begin their career as kamikaze warriors, however, Project Pigeon was cancelled. Skinner also articulated his deep belief that freedom is but an illusion, and a dangerous one at that, instilled in us by people who already control our behaviour. In his view, we cannot afford the freedom to go to war, destroy the climate and maltreat other people. Operant conditioning of proper behaviour, not freedom, is the path towards a better world.

In our conversations, I found Skinner to be one of those influential scholars who have developed one big system into which they squeeze every idea encountered. His techniques work well, particularly in situations where one has control over others, be it pigeons enclosed in a box or humans in similar situations. But they are not the sole key to human nature, or to making the world a better one. Today his philosophy reminds me of the promises now made by some tech companies and advocates of big nudging that, to better the world, all we need to do is give them access to all our data, turn our homes into smart boxes and let them surveil and modify our behaviour. That is not just an analogy; the techniques are astonishingly similar.

Intermittent Reinforcement

Back to the professor in my class. When the students stopped nodding, the professor's behaviour gradually faded away. How could they have made the professor continue to spend more time on the right side of the classroom? How quickly the behaviour faded was under the students' control: if they had nodded every single time the professor was on the right side of the classroom and then suddenly stopped, he would also have soon stopped spending most time on the right side. This loss of external control is called *extinction*. However, if students had only occasionally nodded when the professor moved to the right, then his behaviour would have continued much longer. This technique is called *intermittent reinforcement*. What it means is that reinforcement of the desired behaviour is irregular, not constant: not every time, or every second or third time, and so on. Reinforcement is not predictable. Sometimes the behaviour is reinforced, sometimes it isn't.

behaviour → intermittent reinforcement → increased frequency and persistence of behaviour.

Intermittent reinforcement is the way to build up lasting behaviour.[3] The hungry pigeon in the Skinner box pecks more frequently and faster when it does not get a food pellet every time, but at irregular intervals. Similarly, irregular reinforcement can be used to develop persevering and hard-working behaviour, but also to get people hooked on smartphones or slot machines.

HOW TO GET USERS HOOKED

Assume you are a software engineer, and your company pays you for increasing customer satisfaction. Its business model is 'users pay with their data', and your customers, say the advertisers, want users to spend as much time as possible on an app for maximum exposure to their ads. How would you proceed? The answer is to program inter-mittent reinforcement. This is how it works:

Step 1: Identify the behaviour you want to increase: time spent on a site, number of clicks, click-through rate, number of posts, or something else.

Step 2: Identify a positive reinforcement that can build up and control this behaviour. Social media have no food pellets, drinks or hugs to offer as reinforcement. But they can use another currency: social approval and the dopamine shots one gets from being accepted as a member of a group. Thus, social approval is a potential reward to make users spend more time on a site.

Step 3: Divide the reinforcement into small, countable units. Social approval works best for getting users hooked if it comes in small dis-tinct units, like the food pellets in Skinner's experiments.

Step 4: Introduce intermittent reinforcement. This spreads reinforce-ment in an unpredictable way over time and keeps users watching, clicking or posting.

So what positive reinforcement could you introduce? Nodding would be difficult. But think about nodding as notifications or, even better, 'likes'. These come in distinct units, and at irregular times.

The 'Like' Button

In the first versions of Facebook, little existed that would bind users to the site. People sent their messages, and that was it. In later versions, comments on others' posts were possible, which acted as rewards for checking one's site. Positive comments are reinforcers. The real break-through came when the 'like' button was introduced in 2009. Unlike comments, which may have sarcastic undertones and require evalua-tion, the 'like' button resolved all ambiguity. It was even simpler than a number between one and ten. A 'like' is a 'like', just as a food pellet is a food pellet. It is even possible to count them, along with the number of followers, which makes social comparison as simple as comparing two numbers. 'Likes' do not necessarily follow every act of checking in; reinforcement is intermittent. The 'like' became the ideal unit for re-inforcement that, together with comments, could control the behaviour of users:

checking social media $\rightarrow$ intermittent reinforcement by 'likes' $\rightarrow$ increased frequency and persistence of checking.

In this way, several behaviours – checking, scrolling, clicking and posting – are influenced by 'likes'. The impulse is to check constantly because one never knows when the next 'like' will come. This behaviour is almost automatic; people continue to scroll and click, just once more, even when they believe it's a waste of time. Day after day, millions of people spend hours posting pictures on Instagram, waiting expectantly for feedback, and counting the 'likes' they get. 'Likes' become hugs. Several years ago, in fact, designers at MIT Media Lab made headlines after developing a smart vest that gives you a hug for each 'like' you get on Facebook.[4]

For instance, one might assume that if users get a large number of 'likes', they might slow down and enjoy their fame. Skinner's theory instead predicts that the more 'likes' users get, the more frequently they will post, which decreases the time between successive posts. That is exactly the pattern that was found in an analysis of over 1 million posts on Instagram and other social media platforms.[5] The number of 'likes' controls users' frequency and timing of posting. Other studies concluded that the brain regions activated by 'likes' closely overlap with those activated by non-social awards such as food, just as with Skinner's food pellets.[6]

Before email and social media, one of the ways people maintained contact with others was by writing letters. The letter carrier delivered the letters at a certain time of day, say at noon, so people checked their mailbox once a day. This corresponds to what is called a *fixed-interval reinforcement* schedule, which leads to one spike of behaviour and then nothing until the next day. Many a person expectantly peered out the window with anticipatory joy, waiting for the delivery of letters or packages, but once they arrived, that was it for the next twenty-four hours. Messages via email or social media sites, in contrast, can arrive at any time, 24/7, and arrive irregularly. This design produces intermittent reinforcement, which leads to constant checking behaviour. It would correspond to a postal system in which several letter carriers might turn up at any time of day or night, carrying only one letter or package each.

It might seem that Facebook deliberately went through steps 1 to 4 above and designed the 'like' button in response. Yet that was not so. As with many discoveries, Facebook appears to have serendipitously stumbled over the 'like' button while trying to solve another problem. When the site grew in popularity, posts were overrun with comments stating little more than that someone liked it. The 'like' button was originally intended as a means of cleansing the site from this wave of redundant comments. Only later did it become clear what a treasure they had unearthed.

The Tools of Attention Control Technology

'Likes' are the glue that keeps people hooked. But not the only one. Social media sites run experiment after experiment to find out how to keep users bonded with the screen. Sean Parker, the first president of Facebook, explained the goal of social network platforms: 'How do we consume as much of your time and conscious attention as possible?' To do so, he continued, whenever someone likes a post, we 'give you a little dopamine hit' to encourage you to upload more content: 'It's a social-validation feedback loop ... exactly the kind of thing that a hacker like myself would come up with, because you're exploiting a vulnerability in human psychology.'[7] Dopamine is one of about twenty major neurotransmitters that carry urgent messages between neurons, nerves and other cells in the body – like bike couriers weaving through heavy traffic. It becomes active when anticipating or experiencing rewarding events, such as when we bite into delicious food, have sex and receive social approval.

Here are a few ingenious techniques to capture users' attention and time, some of which are so common that we don't notice them any more.

News feed. Sites like Facebook began as a directory of profile pages on which users could list their favourite bands or post pictures. Users visited their friends' homepages from time to time to view their updates, which were relatively minor. In 2006, when Facebook was two years old, it announced a facelift called the *news feed*. The announcement bore the smell of its dorm room origins: 'It updates a personalized list of news stories throughout the day, so you'll know when Mark adds Britney Spears to his Favorites or when your crush is single again.'[8] Hundreds of thousands of users protested against this new technology that turned their private messages into the fodder of mass consumption.[9] But technology won and replaced users' value of privacy with the desire to receive as much attention as possible, not only from friends but from anybody on the globe. What the Facebook announcement neglected to mention, however, was that the news feed did not show all posts but used an algorithm to select them. The first algorithms were based on intuition about what people liked, giving five points for a photo or one point for joining a group, and multiplied this score by the number of friends involved in the story.[10] With the help of the 'like' button, which provided a direct measure of what people liked, this crude algorithm eventually morphed into a top-secret machine learning system that determines what content a user can easily see (because it is placed near the top of the news feed), what content is hard to find (placed far away from the top) and what content the user will not see at all (because the algorithm decided the content is not relevant for the user). As a result of the news feed, users spend more time on the site.

Notification systems. 'Likes' feed into a notification system, which is a control feature to bring users back to the site. The moment someone likes a post, a comment, or comment within a comment, an alert appears that can be clicked on. Over time, Facebook increased notifications; the more notifications, the more frequently people check in.

Delay 'likes'. Notification algorithms have been reported to sometimes withhold 'likes' so that the person who makes a post initially does not get any 'likes', or only a few, and may be disappointed. Only later are the 'likes' sent in larger bursts. This delay amounts to an amplification of intermittent reinforcement to make people stay on even longer.[11]

Auto-play. In a cinema, you pay for the film, watch it and leave after it ends. On YouTube, after you watch a video, a related video automatically begins in order to keep you watching and exposed to as many advertisements as possible. According to YouTube, the average session on mobile devices lasts more than an hour, and 70 per cent of all watching time is controlled by the recommender system, including auto-play.[12] People make few choices themselves. Not only does

YouTube's recommender algorithm lure viewers into spending more time on the screen than intended but it can also lead them towards extreme and unscientific viewpoints.[13] That is, the fewer choices people make, the more likely they end up with untrustworthy information.

Snap streaks. A streak is the number of consecutive days a user and a friend have sent each other a 'snap', that is, a photo or video. Platforms such as Snapchat display the number together with icons such as a fire emoji. The hook is that the number drops to zero if a day is missed. This feature nudges users to keep responding to their friends; not doing so can cause disappointment and anger. As a consequence, users tend to send reminders to their friends that they are awaiting a reply. Diehard users have continued their streaks for more than 2,000 days.[14] Snapchat also awards points for every snap sent or received. A low score is considered embarrassing. And there are virtual trophies, such as specific emojis for sending specific kinds of snaps. All these features keep users sending snaps and spending more time on the platform. The average Snapchat user sends thirty to forty messages every day.[15]

Mindless games that require constant attention. In the Facebook game FarmVille, players have to tend a farm. There are set time limits, such as if you don't return to the game within sixteen hours to harvest the rhubarb, your fields will be riddled with withered stalks.[16] In 2010, the game boasted over 80 million monthly active users, over 30 million of whom were playing it daily. Some of them spent not just their time but also money on virtual farming (the game is free, but if you purchase certain features, you are able to farm better). *Time* named the game one of the '50 Worst Inventions' in recent decades for consisting of mindless chores on a digital farm and for having the most addictive design among Facebook games.[17] The contents of an addictive game are irrelevant. Video game designer Ian Bogost learned this lesson when he created a parody of FarmVille to lay bare its mindless and repetitive character. The game was called Cow Clicker. Players could click on a picture of a cow, the cow said moo, and players earned another click in order to be able to click on a cow again in six hours. Clicking earns clicks, that was it. The six-hour span made the players keep returning to the game, although the time could be reduced for a fee. Players could invite friends to click on their cow, and, when they did, they all received another click. Each time they clicked on a cow, this was announced to their friends on Facebook. The message read: 'I'm clicking a cow.' Bogost had expected Cow Clicker to have a short life because of its ludicrousness. Instead, within weeks it achieved a cult status, and the number of players grew to tens of thousands. In the end, Bogost shut the game down in desperation, an act he called *Cowpocalypse*.[18]

Loot boxes. Many video games offer users the chance to buy virtual loot boxes, which may contain useful resources, such as weapons and armour. Like the buyers of real loot bags of old, most of the time, users find crap in the box, but occasionally something really good. This intermittent reinforcement fosters excitement and surprise and keep users purchasing more boxes. A survey of over 7,000 gamers found evidence for a link between the amount spent on loot boxes and the severity of their gambling problem.[19] The UK's National Health Service warned that this randomized reward structure sets up kids for gambling addiction, and some countries have regulated or banned the sale of loot boxes.[20]

Each of these techniques is designed to hook users to a site: to make it difficult to leave a platform and compelling to return to it. For many of us, the effect is a mixture of feeling good, a favorite pastime and a waste of time and attention. For others, the result is addiction: a feeling of loss of control and a constant craving for positive reinforcement.

The designers of these attention techniques are well aware of the consequences, as are the heads of digital companies, who place strong restrictions on their own children's internet use. As Tim Cook, CEO of Apple, explained: 'I don't have a kid, but I have a nephew that I put some boundaries on. There are some things that I won't allow; I don't want them on a social network.'[21]

The Power of Your Smartphone

You might object that paying attention to your smartphone is always a deliberate decision, for instance, because you're expecting a message. And if you don't want to bother with messages, you simply turn the phone off. You feel in control. But are you?

This situation was tested in an experiment with over 500 undergraduates.[22] One group was asked to leave all of their belongings in the lobby, including their smartphones, before entering the test room. A second group was instructed, after entering the test room, to put their phones away in their pockets or bags. A third group was instructed, after entering the test room, to place their phones face down on the desk, for use in a later study. All participants were asked to turn off the ring and vibration settings. Then they were all given standard tests of attention and intelligence, such as completing a series of maths problems while simultaneously remembering a letter sequence. Because nobody's smartphone could ring or vibrate, its location should have had no impact on the students' performance. Yet one group performed better than the others in every single task. It was the group whose smartphones were in the other room. Those who had their smartphone on the desk performed worst. The nearer the smartphone, the stronger its claim over the owner.

Would that still happen with smartphones that are not only silenced but turned off completely? In a new version of the same experiment, turning the smartphone off made it no less distracting. Its mere presence was again enough. After the experiments, the students were asked whether they thought the location of their smartphone had any impact on their performance. The vast majority believed that it did not. They were unaware that the phone controlled their attention. Ironically, those who reported they would have trouble getting through a normal day without their phone suffered most from its brain drain.

This study suggests that the mere presence of students' mobile devices in schools and universities, *even when they are not activated*, may undermine attention, learning and test performance. Unless the devices are needed in class, leaving them in a different room is the wisest strategy for learners.

Smartphones are not the first technology to demand our attention; TV, radio and the regular phone have been accused of doing the same. My point here is that smartphones can reduce the ability to concentrate even when they are silenced or shut off, and that few are aware of this phenomenon. The problem is not technology, it's whether we understand its impact on us and whether we learn to regain the upper hand. Many are more intimately attached to their phone than to their friends and family. In a survey of 500 adult

Americans, two-thirds said they sleep with their phone at night, and almost every second person would rather give up sex than their mobile phone for a year. The vast majority – three-quarters – consider themselves addicted to their phone.[23] The result is a permanent state of distraction, of not being able to pay full attention to other tasks and use one's intelligence at full capacity. If you need to concentrate on something else, put the phone away – far away. As the old saying goes: out of sight, out of mind.

IS SOCIAL MEDIA ADDICTION LIKE GAMBLING ADDICTION?

Throughout her pregnancy, Isabella, a thirty-eight-year-old living in Las Vegas, had gambled, losing every dollar she owned. She continued until days before giving birth to her son. For her evening therapy group, she wrote about how most days she would spend some sixteen hours in a chair in front of a slot machine, before and after giving birth, with people smoking around her. She barely ate a thing because she did not want to lose any time at her machine:

> Even after he was born I couldn't stop gambling. I'd leave him at home with my sister for hours and hours. Later, after losing everything, there would be stains all the way down to my hips from the leaking of my breasts. He'd be at home hungry, and I'd be gambling it all away. Now I'm trying to stop gambling, but I get so bothered by the machines when I get baby formula at the store. I try to close my eyes and get past them, but it doesn't always work.[24]

In Las Vegas, slot machines are not only waiting in casinos, but also beckon players at the entrances of gas stations, supermarkets or drug stores. Isabella could hardly avoid the sight of them.

Is addiction to gambling similar to addiction to social media? There are indeed similarities. The first similarity is the goal of the companies that provide the machines. In her brilliant book *Addiction by Design*, Natasha Dow Schüll describes the efforts of slot machine engineers and developers to keep people glued to the machine. As game designer Nicholas Koenig explains, the hidden algorithms are critical for getting players addicted: 'Once you've hooked 'em in, you want to keep pulling money out of them until you have it all; the barb is in and you're yanking the hook.'[25]

To meet this goal, slot machines have become 'personalized'. Two machines that look similar from the outside may have different algorithms that fit different customer types. For instance, *escape players*, who want to escape from the uncertainties of their lives by spending as much time as possible at the machine, will likely get hooked on machines that are programed to dispense little payouts at random points in time. *Jackpot players*, in contrast, are not interested in little payouts. They are willing to lose big in order to win big and prefer machines with rare but high payoffs. For escape players, video poker has become the favourite game, where they can spend about two hours on the machine for every $100 lost, about double the time that can be spent on regular slot machines for the same price. That, by the way, is more expensive than recreational drugs.[26] Reinforcement occurs more frequently but, as with the food pellets in Skinner's experiments, in small units, which maintains a high frequency of gambling behaviour. The gambling industry's term for this business model is 'Time on Device' (or TOD, for short).[27] Thus, the common business model of both slot machines platforms and social media platforms is to capture as much of a person's time as possible.

The second similarity is the use of intermittent reinforcement. It keeps people scrolling though tweets and clicking through photos of friends of friends, even if there is nothing particularly interesting and they know they will have a 'lost time' feeling afterwards. People also grow addicted to slot machines through unpredictable shots of dopamine. Wins come after a random number of games, which leads to a steady and high frequency of playing. As Isabella perceived, the machines at the store exert control over her behaviour – they make her sit down and play. Intermittent reinforcement is powerful, but some people more easily fall prey to it, depending on other influences. In the case of Isabella there was a history of an abusive, alcohol-dependent father and additional factors over which she had no control.

But there is also a difference between gambling and social media. Slot machines resemble 'Skinner boxes', named after the boxes in which Skinner trained pigeons, a lonely bird allotted to each box. Intermittent reinforcement keeps the pigeon pecking at a key and the gambler pushing the buttons, which sometimes leads to a pellet or money as a reward. People addicted to social media find themselves in a different situation: the very point of social media is being connected, gaining social approval and making social comparisons. The 'likes' provide an easy currency to see the extent to which one is accepted; a post with zero 'likes' is equivalent to public condemnation. You might have asked yourself why the people who broke into the Capitol in 2021 posted selfies and thereby publicized identification photos that led to their arrests. They may not have been simply dim-witted; many were perhaps continuing their perpetual quest for the positive re-inforcement of 'likes'. To post means to be seen, to play a slot machine does not.

Addicted gamblers are often ashamed of their addiction. They play alone and do not communicate with others. Even when gamblers sit next to each other, there is little if any social interaction. In one case, a surveillance camera was accidentally directed at a man at the tables who suddenly collapsed on to his neighbour, in the throes of a heart attack. The unconscious victim was literally lying at other players' feet, his body touching the bottoms of their chairs. Yet all of the neighbouring gamblers continued to play, without batting an eyelid.[28]

Many among us find it hard to understand why Isabella and others like her spend their lives in the machine zone. Some researchers think these people cannot calculate probabilities. That explanation misses the point: experienced gamblers are highly sensitive to probabilities, even to differences between personalized machines that look the same. Others believe that gamblers are driven by the urge to win. Yet addicted gamblers do not necessarily play to win. They play simply in order to spend time with the machine. Their behaviour is under the sway of the machine's intermittent reinforcement algorithm. As the mother of an eleven-year-old boy explained, when she wins on video poker, she just puts the money back into the machine. 'The thing people never understand is that I'm not playing to win.' Why does she play? 'To keep playing – to stay in that machine zone where nothing else matters.'[29]

10

Safety and Self-Control

'*Not being able to control events, I control myself.*'
Michel de Montaigne[1]

'*Control yourself or someone else will control you.*'
Anonymous

A mother addicted to online video poker is under the control of the software's intermittent reinforcement, which makes it hard for her to leave the site to spend time with her family and may empty her bank account. A young man eager for attention turns to increasingly violent behaviour, fuelled by positive reinforcement on various social media platforms.[2] Staying in control, or getting it back, is not always easy. Ever since Homer recounted the story of Odysseus, who asked his sailors to bind him to the mast in order to avoid being lured by the sirens' sweet but deadly song, people have thought of numerous ways to stay in control. Some make a pledge to their beloved late mother or father, or to a friend. Others turn to Gamblers Anonymous or phone addicts anonymous, or find a buddy with whom they can together limit the time spent on online gambling, internet porn, or shooting games designed to be addictive.

Staying in control is not only difficult, it is made more difficult by technological design. Similarly, cigarettes have been designed to be addictive by the addition of certain chemicals that are redundant for the mere pleasure of smoking, and slot machines are designed to keep gamblers playing even if they would feel better if they could stop. The tobacco industry, the machine gambling industry and tech companies have all been asked by health organizations to stop exploiting human vulnerability. And, to some degree, tech companies have complied by promoting apps that allow notifications to be turned off, limit who can see the 'likes' or remind users to take a break.

In this chapter, we look at how to foster digital self-control. Self-control does not mean staying clear of games and snubbing distractions. It means being able to stop when one would actually prefer to be doing something else, knowing that one will regret the time spent that way afterwards, or when the activity threatens one's health and that of others.

DISTRACTED DRIVERS

Distracted driving occurs when you take your eyes from the road, your hands from the wheel or your mind off the task of driving safely. That happens when you reach for your phone, text while driving, check emails, take a photo and post it or watch a video, but also when you turn to reach for a bag of potato chips in the back seat. Multi-tasking behind the wheel has become deadly normal. It kills far more people than terrorists do. According to the Centers for Disease Control and Prevention, about eight people are killed in the US in crashes involving distracted drivers every single day.[3]

The Last Text

It was Christmas Eve, and the young woman was eager to get home. But she never arrived. With only a few miles to go, she speeded without braking straight into an eighteen-wheeler. The street was dry, the visibility was good, there was little traffic, and the firemen at the scene of the accident wondered how it could have happened. When her body was carried out of the wreck, they found an intact mobile phone lying on the floor of the car. It displayed the woman's last message: 'I'll be right back.'[4]

It's 8:14 p.m. on June 21, 2014, and Laura is driving her Mazda 3 north on Route de la Station in L'Isle-Verte. She sends a text message to her friend. Two minutes later, a reply comes buzzing on Laura's iPhone and she opens the messages while the car approaches a rail crossing at the crest of a hill. The crossing's red lights flash, its bells clang and the oncoming locomotive sounds its whistle four times. But Laura never slows down. The train barrels into Laura's car at 64 kilometers an hour.[5]

Hi. My name is Jenna. Some could say I don't really have a story. I've never lost anyone close to me to a texting driver. In a way I do have a story. I was in the car a few weeks ago, when I saw a man in a red car texting while he was driving beside us. He suddenly swerved and nearly hit us. He almost hit my side. My father had honked furiously, he almost lost his only daughter. And you know the worst part? After the man looked up with an apologetic look on his face, he went right back to texting! I bet he killed someone that day. Stop texting and driving, I'm only 12. I'm too young to die.[6]

Typically, the victims of distracted driving die for no good reason. The distracting messages sent and received are trivial. People die because of the urge to reach to the phone, which is controlled by intermittent reinforcement. How can we regain control? One way is to take half an hour and listen carefully to those who were unlucky. Years ago, AT&T approached the legendary German filmmaker Werner Herzog to make a documentary about texting and driving. Herzog agreed and created the haunting movie *From One Second to the Next*. Victims and wrongdoers openly talk about the disaster they experienced or caused. A mother whose boy has been paralysed recounts how their lives have been destroyed, as does a young man who killed three little children while texting 'I love you' to his wife. One case Herzog did not get the rights to cover was that of a young man who was writing a message to his girlfriend and steamrolled a child on a bike. His girlfriend was sitting next to him in the passenger seat.[7]

As well as being shown in numerous high schools, *From One Second to the Next* can be seen on YouTube. After watching it, I looked at the viewer count. It was a low five-digit figure. By comparison, *How to Tie the Perfect Bow Tie* or *How to Apply Eyeliner* videos easily get millions of views.

Multitasking

Multitasking means performing two or more tasks at the same time, each of which demands attention. Texting while driving is an example. Breathing while driving is not, because breathing happens automatically. Attention is the crucial limited resource. The *fundamental law of attention* is this: [8]

If you perform a task that requires attention and then simultaneously perform a second one, your performance on the first task deteriorates.

Multitasking is no big deal when mowing the front lawn while listening to a podcast or watching a movie while chatting with a friend. But, in a car, we are operating a potentially deadly weapon. Despite the steady stream of victims, many drivers are of the opinion that the fundamental law of attention does not apply to them because multitasking has become second nature. Psychological studies show that this popular belief is unfortunately an illusion.

For instance, one study compared frequent multitaskers with rare multitaskers. Those who were used to multitasking were found to be more easily distracted by irrelevant information, had a worse memory and were slower at changing between tasks. [9] All of these are abilities at which seasoned multitaskers should excel. But aren't there at least a few exceptional people who are not subject to the law of attention? That question was addressed by a study in which students had to solve simple memory and maths problems using a hands-free headset in a driving simulator. As usual, their performance in four tasks – brake reaction time, keeping distance, memory and maths – dropped in comparison to their performance in each single task. An individual analysis showed that this result held for all 200 students, except for five who were reported to have 'absolutely no performance decrements in multitasking' and were celebrated as 'supertaskers'. [10] Are they really? When checking the study, I found that, contrary to what was suggested, four of these five supertaskers actually performed worse in one of the four tasks. That leaves one out of 200 students. Yet that individual might well be a chance oddity. For instance, if you ask 200 people to roll a dice four times, it is not unlikely that one will happen to roll 'six' four times in a row. That alone does not prove that someone is immune to the laws of chance; this 'supertasker' would need to be further tested to rule out chance.

All in all, a large amount of research has shown that attention is a limited resource, and that performing additional tasks that require attention lowers the quality of performance on the original task. Practising multitasking cannot overrule this law of attention and turn us into supertaskers.

Hands on the Wheel, Eyes on the Road

Why do people text while driving? If you ask teens, some may retort that adults do it too. And they are spot-on. In a US national survey, parents were asked about texting and driving. Half of them were mothers, the other half fathers, all of whom had driven their own child in the previous thirty days.[11] When asked, 'Do you think that you can safely text and drive?' most said 'Never.' But when asked about their actual behaviour, most admitted that they had read and written texts while driving in the past month. Intermittent reinforcement and shots of dopamine have taken control of their behaviour against better understanding. To assist parents, paediatricians and nurses should routinely ask them about texting while driving their child. Yet only one out of four parents in the survey reported that their paediatrician had ever broached the topic.

As mentioned, distracted drivers kill about eight people in the US every day, orders of magnitude more than terrorists do. In spite of this daily death count, many drivers continue to text on the road. Is there a cure for this? One way is to resort to strategies such as putting the phone out of sight and reach when in the car. There are also websites where individuals can officially take the pledge that they will pay full attention to the road and not use a phone while driving or give in to other distractions. Many people have resorted to digital technology itself to counter their urge to text on the road and purchased an app that detects driving, blocks all incoming and outgoing messages and responds with automated messages without alerting the driver. In the national survey, one out every five parents reported using such a self-control app. These apps are safer than smartphones that text via voice command. The latter allow you to keep your hands on the wheel but take your mind off the road. They can provide a false sense of safety.

Safety issues are not limited to the road. While preparing for landing in Singapore, the crew of a Jetstar Airbus A321 heard noises associated with incoming text messages from the captain's mobile phone.[12] The first officer, who was flying the plane, repeatedly asked the captain to complete the landing checklist, but the captain was preoccupied with his phone and did not respond. The aircraft had to make a go-around because the landing gear was not deployed in sufficient time. Distraction due to texting has also been reported as contributing factors to helicopter crashes in Florida and Missouri. In Colorado, the pilot and the passenger of a Cessna 150 took selfies using a flash at night, and the National Transport Safety Board concluded that this action contributed to the subsequent crash of the plane that killed both occupants. In response, several countries have prohibited pilots from using electronic devices for personal reasons while on duty.

DISTRACTED PARENTS

One day, a Yale graduate student in economics took his son to the playground. The very moment he looked down to check his phone, his son fell. It wasn't a serious accident, but it provided the young economist with a hypothesis. When AT&T rolled out its 3G networks across the US in 2008, he was given an opportunity to test it. AT&T rolled out its service at different times in different regions, which allowed for a natural experiment. Region by region, as smartphone adoption rose, he found that emergency units reported an increasing number of injuries for children under five, such as broken bones and concussions.[13] That was consistent with what had happened at the playground but could of course be caused by something other than distracted parents. The economist set out to find out who or what was driving these injuries. He found that the increase happened when parents watched their children at public playgrounds, at pools or at home, but not when teachers or coaches supervised the children. Similarly, the German Lifeguard Association issued a warning that an increasing number of parents are fixated on their smartphones instead of supervising their children on pools and beaches, risking the hazard of a child drowning before they notice.[14] Drowning can be fast and silent.

The sight of parents distracted by their mobile phones in the company of their children has become normal. Like the Yale student, some parents sit on playground benches early in the morning, scrolling and clicking, absent to the fact that their little child has no one to play with. Others push buggies while gazing at the phone screens rather than at their babies seeking to make eye contact with them. Children complain, beg and try to make the phone go away. As the story goes, a five-year-old hid his mother's Blackberry so that she would talk to him, and another boy got so upset that he flushed his father's iPhone down the toilet. But, not much later, the same parents will likely complain that their children themselves are glued to the black mirror.

Sean Parker, former president of Facebook, once commented on the use of Facebook: 'God only knows what it's doing to our children's brains.'[15] Parker was talking about children's excessive use of social media. But parents' use can have a similar impact on their children's development. Leaving aside the question of how harmful excessive use of digital media actually is, there is an undeniably direct effect: the more hours parents spend on the phone, the fewer hours are available for parenting and bonding. What this loss of time together does to children's development is less well understood. The result can be physical damage, such as noticing too late that children are about to injure themselves, and psychological damage, such as children developing feelings of not deserving attention.

Half of US teenagers said that their moms or dads are distracted by their phones while the teenagers try to talk to them, and many wish their parents would spend less time on the phone. One in four teenagers believe that their parents are addicted to their phones.[16] Teens with distracted parents also feel that their parents express less warmth, a possible cause of teen anxiety and depression. Yet, as mentioned before, these studies report correlations, not causes. Parents appear to notice when using a phone that their children are not as relaxed and more easily upset, but some continue anyway. These children get the signal that whatever their parents do on their smartphone is more important than they are.

Conversely, when parents watch what children do, this sends a signal to children that what they are doing is important, and they try harder. Children even perform better at sports when their parents are watching than when parents are on their phones. In general, children need attention in order to develop their skills. That is also the key to early language learning. In one study, thirty-eight mothers taught their two-year-olds two novel words, with one minute of teaching time for each word. One of these periods was interrupted by a mobile phone call, the other not. If the period was interrupted, the remaining time was always added afterwards, so that the total time spent on teaching each word remained identical. When the teaching was not interrupted, children learned the word; when teaching was interrupted, they did not.[17]

Studies also show that the best parents can do for early language development is to read stories aloud to their children and keep going even after a child can read. In contrast, when watching baby videos such as *Baby Einstein* and *Brainy Baby*, children under the age of two learn less than by listening to a person.[18] These allegedly smart early language-learning programmes are designed primarily to grab kids' attention and do not deliver what they promise.

Daddy, Where Does the Phone Sleep?

Intermittent reinforcement makes quite a few people check their phone more often than they say they really desire. For some, this urge cannot be resisted during yoga, a religious service or a funeral. A dopamine shot may become more important than the goal to relax, to pray or to commemorate a deceased friend. To regain self-control, building up new habits may help. Research indicates that self-control measures attenuate the relationship between use of electronic media and loss of sleep.[19] And these should be learned as early as possible. Some parents have agreed on smartphone-free time or space with their children; others agree on having no phone at the table during meals. Others again have bought or built a cute little bed along with their child's first smartphone (figure 10.1). Before getting ready for bed, the child can put the phone into its own little bed outside the child's room. This creates a habit that can help prevent children from spending their nights texting, posting and watching videos under the blankets. Both phones and humans reload while asleep.

FIGURE 10.1: Smartphone bed. Children learn the habit of putting their phone in its little bed before getting into their own. While 'sleeping', the smartphone – like a human being – is loaded with energy.

These habits and devices define the culture in a family and can be adapted to the specific needs of its members. Whatever the rules agreed upon, they should hold for parents and children equally. There are no limits to creativity. In the hallway of a friend's home I discovered a bag hanging on the wall with eight pockets, inviting guests to leave their phones there in order to foster a good dinner conversation. If you truly want to spend *less* time on the phone and *more* time on personal relationships with children, friends and family, there are plenty of means to make this possible.

USE IT OR LOSE IT

In the early hours of 1 June 2009, Air France Flight 447 was on its way from Rio de Janeiro to Paris. It was business as usual: passengers were sleeping, dozing, reading or watching a video. The route crossed the intertropical convergence zone, passing through the top of a powerful thunderstorm. At 2:02 a.m., after a short briefing, the captain took a break. His two co-pilots took over the plane. Twelve minutes later, the plane plunged into the Atlantic Ocean, killing all 228 people aboard.

What had happened? Four minutes before the crash, the autopilot disengaged. It disconnected because the air-speed sensors iced over, and it no longer had reliable data. The two co-pilots were forced to fly the plane manually, without reliable indicators of air-speed. Within a fraction of a second, the crew found itself in one of the most dangerous crisis scenarios. Neither of them had ever received training on how to fly the plane in this situation at cruise altitude. What made it worse, at the moment when the autopilot disengaged and the plane rolled to the right, the pilot flying reacted with a correction to the left that was too extreme for high altitude and destabilized the plane. At high altitudes, the air is thin, and smaller manual corrections are needed than at low altitudes. The pilot flying also tried to put the plane into a climb, which caused it to lose speed. That initiated two loud *stall* warnings in the cockpit. 'Stall' means that the minimal speed necessary to keep the plane flying is no longer obtained, and the plane plunges. Pilots are trained to put the nose of the plane down in such a situation to gain speed again. But the black-box record showed that the pilots were confused about what was going on. The aircraft fell like a stone from the sky. One can only imagine what the terrified passengers and crew experienced in the final moments. The last recorded speed before impact was just over 120 miles per hour.

The final report of the investigation pointed out a lack of training in manual flying at high altitudes as a contributing factor to the disaster. In the course of increasing automation of planes, basic flying skills were insufficiently taught.[20] The disaster of Flight 447 had many causes, some of which remain uncertain, but one thing is clear. The crash was entirely unnecessary.[21]

Automation for Regular Events, Humans for Unexpected Events

Airlines and plane manufacturers were among the first to move towards autopilots. Automation can increase safety in situations that are stable and predictable, as in regular high-altitude cruising, but routinely relying on it can result in pilots who have little experience what to do if the autopilot fails. The Air France Flight 447 crash and similar accidents indicate that pilots have become too dependent on computerized systems and may not know what to do when unexpected things happen. In response, the US Federal Aviation Administration released a 'safety alert for operators' in 2013. It recommended that airlines instruct their pilots to spend less time flying on autopilot and more time flying by hand and sight.[22]

Like the Aviation Administration, the US Navy has realized that growing dependence on automation can be fatal. Around 2000, the Navy had begun to phase out training its service members to navigate by the stars or use sextants and charts in favour of electronic navigation systems, such as GPS.[23] After the initial enthusiasm that perfect computer technology can replace imperfect human judgement, the Navy realized that in a war satellite signals are likely to be hacked or jammed, and that satellites may even be shot down. Meanwhile, the Naval Academy has now gone back to basics and trains its members to use their own brains.

As we have seen in Chapter 4, automated cars share the same problem. Computers can take over an ever-increasing number of routine tasks, such as parking and overtaking on highways, but when something unexpected happens, a human driver is needed to step in. Unlike the pilots of Air France 447, human drivers have even less time to react, often only a few seconds or fractions of seconds. This is why alert drivers are needed in regular traffic. Outsourcing driving skills to onboard computers and sensors does not relinquish this need. As mentioned earlier, one way out is to build closed and controlled highways or cities that are adapted to the limited capability of automation. This option, however, does not appear as easy for aviation. The general dilemma follows from the stable-world principle: outsourcing navigation skills works as long as everything goes according to plan, but alert and trained humans are required for situations where something happens out of the blue. This dilemma is known as the *automation paradox*:[24]

> The more advanced an automated system, the more crucial an experienced and attentive human controller.

A similar dilemma exists with GPS systems. They are immensely useful for driving or walking. But relying on them routinely in everyday life reduces the development of spatial reasoning, including navigation ability and the ability to form a mental map of the environment.[25] When we use GPS all the time, our brain doesn't bother to build a cognitive map of our surroundings. We hardly know where the river or lake is, or where north or south are. When the phone battery unexpectedly dies, we will not know where the restaurant is where we are supposed to meet our friends, and since we have not memorized the phone numbers of our friends either, we are lost. We might not even know how to get back to our Airbnb. In a world of certainty, where GPS always works without a hitch, our spatial sense and memory could be outsourced and dispensed with. In the real world, GPS can fail. It already failed for more than twelve hours in 2015 due to failures in the satellite network.[26] It may get a bug, run out of batteries or become the victim of an international hacker attack.

Using GPS started as an option. It helped to navigate through new and unknown territory. Overusing this option leads to a vicious circle. Previous skills – reading a map, knowing where north is, memorizing street signs, noticing landmarks – become underused or are lost entirely. That, in turn, makes people more dependent on the system. When something unexpected happens, then there is no option left. To break this circle, it can be helpful to develop habits that allow the advantages of GPS technology to be used without losing all of one's own navigation skills. Some people use GPS only for finding new locations, but then exercise their spatial memory to find old ones. Others use GPS while walking but turn the audio off.

Trying to find old locations with your own spatial sense keeps it engaged and alive. Heedlessly following audio commands such as 'turn right now' and doing precisely what one is told is the worst for fostering a spatial sense. Astounding stories have been reported about people making a trip to pick up some groceries and ending up hundreds of miles from their destination.[27] As a famous scientific study with London taxi drivers has shown, developing a sense of navigation changes your brain. These taxi drivers who had no GPS developed alterations in their brain functions as they learned to navigate. The brain is like a muscle: it needs to be exercised. Use it or lose it.

11
Fact or Fake?

'Children must be taught how to think, not what to think.'
                                                    Margaret Mead[1]

*'Instead of seeking to outperform the human brain, I should
have sought to understand the human heart.'*
                                    Kai-Fu Lee, former head of Google China[2]

We think it is easy to tell a fact from a fake. Sometimes it is, but at
other times it can be extremely tough – particularly if a narrative
contradicts one's own experience. The seventeenth-century English
philosopher and physician John Locke told this story:[3]

> And as it happened to a *Dutch* Ambassador, who entertaining the King
> of *Siam* with the particularities of *Holland*, which he was inquisitive
> after, amongst other things told him, that the Water in his Country,
> would sometimes, in cold weather, be so hard, that Men walked upon
> it, and that it would bear an Elephant, if he were there. To which the
> King replied, *Hitherto I have believed the strange Things you have told
> me, because I look upon you as a sober fair man, but now I am sure
> you lie.*

Locke was a founder of empiricism, the claim that all our knowledge, except possibly logic and mathematics, stems from experience.
He distinguished between certainty (knowledge) and probability (rea-
sonableness). If you have seen a man walking on ice, this is knowledge,
not probability. If you haven't, it is probability. For Locke, probability

depends on two factors: conformity with one's own experience and the testimony of others' experience. If the King of Siam, who has never seen water turning into ice, is told that the Dutch can walk on it, this report contradicts his experience, and all depends on the credibility of the witnesses: their number, integrity and skill, and the existence of contrary testimonies. There was only one witness, the ambassador, and so the king concluded he was a liar.

Throughout history and on to the present day, telling fact from fake has remained a challenge. Even if we know by hindsight, we often cannot know by foresight. Consider another historical example. In the year 1515, the German master painter Albrecht Dürer carved a woodcut of a rhinoceros (figure 11.1, left). Dürer had never seen this animal with his own eyes; he relied on a sketch and a newsletter sent by a merchant from Lisbon. Similarly, relying on the testimony of others, the English cleric Edward Topsell carved a woodcut depicting a unicorn (figure 11.1, right).[4]

Imagine you were born in Dürer's hometown of Nuremberg in 1616, the year the Roman Inquisition demanded that Galileo abandon his belief that the earth and planets revolved around the sun. You grew up in a time when facts were decided by religion rather than science, and travelling far from home was strenuous. Thanks to the invention of the printing press, you were able to see these two woodcuts. Would you have believed such animals really exist? A huge animal with a horn on its nose and a massive protective armour that

FIGURE 11.1: Which one is a real animal? Albrecht Dürer's woodcut of a rhinoceros from 1515 and Edward Topsell's woodcut of a unicorn from 1607.

surpasses the heaviest battle horse? Or this slender horse-like animal with a very long thin horn? Unicorns had at least been painted before, most famously by Leonardo da Vinci, and its long horns had been found and exhibited (these were in fact narwhal horns, but people then had never seen a narwhal either). Your conclusion might have been that both animals are equally plausible, or implausible.

The cases of frozen water, the rhinoceros and the unicorn illustrate how difficult it can be to tell fact from fiction. After the printing press was invented, Europe witnessed a wave of fake news on printed broadsides and pamphlets. Each revolution in communication technology, from the printing press to the internet, has opened new gates for a flood of disinformation. One might object that modern technology has made it easier to sort out the fakes from the real thing. If photography had then existed, the ambassador of Holland might have convinced the king by showing him a photo of people skating on hard water. Yet photos themselves provide no failsafe proof. Already in 1917, two Yorkshire girls aged ten and sixteen took photographs of themselves with tiny fairies dancing around their heads.[5] Arthur Conan Doyle, the creator of Sherlock Holmes and, unlike his famous character, a staunch believer in spiritualism, was convinced that these photos were genuine. Speculation is still rife about how the girls got the fairies into the pictures; they never disclosed their technique. With today's software technology, photos and videos can easily be edited by everyone. In a *deepfake*, a person in an image or video is replaced with someone else's face or body; this can already be done live, such as during a Zoom meeting. Or what politicians say in a video can be altered, literally putting words into their mouth. In fact, as technology advances, it may grow increasingly difficult to separate truth from edited truth. That also means that people need to become smarter in understanding who is behind a message, photo or video, and in evaluating the trustworthiness of content.

Fact checking has become a buzzword, and currently over one hundred fact-checking projects around the world are in operation. International Fact-Checking Day appropriately takes place straight after April Fool's Day, on 2 April. Yet facts alone are not synonymous with the truth; the facts can be 100 per cent right, but the story can still be misleading, if driven by a hidden agenda. And who checks the fact checkers? For instance, when the now-defunct conservative magazine the *Weekly Standard* became an approved fact checker at Facebook, progressive watchdog groups protested, having previously criticized the *Weekly Standard* for pushing false claims about Obamacare.[6] What we have today are some fact-checking organizations accusing others of being partisan fact checkers.

FAKES

In George Orwell's *Nineteen Eighty-Four*, Winston Smith is an employee of the Ministry of Truth, whose mission is to propagate lies. Winston's greatest pleasure in life is his work, which entails altering unkept promises and false predictions made by Big Brother to fit the current facts. When the Ministry of Plenty, which maintains a regime of scarcity and starvation, reduced the chocolate ration after promising that it would not be lowered, Winston converted the promise into a warning that there might be a reduction. When the Ministry of Peace, which engages in warfare, predicted no invasion on the South Indian front by Eurasian enemies but then it happened, that paragraph in Big Brother's speech was turned into a prediction of the invasion. Minute by minute, the past is updated in newspapers, books, posters, films, soundtracks and photographs. Big Brother is never wrong.

In the pre-internet setting of Orwell's book, the Ministry of Truth employs thousands of employees to collect all copies of newspapers or books, destroy them and replace them with the altered versions. Today, digital technology enables every individual to alter evidence, photos and videos in a way that the forgery is hardly detectable. No Ministry of Truth is needed. As a consequence, the distinction between what is real and what is fake blurs. And that is not because people have to trust the testimony of others when they have not experienced an event themselves, as John Locke thought. Even after seeing a picture or video on the internet, we can no longer be sure to what degree it represents reality. Editing pictures of oneself has become normal conduct. The social media overflow with photos of beautifully optimized faces and bodies that may make those with a less spectacular physiognomy feel inferior, and in turn induce them to optimize their own photos. Manipulation has become so normal that unedited photos are often specially marked in social media as 'no filter'. When adolescent girls aged fourteen to eighteen were shown pictures of peers in which body parts appeared artificially slender, they found these pictures more 'natural' than unedited ones – even though the girls were perfectly aware that the pictures had been manipulated. [7] When the meaning of a term changes, thinking changes. Artificial is Natural.

People spread fake pictures or fake news for mundane reasons such as social comparison and getting attention and 'likes'. But they also do so to exclude and punish social groups. These motives are political and nothing new. When the Black Death hit Europe in the mid-fourteenth century, Jews were accused of deliberately poisoning the wells and were massacred in Toulon, Barcelona, Basel and the rest of Europe. In Strasbourg, they were burned alive as a preventive measure before the plague had even arrived. Jews were also accused of slaughtering Christian children and using their blood for religious rituals, a myth renewed by QAnon and other twenty-first-century conspiracy communities. [8] The Covid-19 pandemic provided a new fertile ground for blaming other cultures. At the beginning of the pandemic, citizens of Asian descent were attacked in many non-Asian countries, and Chinese restaurants reported a drop of 50 per cent in business as customers shunned them. Rumours and stigmas spread rapidly through social media, with claims that Chinese cookies, rice and Red Bull were contaminated with the virus, and that the whole Covid-19 pandemic was a conspiracy against Trump to drag him down in the presidential election. [9] Conspiracy theories have led to lower acceptance of masks, social distancing and vaccines during the pandemic and have had a disastrous impact on HIV prevention, Zika and Ebola in the past.

I Have Said It Thrice

Before the Brexit referendum, Boris Johnson explained to the British how they had become the victims of the European Union, a bureaucratic monster that chains free markets and suffocates its citizens with ludicrous rules. One of the silly rules, he wrote in the *Telegraph*, is that children under eight aren't allowed to blow up balloons. Another one is that you can't recycle a tea bag.[10] Months before the Brexit vote, when questioned during a parliamentary Treasury Committee hearing as to which EU regulations actually stated this, Johnson bluntly told the committee chairman that it says so on the website of the European Commission. The chairman, however, had the toy safety requirements in front of him, and there was no such rule – no ban on blowing up balloons, not even a requirement that parents should be present. The safety requirement merely asked for warning labels on the packaging that children under eight can choke on balloons. Johnson had fabricated the story. When the chairman also pointed out that there was no EU legislation that forbids recycling tea bags, Johnson had to admit that this decision was in fact taken by the local Cardiff City Council. But what about the coffins? Johnson had also told the public about ridiculous European legislation governing the weight, dimension and composition of coffins, another myth. Or prawn cocktail crisps? According to Johnson, one of the biggest threats to the freedom of the British food industry was the EU ban on prawn cocktail flavour crisps. He told the tale of bravely travelling to Brussels to confront the bossy female bureaucrat responsible for outlawing them, a symbolic humiliation of British democracy. In his own words, 'we will die in the last ditch to preserve the prawn cocktail flavour crisp'. Once again, no such EU ruling existed, and probably also no such woman, as he had made up many of his stories about Brussels.[11] Yet in the end, that did not matter. The fairytales paid off.

Why would people believe in fake news? The common answer is that people are stupid, not interested in evidence and want to have their opinions confirmed. That may be true in some cases, but there is a more interesting explanation based on a fundamental psychological law:

> *Reiteration effect*: The more frequently an assertion is repeated, the more believable it becomes, independent of whether it is true or false.

In Lewis Carroll's poem 'The Hunting of The Snark', the Bellman proclaims: 'I have said it thrice: What I tell you three times is true.'[12] The reiteration effect works with political news that confirm our prejudices, but surprisingly also with neutral news and trivia. I discovered this myself in an experiment I conducted where participants were given assertions to read such as 'The People's Republic of China was founded in 1947' and 'There are more Roman Catholics in the world than Muslims.'[13] For each assertion, participants had to express their confidence in whether it was true. Two weeks later, they were given a new set of assertions containing some of the old ones. The same procedure was repeated another two weeks later. Participants' belief in the repeated assertions increased with every repetition, whether they were true or not.

Note that the reiteration effect assumes lack of knowledge. Someone who knows for sure that the People's Republic of China was proclaimed in 1949 by Mao Zedong after the Chinese Civil War ended will not be influenced by repetitions of a false fact. In general, the larger people's ignorance about a topic, the more likely they will be subject to the reiteration effect. Predictions about the future are always uncertain, and here reiteration has a fertile field for persuasion – and for influencing what will happen. The Roman statesman Cato is said to have reiterated his call to destroy Carthage at the end of every one of his speeches until his call became reality. The Russian revolutionary Vladimir Lenin, among others, is reported to have said that a lie told often enough becomes a truth. In the social media, a fake news cascade begins with a rumour and continues when others propagate the rumour by retweeting it. As a consequence, people may hear the same message repeated several times, and the reiteration effect kicks in. Each time the news sounds more believable, until we firmly believe it.

Yet repetition alone is not the entire story. Five repetitions are more powerful if they come from five different people than from the same person. Some of these five people may even be social bots. These algorithms present themselves as people in order to influence human users on social media. Coordinated networks of bots, called botnets, can be effective in spreading messages to real users. In one study, a botnet spread Twitter hashtags such as #getyourflushot, to encourage users to vaccinate, and #turkeyface, for photoshopping a celebrity's face onto a turkey.[14] Within a short time, 25,000 human users followed the botnet, most of them following several bots. Human users were influenced by how many different bots repeated a message, not just the number of times a message was repeated. In this way, the spread of news in the social media differs from the spread of a virus in infectious diseases. While the chance of getting infected increases with each exposure to the virus, no matter whether it is from the same or a different infected person, the chances that information spreads through Twitter depend crucially on both the number of repetitions and the number of different people or bots that repeat the content.

When we talk about fake news, we tend to think of politicians' lies or far-fetched conspiracy stories such as that the SARS Corona-2 virus was genetically engineered by a Chinese biological weapons programme, caused by the electromagnetic fields of the 5G mobile networks or manufactured by Jews to cause a global collapse of the stock market and profit from insider trading. Yet we hardly notice the mass of 'normal' fake news. It is much subtler than plainly wrong facts and sometimes not even deliberate, but inadvertently dreamed up.

Blunders

One source of unintentional fake news is blunders. A blunder is due to someone making a mistake because of neglecting to think or read a source carefully. They may not be deliberate fakes, but they can be equally misleading. Often, a reader can immediately see that some news must be a blunder, even if they'd like the story to be true. If you enjoy jogging, for example, you might be receptive to this media headline about a study on longevity:[15]

For every hour of daily jogging, you live seven hours longer.

To invest one hour and gain seven – what more can you ask for? As a passionate jogger, you can start calculating how much longer you will live than the couch potatoes in your neighbourhood. But pause to think for a moment. If that claim were true, we could literally run ourselves into immortality. Jogging, say, four hours a day would mean living twenty-eight hours longer. That is more than a twenty-four-hour day, and thus our life expectancy would increase each day. Clearly something is wrong here. Indeed, the original study made no such claim. What it said was that this effect holds for two hours of jogging per *week*, not for more. More precisely, the seven-hour figure was estimated this way: a group of joggers aged forty-four, who run for two hours per week, spend a total of 0.43 years running by the age of eighty and win 2.8 years of increased life expectancy. These are the numbers that were translated into the headline proclaiming one hour of running for seven hours of living longer. More running is not necessarily better. On the contrary, excessive running can increase the risk of heart disease and shorten one's life.

The jogging headline is easily shown to be false – it just requires a bit of thought. Alternatively, one can switch from the website that featured the headline to more trustworthy sources on scientific studies, such as the *New York Times*, where one can find the correct claim that the gain in life expectancy is capped at around three years.[16]

FAIRYTALES ABOUT ALGORITHMS

Much of what you hear about AI is also riddled with fake news, often subtle, preying on awe or fear to capture your attention or to sell a product. The entire history of AI has been soaked with over-inflated promises and hopes, not so unlike those in stock markets that lead to bursting bubbles. The big downs in this rollercoaster ride were the 'AI winters' of the 1970s and 1980s, where funding, along with the reputation of AI, collapsed. As a result, AI became a dirty word for quite some time. For instance, when the supercomputer Watson was created in 2011, IBM did not call it AI but 'cognitive computing', fearing that otherwise no one would take Watson seriously. Since then, we have seen true advances in deep neural networks and computing power, but also unqualified, glorified claims about the general superiority of technologies over humans. Many of these tall tales are motivated by making profit, getting funding or wishful thinking. Promises about the future are cheap but hard to evaluate. One can always say, if it's not now, it will be soon.

There is another, more subtle and interesting form of hype. It works by using terms the audience likely misunderstands, and by rewriting the past. This technique recalls Winston Smith's attempts at the Ministry of Truth to alter reality in order to create the impression of an omniscient Big Brother. I will briefly describe only a few cases, but the general message is to beware of extravagant claims. The first uses a method of persuasion that has stood the test of time in centuries of advertisement: to describe a product by using a term that that suggests properties it doesn't have.

Full Autonomy

As we saw in Chapter 4, the Society of Automotive Engineers distinguishes five levels of automation in cars, from cruise control (Level 1) to self-driving cars (Level 5), that is, cars that drive safely everywhere and in all traffic conditions without a human actively monitoring their operations. These levels are not the same. Nevertheless, car manufacturers often call their Level-2 or Level-3 cars 'self-driving' in advertisements, which tends to be repeated in the media. Take Tesla, whose marketing claim since 2016 has been that 'all Tesla cars being produced now have full self-driving hardware'[17] and whose owner, Elon Musk, promised 'full autonomy' by 2018.[18] At the same time, the advertisements correctly add that the system needs active monitoring by the driver, or that the proper software has yet to be developed. The expression 'full self-driving hardware' means that the computers can steer, brake and accelerate; but the main problem is having the intelligent software. By reiterating the terms 'full autonomy' and 'self-driving cars', more and more people have begun to believe that these vehicles are actually on the roads. This confusing and suggestive language has been noticed and led to lawsuits. For instance, the German Centre for Combating Unfair Competition has sued Tesla for making false promises to consumers.[19] The Centre, it should be mentioned, represents more than 1,000 companies, including Tesla's competitors Audi, BMW, Daimler and Volkswagen.

Why don't companies advertise the amazing progress in Level-2 driving that might eventually lead to full Level-3 driving? Car engineers can be proud of this new technology. Honesty and modesty might be the wiser option. It could avoid more reputational damage the moment people begin to notice that the words do not mean what they were led to believe.

Curing Cancer

A favourite turf of AI hype is healthcare. A case in point is IBM's marketing of Watson for Oncology which, as Chapter 3 explains, has little to do with what the computer is actually able to do. In the words of Peter Greulich, a former IBM manager, 'IBM ought to quit trying to cure cancer. They turned the marketing engine loose without controlling how to build and construct a product.'[20] Commercial companies have vested interests in selling their products, and IBM's marketing team has been quite successful in creating the illusion that Watson can cure cancer. They have been so successful that authors of popular books on AI have become company salespersons.

A second classic rule of persuasion is to present the reader with a false set of choices. You are told that the most important medical decisions are increasingly based on computers such as IBM Watson, and that these know you better than you and your doctor can. The only downside is that the AI will have to know everything about you and also will decide what is best for you. You can no longer make decisions about what you eat and what treatment you get because that's the very point. Here is your choice:

- Maintain your privacy and free decision in healthcare *or*
- Get access to far superior health care.

The logical conclusion, we are told, is that most people will choose superior healthcare and surrender to AI authority.[21] That may well be, but the choice is a wrong one. It reminds me of financial advertisements that ask us to choose between managing our own money badly or handing it over to a portfolio manager who will make far superior investments. That choice is wrong because studies have found no evidence that, on average, portfolio managers will increase your wealth more than you on your own.[22] It's an advertising ploy, aimed at increasing the managers' own wealth. Just as the financial ad discourages you from taking responsibility for your own wealth, authors who pose medical choices like the one above discourage you from making your own informed choice – and, to add insult to injury, young people from considering studying general medicine.

As I argued in Chapter 3, we can reap the benefits of AI to patients' health only if the two existing chronic diseases of healthcare systems – conflicting interests and risk illiteracy – are faced head on and cured. Otherwise, AI will be gamed and able to contribute little to patients' health. A supercomputer alone does not help patients. AI is always AI designed and marketed by people. To believe that mere computing power and smart algorithms by themselves will generate superior healthcare is an illusion. It means failing to understand that diseases are more complex and healthcare systems are more dysfunctional than many computer scientists anticipate.

So far, we have seen two classic methods of persuasion: using deceptive terms and presenting wrong choices. Another method is to use a well-known success story and refashion it so that it appears to support one's favourite message: that algorithms lead to superior decisions.

Moneyball

Moneyball, the 2003 US bestseller by Michael Lewis that spawned a movie starring Brad Pitt, tells the story of Oakland A's general manager Billy Beane and how he led his baseball team to greatness on a shoestring budget. The second hero is Bill James, a statistician, and their shared insight is that baseball can in essence be reduced to data and algorithms, which they call 'sabermetrics'. According to Lewis, for more than a century, managers and general managers relied on their guts or educated guesses for spotting future major league baseball players.[23] Beane in contrast, introduced an algorithm to spot 'sleepers', that is, unknown or underrated talents: 'It is simply a matter of figuring out the odds, and exploiting the laws of probability.'[24] In Lewis's account, the players recruited by algorithms were decisive for the Oakland A's success in the early 2000s.[25] In baseball, there is a long debate between relying on the intuition of experienced scouts for picking players and on statistical number crunching.[26] *Moneyball* argues that the revolutionary use of baseball statistics changed the game, one of the great victories of algorithms over expert intuition.

Hollywood is famous for stretching the truth into melodramatic stories. Baseball experts noted that Lewis likewise did not let the facts stand in the way of a good story. Among those facts, the relevant one here is that players selected by algorithms and featured by Lewis actually played relatively little part in Oakland's success. The team thrived primarily because of three superb pitchers known as the Big Three, all of whom were discovered by traditional scouting methods based on intuition and judgement, not by algorithms:

> At the heart of the pitching staff were three dominant starters: Mark Mulder, Tim Hudson, and Barry Zito. All three were early-round picks, highly scouted, and well regarded – Mulder and Zito were selected in the top ten of their respective drafts. This was hardly a case of Beane's spotting sleepers ... because of nuanced numbers. Indeed, Michael Lewis does not suggest that sabermetrics had anything to do with Beane drafting the three studs who led Oakland to greatness. Indeed, he virtually ignores them. Lewis devoted a few paragraphs to the Big Three (making the strained claim that Beane appreciated them for quirky reasons), quickly dropping them and transitioning to an entire chapter on ... Chad Bradford.[27]

Bradford was a pretty good relief pitcher but performed nowhere close to the Big Three in innings, wins or savings.[28] In fact, after Oakland A lost their Big Three pitchers, the team's successful run between 1998 and 2003 plopped. Lewis's account of the supreme wisdom of algorithms is a well-told story. But it is a fiction, conveniently leaving out the facts that do not fit its narrative. Nevertheless, it has become a staple example used by gifted storytellers and popular writers who want to convince us that AI will soon replace human judgement in all domains, even in ill-defined ones such as spotting future top baseball players.[29] The better alternative would be to ask how baseball statistics and expert intuition can be combined to make better decisions, but that would be a difficult question and not the fabric for a grand tale of heroic success.

The story about Oakland A's success illustrates a genre that twists the evidence to create the impression that algorithms have been the key to better decisions in situations where they play little role. Such hype helps to sell popular books but does not help us understand the actual potential and limits of AI.

PERSONALIZED ADS: A BUBBLE
ABOUT TO BURST?

Google earns about 80 per cent of its revenue from ads, and Facebook even 97 per cent. The advertisers pay these astronomical sums. Therefore, one might expect them to have carefully checked whether the return on their ads justifies the costs. While at Google, Eric Schmidt assured advertisers that they pay only for what works: 'Our business is highly measurable. We know that if you spend X dollars on ads, you'll get Y dollars in revenues.'[30] Yet there is increasing evidence that this is not the case; rather, it seems unclear in many cases whether personalized ads actually pay.

Every time you search for information about a product online, manufacturers and retailers can bid for paid ('sponsored') *search ads* that are placed above the unpaid ('organic') search results. Which company wins the bid is determined by an automatic auction. Google and others earn money by every click on the sponsored ad, but not if you click on the organic result. In addition, when you read online content such as sport, advertisers can bid to have *display ads* shown on the pages being read. These targeted ads are considerably more expensive than non-targeted advertising. They require that the platforms collect as much data about you as possible, in order to predict your clicks. This collection and analysis of personal data is the heart of surveillance capitalism. But there are now a number of reasons to suspect that this system fails to deliver what has been asserted and rather resembles a bubble that may burst.

Do Sponsored Ads Pay?

When Steve Tadelis, a professor of economics at the University of California, Berkeley, spent a year at eBay, its marketing consultants spoke of how profitable their ad campaigns were. The most successful method was *brand keyword advertising*, he was told. If a search includes a brand keyword, such as 'eBay motorcycle', Google, Bing and other platforms offer to place a paid link to the brand, here eBay, at the top of the organic search results. The consultants asserted that eBay earns $12 for each dollar spent on brand keyword advertising.[31]

Together with two economists at eBay, Tadelis conducted a number of experiments to measure the actual returns. In each experiment, eBay halted brand keyword advertising (on Google, Bing and Yahoo!) in one set of cities while continuing advertising in others. If the sponsored ads actually worked, eBay's earnings should decline in the periods where the ads were removed. But it didn't. Nor did earnings drop when eBay halted bidding for *non-brand keywords*, such as 'cell phone' and 'used gibson les paul'. Only new and infrequent users were influenced by ads, not more frequent users. Tadelis and his coresearchers calculated that eBay by no means earned $12 per dollar spent, as was claimed, but instead lost 63 cents for each dollar spent.[32] Having learned that they were actually losing money on these ads, eBay struck brand keyword advertising from its marketing budget.

Unlike the economists, the marketing consultants were looking at correlations, not causes. Say you run a well-known coffeehouse and hire two people, Jack and Joe, to hand out coupons in order to attract customers. Soon, half of the customers arrive with coupons distributed by Jack, but few with those distributed by Joe. You might well conclude that Jack's marketing strategy or charisma is superior and has led to some 50 per cent of sales. Yet, unlike Joe, who went downtown to give away coupons, Jack stood by the coffeehouse and gave coupons to those people in front of it.

Just as most of the people who arrived with Jack's coupons in hand would have visited the coffeehouse anyway, 99.5 per cent of the users ended up on eBay's website without the paid link. All they needed was to click on the 'organic' link to eBay or to go directly to eBay's website. Note that eBay has to pay Google only if you click on the sponsored link, not if you click on the organic link, which is typically just below it.

It is likely that other well-known brands would obtain similar results, but that remains conjecture because experiments on the topic are rarely conducted. An experiment with a less well-known brand, Edmunds. com, a source for automotive information, reported that when brand keyword advertisement was shut off, only half of its normal traffic flowed through the organic search link. The other half likely landed on websites of competitors, who sneakily bid on the keyword 'Edmunds'.[33] Yet, unlike the eBay experiment, this study could not provide precise measurements of the returns over investment. Thus, companies with low brand recognition might profit from brand keyword advertising, if only to protect themselves from competitors who might otherwise draw away their customers. But that is like being forced to distribute coupons in front of your coffeehouse because otherwise your competitors will stand there and distribute their own coupons.

The general lesson in face of the eBay experiments is that companies should run their own experiments to find out whether their ads actually pay. But even among those firms whose branded keyword ads were not regularly purchased by competitors (large firms like eBay), only one out of every ten stopped brand keyword advertising, and mostly without doing an experimental study. The majority of firms just continued conducting business as usual.

You might wonder why. It is in the best interest of a company to know how effective their advertising is, but that does not necessarily apply to its marketing department. The department can secure a larger budget and more personnel if their campaigns are seen as brilliant. It also competes with the print and TV marketing group, which provides another internal conflict of interest. Besides conflicts of interest, the prevailing reliance on correlations rather than experiments leads to overblown estimates of campaign effects.[34] For instance, Google shows its customers how to calculate the return over investment in a way that leads to these inflated estimates.[35]

Do Display Ads Pay?

In an analysis of twenty-five large-scale digital advertising field experiments from well-known retailers and financial service companies, researchers from Google and Microsoft concluded that it is nearly impossible to measure the returns of advertising.[36] Contrary to Eric Schmidt's claim, if the ads have an effect, these are so often so tiny that it is difficult to prove their existence. Similarly, an experiment with 1.5 million customers of a nationwide US retailer showed that displaying ads for a clothing line resulted in only tiny and insignificant effects on increased purchases, with one exception.[37] For customers aged over sixty-five, sales increased by 20 per cent due to advertising, but almost all of these elderly customers went to bricks-and-mortar stores as opposed to ordering online. Two follow-up experiments didn't find an overall increase in purchases either.

Adding to the uncertainty is the likelihood that display ads are no longer as effective as they might once have been. First, users today pay less attention to ads. Since 1994, for instance, when the first banner ads were displayed, the click-through rate has plunged from a remarkable 44 per cent to 0.46 per cent in 2018.[38] Second, many consumers are annoyed by the steady flood of ads and increasingly rely on ad blockers. And third, advertisers face click fraud. Entire botnets and human 'click farms' are employed to deliver click-throughs on ads in order to make campaigns look better than they really are. These services are even hired by crafty advertisers to click on the ads of their competitors in order to mislead them about the effect of their ads and increase their costs, thereby depleting their budget. Studies estimated that more than a quarter of website traffic showed non-human signals, and that more than half of all ad dollars spent on display ads were lost to fraud.[39] The upshot is that advertising platforms profit from ad fraud, including from every false click.

All in all, there is considerable uncertainty about whether and when sponsored and display ads increase sales, and, if they do, whether such an increase justifies the increased costs. Diminishing attention, ad blocking and fraud tilt the scale against the widely claimed great benefits for the advertiser. This recalls another situation in the years before the financial crisis of 2008, where the big global rating agencies gave AAA ratings to banks' toxic mortgages, which allowed banks to sell these for exaggerated prices. The rating agencies were not neutral: the banks paid them for the perfect grades, just as advertisement agencies profit from overstating the value of ads. The high prices for ads were one of the reasons why eBay began to check what they were actually getting for their money.[40]

If a sufficiently large number of companies followed eBay's lead, rose above their internal conflicts of interest and conducted their own experiments, the advertising bubble might well follow the fate of the pre-2008 financial bubble. That would not only be beneficial for the advertisers' budgets, but also have the potential to change society at large. For one, it would free the brainpower of bright young researchers who currently focus on predicting clicks, so that they can apply their talents to something more useful.

Crucially, if further experiments confirm that many ad campaigns do not deliver the promised return on investment, more companies might reconsider spending huge amounts on such personalized ads with little return. The pay-with-your-data model would crumble and, with it, the desire of tech companies to sell our attention and time. It would bring about the end of ad-based surveillance capitalism as we know it.

CHECKING TRUSTWORTHINESS

Checking the trustworthiness of sources entails more than checking facts. It requires digging out who is behind the information we get, what the underlying intentions are and whether the information is correct. Traditionally, investigative journalists have been the gate-keepers of trustworthy news. But their number has been dwindling since the rise of large media conglomerates in the 1980s, for whom publishing the truth about corruption or corporate crime may not be in their best financial interest. Advertisers have reduced spending with media that reported unfavourable details about their business practices. The rise of social media further contributes to the classical media's loss of control, with positive and negative consequences. On the one hand, people can report on issues such as corruption and violations of human rights not covered by media conglomerates. On the other hand, everyone can easily spread rumour, lies and hoaxes. Now, all of us are called to be our own investigative journalists. How many of us are ready?

Digital Natives

It is widely believed that being fluent on social media is equivalent to being able to navigate through the tricks and traps of the internet. Digital natives know how to keep multiple information on their finger-tips, fluidly switching between TikTok and Snapchat while texting a friend and uploading a selfie to Instagram. With hours of online experience every day, so one might think, skills to judge the credibility of information evolve naturally.

To see how skilled at this digital natives actually are, Stanford researchers assessed some 900 students from middle school, high school and college across twelve US states.[41] They asked the students to evaluate online sources via questions such as 'What is the evidence?' and 'Who is behind the information?' For instance, middle schoolers read an online article entitled 'Do millennials have good money habits?' written by a bank executive and sponsored by Bank of America, which argued that many millennials need help with financial planning. Then they were asked to think about one reason why they might not trust the article. Surprisingly, most students did not consider authorship or sponsorship and the resulting conflict of interest as grounds for scepticism. In another test, they were asked to look up the homepage of the online magazine *Slate* and determine whether its content was an advertisement or a news article. The middle schoolers could easily identify traditional ads with coupon codes. But over 80 per cent believed that a native (paid) ad clearly identified with the words 'sponsored content' was a real news story.

Are high school students better at evaluating online content? In that study, they were asked to evaluate two Facebook posts announcing Donald Trump's candidacy for president, one from Fox News and one from a similar-looking fake account. The real post contained a blue checkmark indicating that the account had been verified as legitimate by Facebook. Only a quarter of the high school students were aware of the significance of the blue checkmark, and one out of three found the fake Fox News account more trustworthy.

Another post shown to the high school students, from the photo-sharing website Imgur, featured a picture of malformed daisies along with the claim that the flowers had nuclear birth defects following Japan's nuclear disaster at Fukushima (figure 11.2). The question posed by the experimenters was whether the picture provides strong evidence about the conditions near the nuclear power plant. A naive person would be taken in by the compelling picture, while a critical reader would be more careful and note that there is no proof that the picture was actually taken near Fukushima. As one critical student noted:

> No, it does not really provide strong evidence. A photo posted by a
> stranger online has little credibility. This photo could very easily be

FIGURE 11.2: Nuclear birth defect? Mutated flowers, similar to those in one of the tasks of the Civic Online Reasoning Test.

photoshopped or stolen from another completely different source; we have no idea given this information, which makes it an unreliable source.

But only a minority of the high school students pointed out the unknown source and the lack of evidence. By contrast, three-quarters of them did not question the source or the evidence at all. Their reasoning was in line with the following argument of one student:

This post does provide strong evidence because it shows how the small and beautiful things were affected greatly, that they look and grow completely different than they are supposed to. Additionally, it suggests that such a disaster could happen to humans.[42]

All in all, the vast majority of high school children had never learned to reason critically about posts – despite being digital natives.

What about college students? Along with high school students, they were asked to evaluate whether a particular website was a reliable source of information about the minimum wage and were directed to an article on minimumwage.com entitled 'Denmark's Dollar Forty-One

Menu' (figure 11.3). The article takes up a question raised by the *New York Times*: if Denmark can pay their workers a comparatively high minimum wage, why can't the United States? It argues against raising the minimum wage because that would increase labour costs and make Big Macs cost more. The equivalent of the 'Dollar Menu' in Denmark is $1.41, making Danish fast food restaurants far less profitable. Therefore, the minimum wage would raise prices in the US and eliminate hundreds of thousands of jobs.

The website looks reliable and describes itself on the 'About Us' page as 'a project of the Employment Policies Institute (EPI)', which is 'a non-profit research organization dedicated to studying public policy issues surrounding employment growth'.[43] In response to the article, the *New York Times* reported that EPI 'is led by the advertising and public relations executive Richard B. Berman, who has made millions of dollars in Washington by taking up the causes of corporate America'. A reporter who visited the EPI headquarters found that nobody is employed there; it is just one of many of Berman's online

FIGURE 11.3: Is this a reliable source of information about the minimum wage? One of the tasks of the Civic Online Reasoning Test.

entities. That information, of course, cannot be found on minimum-wage.com. In order to find out, the students would have to exit the website and search for what is known about its sources – a process that is known as 'lateral reading' (as opposed to vertical reading, that is, how we read printed text). Yet, even though that possibility was explicitly mentioned in the instructions, the vast majority of students never ventured beyond the site. Instead, they trusted its appearance and what was said on the 'About Us' page. As one student explained:

> I read the 'About Us' page for minimumwage.com and also for Employment Policies Institute. EPI sponsors minimumwage.com and is a nonprofit research organization dedicated to studying policy issues surrounding employment, and it funds 'nonpartisan' studies by economists around the nation. The fact that the organization is a non-profit, that it sponsors nonpartisan studies, and that it contains both pros and cons of raising the minimum wage on its website, makes me trust this source.

This student reasoned soundly but based solely on how the organization portrayed itself. Less than 10 per cent of college and high school students went beyond the surface appearance of the webpage and were able to critically evaluate the site.

Regardless of what one thinks about the minimum wage, tracking down who is who behind a site reveals its hidden agenda. From middle school to college, however, most students rarely asked who stood behind an online source, did not consider the evidence for the claim presented, and did not consult independent sources to verify the claims. Rather, they took what was said at face value and were captivated by vivid photos and graphic design. Even when encouraged to do an internet search, most did not move beyond the website. All in all, they were easily duped online. Being a digital native does not mean being digitally savvy.

Professionals and Elite Students

That leaves us with the question, surely professionals and students from the best universities are better skilled at evaluating trustworthiness and evidence? To answer this, two of the researchers from the previous experiment rounded up ten professional fact checkers employed at well-regarded news and political fact-checking organizations, whose job is to ascertain truth in digital media, and ten professors of history, whose daily bread is to evaluate the credibility of written texts and the circumstances of their creation.[44] They also enlisted twenty-five undergraduates at Stanford, one of the most competitive universities in the world, located in the heart of Silicon Valley. These students represent our digital future.

Each of the fact checkers, historians and students was given eight minutes time per site to evaluate minimumwage.com and two other websites. All of the fact checkers – but only 60 per cent of the historians and 40 per cent of the students – found out which sponsors were behind minimumwage.com and the Employment Policies Institute. Moreover, the fact checkers were much speedier at doing so, on average within 205 seconds, while those students who also found out took twice as long (419 seconds), with historians in between (361 seconds; figure 11.4).

What was the fact checkers' secret?

Consider the fastest checker. She looked at 'Denmark's Dollar Forty-One Menu' for only six seconds before going to the 'About' tab, where she learned that the site was a project of the Employment Policies Institute, and opened a link to it in a new tab alongside minimumwage.com. After spending just three seconds on the EPI home page, she clicked on their 'About' and read that it was founded in 1991 and is 'a non-profit

FIGURE 11.4: Average time that professional fact checkers, historians and digital natives (Stanford undergraduates) needed to find out who was behind the minimumwage.com website and the Employment Policies Institute. The percentage of members of each group who found the answers is shown on top of the icons for each group, and the average time it took them is shown in seconds (see text).

research organization dedicated to public policy issues'. 'This is profoundly not helpful,' she remarked, and then Googled the EPI. Reading the snippets, she skipped the first results, selected SourceWatch's entry on EPI and quipped: 'So this says it's one of several front groups created by a PR firm.' She scrolled until finding a linked quote from the *New York Times* reporter who had tried to visit the EPI office and found no evidence that it even existed. She clicked on the citation, provided by SourceWatch, and checked the claims by going to the website of National Public Radio, which provided a transcript of an interview with the reporter. Within a space of just two minutes, she discovered that the minimumwage.com and the EPI were not what they appeared to be:[45]

> Obviously, this isn't a legitimate organization, based on the reporting of this *New York Times* reporter. He talks about actually going there, he doesn't see any evidence at all that they actually had an office, there are no employees, all the staff there actually work for the PR firm.

Why did all fact checkers but not all of the students and historians detect the hidden agenda of the website? The answer is that many students and historians used different strategies; in particular, they didn't budge from the landing page and read through it in its entirety. If they did stray from the page, they did so much later in order to click on links that matched their personal interests. All of them no doubt understood that websites are carefully designed and may be financed by groups that promote particular interests, often partisan ones. Yet most lacked the skills to find out. These skills are rules that can be easily learned.

Smart Rules for Judging Trustworthiness

Assume you are contacted by a new website and have limited time for research. The site may ask you to sign up for a movement to decrease the minimum wage, increase tobacco tax, legalize marijuana, sign a petition against gay marriage, donate money to their cause or simply ask you to pass on news. You want to find out whether the site is trustworthy. Here are four rules that professional fact checkers use:

1. *Lateral Reading.* Leave the site early, before reading everything. Take only a brief glance at the content and then move on to other sites to do a background check on its credentials and agenda.
2. *Exercise click restraint.* When you get search results, do not click on the first entry on the first page. Use snippets to search for clues about the site's reliability, that is, scan the entire first page (or even more pages) of results in order to make a wise first click.
3. *Go back and read.* Once you know more about the organization behind the site, read the text carefully with an understanding of the agenda.
4. *Ignore surface features.* Don't pay attention to the design of websites or to top-level domains like .com or .org.

Quickly finding out who is behind a website can be done by first going to 'About' on the site and then leaving the site to do a search of the organization's name, look up independent sources and go from there. This step requires some knowledge of sources and organizations, such as how they are aligned with political parties or with societal issues. Click restraint requires some knowledge of online structures, such as that the first result presented on a search engine is not necessarily the most relevant for your search. Results may make the top of the list because of a vocal group on the net, such as MMR anti-vaxxers, not because of the quality of evidence. Or it is a disguised ad. That first click can be destiny; it may send you on the wrong trail. Always think before you click.

Not-So-Smart Rules

The four rules have been shown to improve students' evaluation of online sources.[46] Yet many digital natives do not seem to be aware of them. Instead, they may be following old advice, which came in the form of a checklist. Consider this widely disseminated list for evaluating web pages, which can be found on hundreds of websites – including the websites of many universities. It asks you to evaluate a page on the basis of five criteria:[47]

Accuracy. If your page lists the author and institution that published the page and provides a way of contacting him/her and . . .

Authority. If your page lists the author credentials and its domain is preferred (.edu, .gov, .org, or .net), and . . .

Objectivity. If your page provides accurate information with limited advertising and it is objective in presenting the information, and . . .

Currency. If your page is current and updated regularly (as stated on the page) and the links (if any) are also up to date, and . . .

Coverage. If you can view the information properly – not limited to fees, browser technology or software requirement, then . . . *You may have a web page that could be of value to your research!*

Or you may not. This checklist does *not* ask the user to leave the page and seek independent information. It assumes that all relevant information appears on the page and that investigating it carefully is sufficient. It deals with features and appearances of websites to which companies can always adapt, while fact checkers' rules deal with critical actions that *we* can take, independent of any modifications made by companies. Versions of this list go back to 1998, the early days of the internet. It can provide clues about reliability, but it is no match for current strategies of persuasion and deception.

In reaction to these kinds of lists, many websites that want to hide their agenda try to fulfil the criteria perfectly. Take, for instance, the minimumwage.com website, which passes all criteria apart from the question of its domain. It lists authors and institution and provides contact information, which satisfies accuracy. There is no advertising, and the information looks objective; thus, it passes the objectivity test. Finally, the site and links are updated, and you can view the information properly without paying a fee, giving a thumbs-up to currency and coverage. Working through this list can provide a false sense of security. The fact checkers succeeded because they knew that the website designers who want to hide their agenda would be careful to satisfy as many items as possible on this standard pre-2000 list.

Governments pour millions into equipping students with digital tools, from tablets to interactive white boards. Equally important, however, are investments in a general curriculum on staying smart in a smart world. Few governments have realized its importance to date.

It comes as little surprise that Finland – which ranks consistently as one of the top countries worldwide with respect to happiness, press freedom, social justice and gender equality, and whose schools consistently excel in international tests of maths, science and language skills – is also at the vanguard of teaching students to tell facts from fakes, pseudoscience from science and gossip from information. Its best-known digital literacy toolkit, called Faktabaari ('FactBar'), is taught from elementary to high school.[48] Finland also launched the award-winning massive open online course 'Elements of AI', available in many languages. Learning in school how to become digitally savvy should not be confined to the land of happy and egalitarian Finns.

THE CEMENT OF SOCIETY

Trust is the cement of a society. In small villages centuries ago, everyone could closely watch everyone else, and people knew what to expect from whom. Little trust was needed, except, as Martin Luther noted, in God.[49] If someone cheated, stole or lied, this person could be identified quickly and punished or excluded from the community. Trust became important when human societies grew larger and more mobile.[50] Merchants trading across countries and continents had to trust – without trust, there is no trade.

The invention of the World Wide Web made our social and economic relations even more dependent on trust. More than ever in human history, we interact with strangers whom we may never meet face to face. Should we trust a person whom we only know through online dating? Should we trust secret algorithms that calculate who should be considered for a job, a loan or social welfare? How many of the five-star ratings of a product we consider buying are genuine and how many are bought? Can we trust social media platforms if their business is to sell our attention and time to advertisers? And what about governments? According to a research team at the University of Oxford, some seventy governments worldwide have built social media misinformation teams to spread lies and conceal truths.[51] Should we just shrug and scroll through the news feed to get another dose of dopamine? We can close our eyes and keep going as a happy consumer, hoping for the best.

The alternative is to become a digitally keen citizen. If homes, factories and cities become smart, why not people? The digital world has made disinformation cheaper and more scalable than ever before.[52] But it also offers tools to find out about the trustworthiness of people and sources. We can get information about what AI can easily do and what it can't and consider how the pay-with-your data business model sells our time and attention. And we can vote for politicians that work together with the public to better understand and regulate the benefits and potential harms of AI. The General Data Protection Regulation of the European Union is a first step towards winning back trust. But even more political courage is needed to translate its general ideal of transparency and dignity into concrete measures. So far, many platforms try to outsmart the regulations, for instance, by making 'accept all cookies' a single click option, while other options require annoyingly extensive scrolling and multiple clicks.

Transparency starts with simple, concrete measures, such as making it easy for people to understand what they actually consent to if they click 'I accept'. Many information platforms hide the answer in lengthy, sometimes twenty-page terms-of-use agreements in a barely decipherable font, which are not written to be understandable. People are offered a choice between two dishonourable options, either to give uninformed consent or to spend hours trying to comprehend these oversized documents before entering a new platform. This forced choice is an affront to human dignity.

I have argued that there is a simple solution to this state of affairs: to require tech companies to replace unreadable documents with a one-pager that honestly and clearly explains what personal information is extracted and sent to which third parties and explicitly asks your consent to the platform becoming the new owner of your pictures and data.[53] To get there, we need engaged policy makers who are willing to fight for this change. But the fight for human dignity continues at a deeper level. Social media platforms are owned by a few immensely rich men who buy up competitors rather than promote market competition. As we have experienced with banks in the financial crisis, these platforms can pose a threat to a healthy democracy by becoming too powerful and too big to fail. A healthy economy thrives from more competitive innovation and less centralization. Rather than moaning to our friends that our children get too little sleep and are depressed by social media, we need to persuade governments to attack the root of the problem, to stop the surveillance business model.[54]

All these are measures that would allow both tech companies and politicians to win back the trust that is lost as people become increasingly aware of the amount of secrecy and misinformation, and the degree to which we are all subject to commercial and governmental surveillance. We should be able to enjoy social media without thousands of engineers and psychologists constantly working on further addiction methods. We should be able to profit from AI in tasks where it delivers better and faster than humans, without being misled to expect that it can predict all of our behaviour and improve all aspects of our lives.

The original dream of the internet was to open the door to the information age. Now we find ourselves in a world that is both an information and a disinformation age. The latter is a serious threat to human evolution: it can erode trust in institutions we have built for the better of all of us, such as government, science, investigative journalism and the justice system. We need to fix the internet; eliminate surveillance business models; resuscitate privacy and dignity. We should be able to look at digital technology with level-headed admiration rather than unwarranted awe or suspicion. To make the digital world a world in which we want to live.

Acknowledgements

How to Stay Smart in a Smart World builds on two earlier popular books of mine, *Gut Feelings* and *Risk Savvy*. *Gut Feelings* made intuition understandable and scientifically respectable, and *Risk Savvy* helped readers cope with risk and uncertainty. *How to Stay Smart* is a guide to staying in the driver's seat in a world increasingly populated by algorithms.

I wrote this book for a general audience to navigate the challenges of a digital world. It is not an academic book but it draws heavily on research, including my own on decision making under uncertainty at the Max Planck Institute for Human Development in Berlin. I am lucky to have the generous and unique support of the Max Planck Society and to profit from its splendid intellectual atmosphere. It's a research paradise. I also would like to thank David and Claudia Harding for their long-term support of the Harding Center for Risk Literacy, which I direct, now located at the University of Potsdam. For those who wish to learn more about the underlying research, I recommend K. Katsikopoulos, Ö. Şimşek, M. Buckmann and G. Gigerenzer (2020), *Classification in the wild* (Cambridge, MA: MIT Press), and G. Gigerenzer (2015), *Simply Rational: Decision Making in the Real World* (Oxford: Oxford University Press). Further pointers to the scholarly literature are provided in the reference list of this book.

I would like to thank Tom Chan, Eli Finkel, Wolfgang Gaissmaier, Sophie Hartmann, Gisela Henkes, Ralph Hertwig, Konstantinos Katsikopoulos, Gary Klein, Brenden Lake, Shenghua Luan, Sarah McGrew, John Monahan, Jean Czerlinski Ortega, Felix Rebitschek, Raul Rojas, Cynthia Rudin, Natasha D. Schüll, Katharina Schüller, Stephen Shladover, Özgür Şimşek, Amy Slep, Isaac Stanley-Becker,

Riccardo Viale, Sam Wineburg, Jason Yosinski and John Zerilli for their many helpful comments. I am also grateful to Josephine Greywoode at Penguin UK for her excellent input. My special thanks go to Rona Unrau, who has edited the entire manuscript and helped me to find sources and to improve draft after draft of the book. Rona has been a wonderful support. I am also thankful to Sarah Otterstetter, who designed the figures. Last but not least, my thanks go to my wife, Lorraine Daston, my daughter, Thalia Gigerenzer, and my son-in-law, Kyle Chan, who provided intellectual input and emotional support over the years spent working on this book, including the extraordinary year of 2020. The coronavirus put a stop to most of my scheduled talks and travel, but in my case the cloud had a silver lining: I suddenly had more time to work on this book.

References

Addiction Resource.net (2020, 5 March). *The average cost of illegal street drugs*. https://www.addictionresource.net/blog/cost-of-illegal-drugs/.

Advisory Council for Consumer Affairs at the Federal Ministry of Justice and Consumer Protection (2017). *Digital sovereignty*. Berlin: Federal Ministry of Justice and Consumer Protection. https://www.svr-verbraucherfragen.de/wp-content/uploads/English-Version.pdf.

Advisory Council for Consumer Affairs at the Federal Ministry of Justice and Consumer Protection (2018). *Consumer-friendly scoring: Recommendations for action*. Berlin: Federal Ministry of Justice and Consumer Protection. https://www.svr-verbraucherfragen.de/en/wp-content/uploads/sites/2/Recommandations-for-action.pdf.

AFP (2020, 26 October). 'Shocking' hack of psychotherapy records in Finland affects thousands. *Guardian*. https://www.theguardian.com/world/2020/oct/26/tens-of-thousands-psychotherapy-records-hacked-in-finland.

Aikman, D., Galesic, M., Gigerenzer, G., Kapadia, S., Katsikopoulos, K. V., Kothiyal, A., Murphy, E., and Neumann, T. (2021). Taking uncertainty seriously: Simplicity versus complexity in financial regulation. *Industrial and Corporate Change* (Vol. 30, pp. 317–345).

Allen, M. (2017, 9 November). Sean Parker unloads on Facebook: 'God only knows what it's doing to our children's brains'. *Axios*. https://www.axios.com/sean-parker-unloads-on-facebook-god-only-knows-what-its-doing-to-our-childrens-brains-1513306792-f855e7b4-4e99-4d60-8d51-2775559c2671.html.

Anderson, C. (2008, 23 June). The end of theory: The data deluge makes the scientific method obsolete. *Wired*. https://www.wired.com/2008/06/pb-theory/.

Anderson, G. (2013, 10 September). What happens to big data if the small data is wrong? *RetailWire*. https://retailwire.com/discussion/what-happens-to-big-data-if-the-small-data-is-wrong/.

Anderson, M., Vogels, E. A. and Turner, E. (2020, 6 February). *The upsides and downsides of online dating*. Pew Research Center. https://www.pewresearch.org/internet/2020/02/06/the-virtues-and-downsides-of-online-dating/.

Anderson, R. (2016, 6 September). The ugly truth about dating: Are we sacrificing love for convenience? *Psychology Today*. https://www.psychologytoday.com/us/blog/the-mating-game/201609/the-ugly-truth-about-online-dating.

Angelino, E., Larus-Stone, N., Alabi, D., Seltzer, M. and Rudin, C. (2018). Learning certifiably optimal rule lists for categorical data. *Journal of Machine Learning Research*, 18, 1–78.

Armstrong, J. S. (2010). *Persuasive advertising: Evidence-based principles*. London: Palgrave Macmillan.

Artinger, F. M., Kozodi, N., Wangenheim, F. and Gigerenzer, G. (2018). Recency: Prediction with smart data. In J. Goldenberg, J. Laran and A. Stephen (eds.), *2018 AMA Winter Academic Conference: Integrating paradigms in a world where marketing is everywhere, February 23–25, 2018, New Orleans, LA. Proceedings* (vol. 29, pp. L-2–L-6). Chicago, IL: American Marketing Association.

Asch, S. E. (1951). Effects of group pressure on the modification and distortion of judgments. In H. Guetzkow (ed.), *Groups, leadership, and men* (pp. 177–90). Pittsburgh, PA: Carnegie Press.

Aschwanden, C. (2016, 6 January). You can't trust what you read about nutrition. *FiveThirtyEight*. https://fivethirtyeight.com/features/you-cant-trust-what-you-read-about-nutrition/.

Awad, E. et al. (2018). The moral machine experiment. *Nature*, 563, 59–64.

Bailey, D. H., Borwein, J. M., Lopez de Prado, M. and Zhu, Q. (2014). Pseudo-mathematics and financial charlatanism: The effect of backtest overfitting on out-of-sample prediction. *Notices of the American Mathematical Society*, 61, 458–71.

Bainbridge, L. (1983). Ironies of automation. *Automatica*, 19, 775–9.

Baltrusaitis, J. (2019, 4 December, updated 2020, 20 June). Top 10 countries and cities by number of CCTV cameras. *Precise Security*. https://www.precisesecurity.com/articles/Top-10-Countries-by-Number-of-CCTV-Cameras.

Baraniuk, C. (2016, 4 February). GPS error caused '12 hours of problems' for companies. *BBC News*. https://www.bbc.com/news/technology-35491962.

Barnes, S. B. (2006). A privacy paradox: Social networking in the United States. *First Monday*, 11(9). https://firstmonday.org/article/view/1394/.

Barra, A. (2011, 27 September). The many problems with 'Moneyball'. *The Atlantic*. https://www.theatlantic.com/entertainment/archive/2011/09/the-many-problems-with-moneyball/245769/.

Barrowman, N. (2014). Correlation, causation, and confusion. *The New Atlantis*. https://www.thenewatlantis.com/publications/correlation-causation-and-confusion.

Begley, S. (2012, 28 March). In cancer science, many 'discoveries' don't hold up. *Science News*. http://www.reuters.com/article/us-science-cancer- idUSBRE 82R12P20120328.

Bennell, C., Taylor, P. J. and Snook, B. (2007). Clinical versus actuarial geographic profiling strategies: A review of the research. *Police Practice and Research*, 8, 335–45.

Benoliel, U. and Becher, S. I. (2019). The duty to read the unreadable. *Boston College Law Review*, 60, 2255–96.

Berg, N. and Gigerenzer, G. (2010), As-if behavioral economics: Neoclassical economics in disguise? *History of Economic Ideas*, 18, 133–65.

Bergin, T. (2018, March 29). How a data mining giant got me wrong. *Reuters*. https://www.reuters.com/article/us-data-privacy-acxiom-insight/how-a-data-mining-giant-got-me-wrong-idUSKBN1H513K.

Berwick, A. (2018, 14 November). How ZTE helps Venezuela create China-style social control. *Reuters*. https://www.reuters.com/investigates/special report/venezuela-zte/.

Best, J. (2013, 9 September). IBM Watson: The inside story of how the Jeopardy-winning supercomputer was born, and what it wants to do next. *TechRepublic*. https://www.techrepublic.com/article/ibm-watson-the-inside-story-of-how-the-jeopardy-winning-supercomputer-was-born-and-what-it-wants-to-do-next/.

Blake, T., Nosko, C. and Tadelis, S. (2015). Consumer heterogeneity and paid search effectiveness: A large scale field experiment. *Econometrica*, 83, 155–74.

Bliss, L. (2019, 5 July). How Utrecht became a paradise for cyclists. *Bloomberg CityLab*. https://www.bloomberg.com/news/articles/2019-07-05/how-the-dutch-made-utrecht-a-bicycle-first-city.

Boden, M. (2008), *Mind as machine. A history of cognitive science*. Oxford: Oxford University Press.

Bond, R. M. et al. (2012). A 61-million-person experiment in social influence and political mobilization. *Nature*, 489, 295–8.

Booth, R. (2014, 30 June). Facebook reveals news feed experiment to control emotions. *Guardian*. https://www.theguardian.com/technology/2014/jun/29/facebook-users-emotions-news-feeds.

Bostrom, N. (2015). *Superintelligence*. Oxford: Oxford University Press.

Brandstätter, E., Gigerenzer, G. and Hertwig, R. (2008). Risky choice with heuristics: Reply to Birnbaum (2008), Johnson, Schulte-Mecklenbeck and

Willemsen (2008), and Rieger and Wang (2008). *Psychological Review*, 115(1), 281–9.

Branwen, G. (2011). The neural net tank urban legend. https://www.gwern.net/Tanks.

Breakstone, J. Smith, M., Connors, P. et al. (2021). Lateral reading: College students learn to critically evaluate internet sources in an online course. *Harvard Kennedy School Misinformation Review*, 2(1).

Breakstone, J. Smith, M., Wineburg, S. et al. (2021). Student's civic online reasoning: A national portrait. *Educational Researcher*.

Breiman, L. (2001). Statistical modeling: The two cultures (with comments and a rejoinder by the author), *Statistical Science*, 16, 199–231.

Brin, S. and Page, L. (2012). Reprint of: The anatomy of a large-scale hypertextual web search engine. *Computer Networks*, 56, 3825–33. (Original work published 1998.)

Britt, R. R. (2015, 1 February). Drivers on cell phones kill thousands, snarl traffic. *Live Science*. https://www.livescience.com/121-drivers-cell-phones-kill-thousands-snarl-traffic.html.

Brockman, J. (ed.). (2019). *Possible minds*. New York: Penguin.

Brooks, R. (2015). Mistaking performance for competence. In J. Brockman (ed.), *What to think about machines that think* (pp. 108–11). New York: Harper.

Brown, A. (2019, 24 June). Couples who meet online are more diverse than those who meet in other ways, largely because they're younger. Pew Research. https://www.pewresearch.org/fact-tank/2019/06/24/couples-who-meet-online-are-more-diverse-than-those-who-meet-in-other-ways-largely-because-theyre-younger/.

Brown, J. (2017, 10 August). Why everyone is hating on IBM Watson – including the people who helped make it. *Gizmodo*. https://gizmodo.com/why-everyone-is-hating-on-watson-including-the-people-w-1797510888.

Brown, K. V. (2015, 19 August). We talked to 24 victims of the Ashley Madison hack about their exposed secrets. *Splinter*. https://splinternews.com/we-talked-to-24-victims-of-the-ashley-madison-hack-abou-1793850144.

Brown, T. (1838). *Lectures on the philosophy of the human mind*. London: William Tait.

Bruch, E. E. and Newman, M. E. J. (2018). Aspirational pursuit of mates in online dating markets. *Science Advances*, 4(8): eaap9815.

Brumfiel, G. (2016, 28 February). U.S. Navy brings back navigation by the stars for officers. *NPR*. https://text.npr.org/467210492.

Brunswik, E. (1956). *Perception and the representative design of psychological experiments*. Los Angeles: University of California Press.

Buolamwini, J. and Gebru, T. (2018). Gender shades: Intersectional accuracy disparities in commercial gender classification. *Proceedings in Machine Learning Research*, 81, 1–15.

Burell, J. (2016). How the machine 'thinks': Understanding opacity in machine learning algorithms. *Big Data and Society*, January–June 2016, 1–12.

Buss, D. (2019). *Evolutionary psychology: The new science of the mind* (6th ed.). New York: Routledge.

Cacioppo, J., Cacioppo, S., Gonzaga, G. C., Ogburn, E. L. and VanderWeele, T. J. (2013). Marital satisfaction and break-ups differ across on-line and off-line meeting venues. *PNAS*, 110, 10135–40.

Cahall, B., Bergen, P., Sterman, D. and Schneider, E. (2014, 13 January). Do NSA's bulk surveillance programs stop terrorists? *New America*. https://www.newamerica.org/international-security/policy-papers/do-nsas-bulk-surveillance-programs-stop-terrorists/.

Calaprice, A. (2011). *The ultimate quotable Einstein*. Princeton, NJ: Princeton University Press.

Carr, N. (2014). *The glass cage*. New York: Norton.

Carroll, L. (2020). *The hunting of the snark*. Copenhagen: SAGA Egmont. (Original work published 1876.)

Centers for Disease Control and Prevention (2020, 6 October). *Transportation safety: Distracted driving*. https://www.cdc.gov/transportationsafety/distracted_driving/.

Chalmers, I. and Glasziou, P. (2009). Avoidable waste in the production and reporting of research evidence. *Lancet*, 374(9683), 86–9.

Chawla, D. S. (2018). The need for digital intelligence. *Nature*, 562, S15–S16.

Chin, C. (2018, 17 August). AI is the future – But where are the women? *Wired*. https://www.wired.com/story/artificial-intelligence-researchers-gender-imbalance/.

Chiusi, F. (2020). *Life in the automated society: How automated decision-making systems became mainstream, and what to do about it*. Introduction. Automating Society Report 2020. AlgorithmWatch/Bertelsmann Stiftung. https://automatingsociety.algorithmwatch.org/.

Cho, E. (2020, 1 May). The social credit system: Not just another Chinese idiosyncrasy. *Journal of Public and International Affairs*. https://jpia.princeton.edu/news/social-credit-system-not-just-another-chinese-idiosyncrasy.

Christl, W. (2017). *Corporate surveillance in everyday life: How companies collect, combine, analyze, trade, and use personal data on billions*. Vienna: Cracked Lab. https://crackedlabs.org/dl/CrackedLabs_Christl_Corporate Surveillance.pdf.

Church, G. M. (2019). The rights of machines. In J. Brockman (ed.), *Possible minds* (pp. 240–53). New York: Penguin Press.

Clayton, V., Sanders, M., Schoenwald, E., Surkis, L. and Gibbons, D. (2020, September). *Machine learning in children's services*. What Works for Children's Social Care. https://whatworks-csc.org.uk/wp-content/uploads/WWCSC_technical-_report_machine_learning_in_childrens_services_does_it_work_Sep_2020.pdf.

Clifford, S., Doane, L. D., Breitenstein, R., Grimm, K. J. and Lemery-Chalfant, K. (2020). Effortful control moderates the relation between electronic-media use and objective sleep indicators in childhood. *Psychological Science*, 31, 822–34.

CNS/ATM (2017). *CNS/ATM Resource Guide* (Chapter 8). Canberra: Civil Aviation Safety Authority. https://www.casa.gov.au/book-page/chapter-8-human-factors.

Cohen, I. B. (1998). Howard Aiken on the number of computers needed for the nation. *IEEE Annals of the History of Computing*, 20, 27–32.

Coleridge, S. T. (1838). *The literary remains of Samuel Taylor Coleridge* (vol. 3), p. 186. London: H. Pickering. (Retrieved from https://archive.org/details/literaryremains003coleuoft/page/186/mode/2up.)

Connolly, K. (2018, 15 August). Child drowning in Germany linked to parents' phone 'fixation'. *Guardian*. https://www.theguardian.com/lifeandstyle/2018/aug/15/parents-fixated-by-phones-linked-to-child-drownings-in-germany.

Copeland, P. et al. (undated) *Google disease trends: An update*. https://storage.googleapis.com/pub-tools-public-publication-data/pdf/41763.pdf.

Coppock, A., Hill, S. J. and Vavreck, L. (2020). The small effects of political advertising are small regardless of context, message, sender, or receiver: Evidence from 59 real-time randomized experiments. *Science Advances*, 6: eabc4046.

Coviello, L., Gneezy, U. and Götte, L. (2017). *A large-scale field experiment to evaluate the effectiveness of paid search advertising*. CESifo Working Paper, No. 6684, Center for Economic Studies and ifo Institute, Munich.

Czerlinski, J., Gigerenzer, G. and Goldstein, D. G. (1999). How good are simple heuristics? In G. Gigerenzer, P. M. Todd and the ABC Research Group, *Simple heuristics that make us smart* (pp. 97–118). New York: Oxford University Press.

Daniel, C. and Palmer, M. (2007, 27 May). Google's goal: To organise your daily life. *Financial Times*. https://www.ft.com/content/c3e49548-088e-11dc-b11e-000b5df10621.

Danielsbacka, M., Tanskanen, A. O. and Billari, F. C. (2020). Meeting online and family-related outcomes: Evidence from three German cohorts. *Journal of Family Studies*. https://doi.org/10.1080/13229400.2020.1835694.

Danziger, S., Levav, J. and Avnaim-Pesso, L. (2011). Extraneous factors in judicial decisions. *Proceedings of the National Academy of Sciences*, 108, 6889–92.

Dastin, J. (2018, 11 October). Amazon scraps secret AI recruiting tool that showed bias against women. *Reuters*. https://www.reuters.com/article/us-amazon-com-jobs-automation-insight-IDUSKCN1MK08G.

Daston, L. (1994). Enlightenment calculations. *Critical Inquiry*, 21, 182–202.

Daston, L. (2017). The immortal archive: Nineteenth-century science imagines the future. In L. Daston (ed.), *Science in the archives: Pasts, presents, futures* (pp. 159–82). Chicago, IL: University of Chicago Press.

Daston, L. (2018). Calculation and the division of labor, 1750–1950. *Bulletin of the German Historical Institute*, 62, 9–30.

Daston, L. (2022). *Rules: A short history of what we live by*. Princeton, NJ: Princeton University Press.

Davis, B. D., Mason, J. C. and Anwar, M. (2020). Vulnerability studies and security postures of IoT devices: A smart home case study. *IEEE Internet of Things Journal*, 7, 10102–10.

Dawes, R. and Corrigan, B. (1974). Linear models in decision making. *Psychological Bulletin*, 81(2), 95–106.

DeMichele, M., Baumgartner, P., Wenger, M., Barrick, K. and Comfort, M. (2020). Public safety assessment: Predictive utility and differential prediction by race in Kentucky. *Criminology and Public Policy*, 19, 409–31.

Deutsches Institut für Service-Qualität (2017). *Kundenbefragung Online-Partnerbörsen* [Survey on dating services]. https://disq.de/2017/20170426-Online-Partnerboersen.html#GesamtP.

Dickmanns, E. D. and Zapp, A. (1987). Autonomous high speed road vehicle guidance by computer vision. *IFAC Proceedings Volumes*, 20, 221–6.

Digital Courage (2016, 26 January). 'Stasi-Barbie' – Der Spion in der Spielzeugkiste ['Stasi Barbie': The spy in the toybox]. Press release. https://digitalcourage.de/blog/2016/stasi-barbie-der-spion-in-der-spielzeugkiste.

Dillet, R. (2016, 13 October). Renault-Nissan CEO Carlos Ghosn on the future of cars. *TechCrunch*. https://techcrunch.com/2016/10/13/renault-nissan-ceo-carlos-ghosn-on-the-future-of-cars/.

Dingus, T. A. et al. (2016). Driver crash risk factors and prevalence evaluation using naturalistic driving data. *Proceedings of the National Academy of Sciences*, 113(10), 2636–41.

Doll, N. (2016, 22 November). Moderne Autos sind Datenkraken [Modern cars are data leeches]. *Welt*. https://www.welt.de/print/die_welt/finanzen/article159665896.

Dosi, G., Napoletano, M., Roventini, A., Stiglitz J. E. and Treibich, T. (2020). Rational heuristics? Expectations and behaviors in evolving economies with heterogeneous interacting agents. *Economic Inquiry*, 53, 1487–516.

Dressel, J. and Farid, H. (2018). The accuracy, fairness, and limits of predicting recidivism. *Science Advances*, 4(1): eaao5580.

Dreyfus, H. L. (1979). *What computers can't do* (revised edn). New York: Harper.

Dyrenforth, P. S., Kashy, D. A., Donnellan, M. B. and Lucas, R. E. (2010). Predicting relationship and life satisfaction from personality in nationally representative samples from three countries: The relative importance of actor, partner, and similarity effects. *Journal of Personality and Social Psychology*, 99, 690–702.

Eames, S. S. (1990). *Barbie Doll fashion: 1959–1967*. Paducah, KY: Collector Books.

Economist (2018, 14 April). What to make of Mark Zuckerberg's testimony. *The Economist*. https://www.economist.com/leaders/2018/04/14/what-to-make-of-mark-zuckerbergs-testimony.

Efrati, A. (2018, 10 December). How an Uber whistleblower tried to stop self-driving car disaster. *The Information*. https://www.theinformation.com/articles/how-an-uber-whistleblower-tried-to-stop-self-driving-car-disaster.

Eggers, D. (2013). *The circle*. New York: Knopf.

Einhorn, H. J. and Hogarth, R. (1975). Unit weighting schemes for decision making. *Organizational Behavior and Human Performance*, 13(2), 171–92.

Elias, J. (2019, 23 October). Alphabet exec says self-driving cars 'have gone through a lot of hype', but Google helped drive that hype. *CNBC*. https://www.cnbc.com/2019/10/23/alphabet-exec-admits-google-overhyped-self-driving-cars.html.

Elliott, J. and Meyer, T. (2013, 23 October). Claim on 'attacks thwarted' by NSA spreads despite lack of evidence. *ProPublica*. https://www.propublica.org/article/claim-on-attacks-thwarted-by-nsa-spreads-despite-lack-of-evidence.

Elsberg, M. (2017). *Blackout*. London: Penguin Books.

Epstein, R. (1995). *Simple rules for a complex world*. Cambridge, MA: Harvard University Press.

Epstein, R. (2013). The truth about online dating. In Editors of Scientific American (eds.), *Disarming Cupid: Love, sex, and science* (Chapter 3.3). New York: Scientific American.

Epstein, R. and Robertson, R. E. (2015). The search engine manipulation effect (S E M E) and its possible impact on the outcomes of elections. *Proceedings of the National Academy of Sciences*, 112(33), E4512–E4521.

ERGO (2019). *ERGO Risiko-Report* [ERGO Risk Report]. https://www.ergo.com/en/Media-Relations/Pressemeldungen/PM-2019/20190912-ERGO-Risiko-Report.

European Commission (2020). *White Paper: Artificial intelligence – A European approach to excellence and trust.* https://ec.europa.eu/info/sites/info/files/commission-white-paper-artificial-intelligence-feb2020_en.pdf.

European Union (2016). *General data protection regulation.* https://gdpr-info.eu/art-5-gdpr/.

Ewing, J. (2020, 14 July). German court says Tesla self-driving claims are misleading. *New York Times.* https://www.nytimes.com/2020/07/14/business/tesla-autopilot-germany.html.

Eyal, N. (2014). *Hooked.* London: Penguin.

Eyal, N. (2019). *Indistractable: How to control your attention and choose your life.* London: Bloomsbury.

Facebook (2020, 29 January). *Facebook reports fourth quarter and full year 2019 results.* Press release. https://investor.fb.com/investor-news/press-release-details/2020/Facebook-Reports-Fourth-Quarter-and-Full-Year-2019-Results/default.aspx.

Farnham, A. (2014, 2 June). Hot or Not's co-founders: Where are they now? *A B C News.* https://abcnews.go.com/Business/founders-hot-today/story?id=23901082.

Federal Aviation Administration. (2013). *Safety alert for operators: Manual flight operations* (SAFO 13002). https://www.faa.gov/other_visit/aviation_industry/airline_operators/airline_safety/safo/all_safos/media/2013/SAFO13002.pdf.

Federal Trade Commission (2019, 25 September). FTC sues owner of online dating service Match.com for using fake love interest ads to trick consumers into paying for a Match.com subscription. Press release. https://www.ftc.gov/news-events/press-releases/2019/09/ftc-sues-owner-online-dating-service-matchcom-using-fake-love.

Ferrucci, D. et al. (2010). Building Watson: An overview of the DeepQA project. *AI Magazine* 31(3), 59–79.

Feynman, R. P., Leighton, R. and Hutchings, E. (1985). *'Surely you're joking, Mr. Feynman!': Adventures of a curious character.* New York: W. W. Norton.

Finkel, E. J., Eastwick, P. W., Karney, B. R., Reis, H. T. and Sprecher, S. (2012). Online dating: A critical analysis from the perspective of psychological science. *Psychological Science in the Public Interest*, 13, 3–66.

Fleischhut, N., Meder, B. and Gigerenzer, G. (2017). Moral hindsight. *Experimental Psychology*, 64, 110–23.

Fletcher, D. (2010, 27 May). The 50 worst inventions: Farmville. *Time*. http://content.time.com/time/specials/packages/article/0,28804,1991915_1991909_1991768,00.html.

Fowler, G. A. (2019, 18 September). You watch TV. Your TV watches back. *Washington Post*. https://www.washingtonpost.com/technology/2019/09/18/you-watch-tv-your-tv-watches-back/.

Fowler, G. A. (2019, 27 December). What does your car know about you? We hacked a Chevy to find out. *Washington Post*. https://www.washingtonpost.com/technology/2019/12/17/what-does-your-car-know-about-you-we-hacked-chevy-find-out/.

Frederik, J. and Martijn, M. (2019). The new dot com bubble is here: It's called online advertising. *The Correspondent*. https://thecorrespondent.com/100/the-new-dot-com-bubble-is-here-its-called-online-advertising/13228924500-22d5fd24

Freed, D. et al. (2018). 'A stalker's paradise': How intimate partner abusers exploit technology. CHI 2018, Montreal, Canada. http://nixdell.com/papers/stalkers-paradise-intimate.pdf.

Geirhos, R. et al. (2020). Shortcut learning in deep neural networks. *Nature Machine Intelligence*, 2, 665–73.

Gendron, S. (2016, 4 May). Croisade contre les textos au volant [A crusade against texting while driving]. *Le Journal de Montréal*. https://www.journaldemontreal.com/2016/05/04/croisade-contre-les-textos-au-volant.

Geraghty, K. and Woodhams, J. (2015). The predictive validity of risk assessment tools for female offenders: A systematic review. *Aggression and Violent Behavior*, 21, 25–38.

Gibbs, S. (2018, 19 January). Apple's Tim Cook: 'I don't want my nephew on a social network'. *Guardian*. https://www.theguardian.com/technology/2018/jan/19/tim-cook-i-dont-want-my-nephew-on-a-social-network.

Gigerenzer, G. (1984). The frequency–validity relationship. *American Journal of Psychology*, 97, 185–95.

Gigerenzer, G. (1991). From tools to theories: A heuristic of discovery in cognitive psychology. *Psychological Review*, 98, 254–67.

Gigerenzer, G. (2001). Digital computer: Impact on the social sciences. In N. J. Smelser and P. B. Baltes (eds.), *International encyclopedia of the social and behavioral sciences* (vol. 6, pp. 3684–8). Amsterdam: Elsevier.

Gigerenzer, G. (2003). *Reckoning with risk: Learning to live with uncertainty*. London: Penguin. (US version: *Calculated risks: How to know when numbers deceive you*. New York: Simon and Schuster, 2002.)

Gigerenzer, G. (2007). *Gut feelings: The intelligence of the unconscious*. London: Penguin Books.

Gigerenzer, G. (2014) *Risk savvy: How to make good decisions*. London: Penguin Books.

Gigerenzer, G. (2021). What is bounded rationality? In R. Viale (ed.), *Routledge Handbook of Bounded Rationality* (pp. 55–69). London: Routledge.

Gigerenzer, G. et al. (1989). *The empire of chance: How probability changed science and everyday life*. Cambridge: Cambridge University Press.

Gigerenzer, G., Gaissmaier, W., Kurz-Milcke, E., Schwartz, L. M. and Woloshin, S. W. (2007). Helping doctors and patients make sense of health statistics. *Psychological Science in the Public Interest*, 8, 53–96.

Gigerenzer, G. and Goldstein, D. G. (1996). Mind as computer: Birth of a metaphor. *Creativity Research Journal*, 9, 131–44.

Gigerenzer, G., Hertwig, R. and Pachur, T. (eds.). (2011). *Heuristics: The foundations of adaptive behavior*. New York: Oxford University Press.

Gigerenzer, G. and Muir Gray, J. A. (eds.). (2011). *Better doctors, better patients, better decisions*. Cambridge, MA: MIT Press.

Gigerenzer, G. and Murray, D. J. (2015). *Cognition as intuitive statistics*. New York: Psychology Press Original work published 1987.

Ginsberg, J. et al. (2009). Detecting influenza epidemics using search engine query data. *Nature*, 457, 1012–14.

Gleave, A. (2020, 27 March). Physically realistic attacks on deep reinforcement learning. Berkeley Artificial Intelligence Research Blog. https://bair.berkeley.edu/blog/2020/03/27/attacks/.

Gleick, J. (1992). *Genius: The life and science of Richard Feynman*. New York: Pantheon.

Gliklich, J., Maurer, R. and Bergmark, R. W. (2019). Patterns of texting and driving in a US national survey of millennial parents vs older parents. *JAMA Pediatrics*, 173, 689–90.

Glöckner, A. (2016). The irrational hungry judge effect revisited: Simulations reveal that the magnitude of the effect is overestimated. *Judgment and Decision Making*, 11, 601–10.

Gordon, B. R. et al. (2019). A comparison of approaches to advertising measurement: Evidence from big field experiments at Facebook. *Marketing Science*, 38, 193–364.

Gorner, J. and Sweeney, A. (2020, 24 January). For years Chicago police rated the risk of tens of thousands being caught up in violence. That controversial effort has quietly been ended. *Chicago Tribune*. https://www.chicagotribune.com/news/criminal-justice/ct-chicago-police-strategic-subject-list-ended-20200125-spn4kjmrxrh4tmktdjckhtox4i-story.html.

Gottman, J. and Gottman, J. (2017). The natural principles of love. *Journal of Family Theory and Review*, 9, 7–26.

Gottman, J. M., Coan, J., Carrere, S. and Swanson, C. (1998). Predicting marital happiness and stability from newlywed interactions. *Journal of Marriage and the Family*, 60, 5–22.

Götz, M., Wunderer, E., Greithanner, J. and Maslanka, E. (2019). 'Warum kann ich nicht so perfekt sein?' ['Why can't I be as perfect?']. *Televizion*, 32(1). https://www.br-online.de/jugend/izi/deutsch/publikation/televizion/32_2019_1/Goetz_Wunderer-perfekt_sein.pdf.

Green, K. C. and Armstrong, J. S. (2015). Simple versus complex forecasting: The evidence. *Journal of Business Research*, 68, 1678–85.

Greenwald, G. (2014). *No place to hide: Edward Snowden, the NSA and the surveillance state*. London: Penguin Books.

Griffiths, J. (2019). *The Great Firewall of China*. London: Zed Books.

Grisso, T. and Tomkins, A. J. (1996). Communicating violence risk assessments. *American Psychologist*, 51(9), 928–30.

Grossman, L. et al. (2011, 28 November). The 50 best inventions. *Time*. http://content.time.com/time/subscriber/article/0,33009,2099708-1,00.html.

Grzymek, V. and Puntschuh, M. (2019). *What Europe knows and thinks about algorithms: Results of a representative survey*. Gütersloh: Bertelsmann Stiftung. https://www.bertelsmann-stiftung.de/fileadmin/files/BSt/Publikationen/GrauePublikationen/WhatEuropeKnowsAndThinkAboutAlgorithm.pdf.

Gunning, D. and Aha, D. W. (2019). DARPA's explainable artificial intelligence program. *AI Magazine*, 40(2), 44–58.

Gururangan, S. et al. (2018). Annotation artifacts in natural language inference data. *Proceedings of the 2018 Conference of the North American Chapter of the Association for Computational Linguistics: Human Language Technologies*, 2, 107–12. https://www.aclweb.org/anthology/N18-2017/.

Halpern, S. (2014, 20 November). The creepy new wave of the internet. *The New York Review of Books*, 22–4.

Hancock, J. T., Toma, C. and Ellison, N. (2007). The truth about lying in online dating profiles. CHI 2007, San Jose, California. https://collablab.northwestern.edu//CollabolabDistro/nucmc/p449-hancock.pdf.

Hao, K. (2020, 4 December). We read the paper that forced Timnit Gebru out of Google. Here's what it says. *MIT Technology Review*. https://www.technologyreview.com/2020/12/04/1013294/google-ai-ethics-research-paper-forced-out-timnit-gebru/.

Harari, Y. N. (2015), *Homo Deus: A brief history of tomorrow*. New York: Harper.

Harari, Y. N. (2016, 16 August). Yuval Noah Harari on big data, Google and the end of free will. *Financial Times*. https://www.ft.com/content/50bb4830-6a4c-11e6-ae5b-a7cc5dd5a28c.

Harford, T. (2014, 28 March). Big data: Are we making a big mistake? *Financial Times*. https://www.ft.com/content/21a6e7d8-b479-11e3-a09a-00144 feabdc0.

Hartmann, S. (2017). Risikobewältigung in der Luftfahrt und in der Medizin – eine vergleichende Untersuchung [Managing risk in air traffic and medicine: A comparative analysis]. Doctoral dissertation. Humboldt University Berlin.

Hauber, J., Jarchow, E. and Rabitz-Suhr, S. (2019). *Prädiktionspotenzial schwere Einbruchskriminalität: Ergebnisse einer wissenschaftlichen Befassung mit Predictive Policing* [The potential of predicting serious burglary offences: Results of a scientific investigation on predictive policing]. Hamburg: Landeskriminalamt Hamburg. https://www.polizei.hamburg/content blob/13755082/74aff9285c340ad260ed65fe912caa17/data/abschlussber icht-praediktionspotenzial-schwere-einbruchskrminalitaet-do.pdf

Hawkins, A. J. (2019, 22 April). Here are Elon Musk's wildest predictions about Tesla's self-driving cars. *The Verge*. https://www.theverge.com/2019/4/22/18510828/tesla-elon-musk-autonomy-day-investor-comments-self-driving-cars-predictions.

Hayes, B. (2006). Gauss's day of reckoning. *American Scientist*, 94, 200–205.

Haynes, T. (2018, 1 May). *Dopamine, smartphones, and you: A battle for your time*. Harvard University. http://sitn.hms.harvard.edu/flash/2018/dopamine-smartphones-battle-time/.

Helbing, D. et al. (2017, 25 February). Will democracy survive big data and artificial intelligence? *Scientific American*. https://www.scientificamerican.com/article/will-democracy-survive-big-data-and-artificial-intelligence/.

Heyman, R. E. and Slep, A. M. S. (2001). The hazards of predicting divorce without crossvalidation. *Journal of Marriage and the Family*, 63, 473–9.

Hirsch, S. and Hirsch, A. (2011). *The beauty of short hops: How chance and circumstance confound the Moneyball approach to baseball*. Jefferson, NC: McFarland & Co.

Hitsch, G. J., Hortaçsu, A. and Ariely, D. (2010). Matching and sorting in online dating. *American Economic Review*, 100, 130–63.

Hofstadter, D. (2018, 30 January). The shallowness of Google Translate. *Atlantic*. https://www.theatlantic.com/technology/archive/2018/01/the-shallowness-of-google-translate/551570/.

Holte, C. H. (1993). Very simple classification rules perform well on most commonly used datasets. *Machine Learning*, 11, 63–91.

Holzinger, A., Biemann, C., Pattichis, C. S. and Kell, D. B. (2017). *What do we need to build explainable AI systems for the medical domain?* ArXiv. https://arxiv.org/abs/1712.09923.

Howard, P. N. (2020). *Lie machines.* New Haven: Yale University Press.

Hsu, J. W. (2015, 2 July). TransAsia pilot shut down wrong engine before Taiwan crash. *Wall Street Journal.* https://www.wsj.com/articles/transasia-pilot-shut-down-working-engine-before-taiwan-crash-1435815552.

Hu, J. C. (2018, 18 December). How one light bulb could allow hackers to burgle your home. *Quartz.* https://qz.com/1493748/how-one-lightbulb-could-allow-hackers-to-burgle-your-home/.

Huang, S. et al. (2020). Social advertising effectiveness across products: A large-scale field experiment. *Marketing Science,* 39, 1142–65.

Isaac, M. (2016, 22 November). Facebook said to create censorship tool to get back into China. *New York Times.* https://www.nytimes.com/2016/11/22/technology/facebook-censorship-tool-china.html.

Islam, M. S. et al. (2020). COVID-19-related infodemic and its impact on public health: A global social media analysis. *American Journal of Tropical Medicine and Hygiene,* 103, 1621–9.

Istituto Superiore di Sanità. (2020). *Characteristics of COVID-19 patients dying in Italy.* Report based on available data from 18 November 2020. https://www.epicentro.iss.it/en/coronavirus/sars-cov-2-analysis-of-deaths.

Joel, S., Eastwick, P. W. and Finkel, E. J. (2017). Is romantic desire predictable? Machine learning applied to initial romantic attraction. *Psychological Science,* 28, 1478–89.

Johnson, B. (2010, 11 January). Privacy no longer a social norm, says Facebook founder. *Guardian.* https://www.theguardian.com/technology/2010/jan/11/facebook-privacy.

Jung, J., Concannon, C., Shroff, R., Goel, S. and Goldstein, D. G. (2017). *Simple rules for complex decisions.* ArXiv. https://arxiv.org/abs/1702.04690.

Kahneman, D. (2019). Comment on 'Artificial intelligence and behavioral economics'. In A. Agrawal, J. Gans and A. Goldfarb (eds.), *The economics of artificial intelligence* (pp. 608–10). Chicago, IL: University of Chicago Press.

Kapoun, J. (1998, August). Teaching Web evaluation to undergrads. *College and Research Libraries News,* 522–3.

Katsikopoulos, K., Şimşek, Ö., Buckmann, M. and Gigerenzer, G. (2020). *Classification in the wild.* Cambridge, MA: MIT Press.

Katsikopoulos, K., Şimşek, Ö., Buckmann, M. and Gigerenzer, G. (2022). Transparent modeling of influenza incidence: Big data or a single data point from psychological theory? *International Journal of Forecasting 38,* 613–619.

Kawohl, J. and Becker, J. (2017). *Studie: DAX-Vorständen fehlt umfassende Digital-Kompetenz und eigene Erfahrung mit Unternehmertum.* Pressetext Hochschule für Technik und Wirtschaft Berlin. https://www.pressetext.com/news/studie-dax-vorstaenden-fehlt-umfassende-digital-kompetenz-und-eigene-erfahrung-mit-unternehmertum.html.

Kay, J. and King, M. (2020). *Radical uncertainty.* London: Bridge Street Press.

Kayser-Bril, N. (2019, 4 November). Facebook enables automated scams, but fails to automate the fight against them. *Algorithm Watch.* https://algorithmwatch.org/en/story/facebook-enables-automated-scams-but-fails-to-automate-the-fight-against-them/.

Kayser-Bril, N. (2020, 17 September). Female historians and male nurses do not exist, Google Translate tells its European users. *Algorithm Watch.* https://algorithmwatch.org/en/story/google-translate-gender-bias/.

Kellermann, A. L. and Jones, S. S. (2013). What it will take to achieve the as-yet-unfulfilled promises of health information technology. *Health Affairs*, 32, 63–8.

Kim, M. (2015, 8 January). Are smartphones causing more kid injuries? *Philly Voice.* https://www.phillyvoice.com/cell-phone-too-deadly-kids/.

Kleinhubbert, G. (2013, 25 November). Abgelenkt [Distracted]. *Der Spiegel.* https://www.spiegel.de/spiegel/print/d-122579480.html.

Koh, P. W. et al. (2021, 9 March). *WILDS: A benchmark of in-the-wild distribution shifts.* ArXiv. https://arxiv.org/abs/2012.07421v2.

Kosko, B. (2015). Thinking machines = old algorithms on faster computers. In J. Brockman (ed.), *What to think about machines that think* (pp. 423–6). New York: Harper.

Kostka, G. (2019). China's social credit system and public opinion: Explaining high levels of approval. *New Media and Society*, 21, 1565–93.

Kostka, G. and Antoine, L. (2019). Fostering model citizenship: Behavioral responses to China's emerging social credit systems. *Policy and Internet*, 12, 256–89.

Kostka, G. and Zhang, C. (2018). Tightening the grip: Environmental governance under Xi Jinping. *Environmental Politics*, 27, 769–81.

Kozyreva, A., Lewandowsky, S. and Hertwig, R. (2020). Citizens versus the internet: Confronting digital challenges with cognitive tools. *Psychological Science in the Public Interest*, 21, 103–56.

Kramer, A. D. I., Guillory, J. E. and Hancock, J. T. (2014). Experimental evidence of massive-scale emotional contagion through social networks. *Proceedings of the National Academy of Sciences*, 111, 8788–90.

Krauthammer, C. (1997, 26 May). Be afraid. *Washington Examiner.* https://www.washingtonexaminer.com/weekly-standard/be-afraid-9802.

Kruglanski, A. and Gigerenzer, G. (2011). Intuitive and deliberate judgments are based on common principles. *Psychological Review*, 118, 97–109.

Kumar, N., Berg, A. C., Belhumeur, P. N. and Nayar, S. K. (2009). Attribute and simile classifiers for face verification. *2009 IEEE 12th International Conference on Computer Vision*, Kyoto, 365–72.

Kurzweil, R. (2012). *How to create a mind*. New York: Penguin.

Lake, B. M., Ulman, T. D., Tenenbaum, J. B. and Gershman, S. J. (2017). Ingredients of intelligence: From classic debates to an engineering roadmap. *The Behavioral and Brain Sciences*, 40: e281.

Lanier, J. (2019, 23 September). Jaron Lanier fixes the internet. *New York Times*. https://www.nytimes.com/interactive/2019/09/23/opinion/data-privacy-jaron-lanier.html.

Lanier, J. and Weyl, E. G. (2018, 26 September). A blueprint for a better digital society. *Harvard Business Review*. https://hbr.org/2018/09/a-blueprint-for-a-better-digital-society.

Lavin, T. (2020, 29 September). QAnon, blood libel, and the Satanic panic. *New Republic*. https://newrepublic.com/article/159529/qanon-blood-libel-satanic-panic.

Lazer, D., Kennedy, R., King, G. and Vespignani, A. (2014, 14 March). The parable of Google Flu: Traps in big data analysis. *Science*, 343, 1203–5.

Lea, S., Fischer, P. and Evans, K. (2009). *The psychology of scams: Provoking and committing errors of judgement* (Report No. 1070). Office of Fair Trading/University of Exeter.

Lee, D.-C. et al. (2017). Running as a key lifestyle medicine for longevity. *Progress in Cardiovascular Diseases*, 60(1), 45–55.

Lee, K.-F. (2018). *AI superpowers: China, Silicon Valley, and the new world order*. Boston: Houghton Mifflin Harcourt.

Leetaru, K. (2018, 5 April). The data brokers so powerful that even Facebook bought their data – but they got me wildly wrong. *Forbes*. https://www.forbes.com/sites/kalevleetaru/2018/04/05/the-data-brokers-so-powerful-even-facebook-bought-their-data-but-they-got-me-wildly-wrong/#3d727faf3107.

Lewandowsky, S. et al. (2020). *Technology and democracy: Understanding the influence of online technologies on political behaviour and decision-making*. EUR 30422 EN. Luxembourg: Publications Office of the European Union.

Lewis, M. (2003). *Moneyball*. New York: Norton.

Lewis, R. A. and Rao, J. M. (2014). *On the near impossibility of measuring the returns of advertising*. Paper presented at the AEA Annual Meeting, 4 January 2014. https://www.aeaweb.org/conference/2014/preliminary.php.

Lewis, R. A. and Reiley, D. (2014). Advertising effectively influences older users: How field experiments can improve measurement and targeting. *Review of Industrial Organization*, 44, 147–59.

Lichtman, A. J. (2016). *Predicting the next president: The keys to the White House*. Lanham, MD: Rowman and Littlefield.

Lin, Z. J., Jung, J., Goel, S. and Skeem, J. (2020). The limits of human prediction of recidivism. *Science Advances*, 6: eaaz0652.

Lindström, B. et al. (2021). A computational reinforcement learning account of social media engagement. *Nature Communications*, 12, 1311.

Liptak, A. (2017, 1 May). Sent to prison by a software program's secret algorithms. *New York Times*. https://www.nytimes.com/2017/05/01/us/politics/sent-to-prison-by-a-software-programs-secret-algorithms.html.

Locke, J. (1975). *An essay concerning human understanding*. Oxford: Oxford University Press. (Original work published 1690.)

Lorenz-Spreen, P., Lewandowsky, S., Sunstein, C. R. and Hertwig, R. (2020). How behavioral sciences can promote truth, autonomy and democratic discourse. *Nature Human Behavior*, 4, 1102–9.

Lotan, G. (2014, 4 August). Israel, Gaza, war and data – The art of personalizing propaganda. *Global Voices*. https://globalvoices.org/2014/08/04/israel-gaza-war-data-the-art-of-personalizing-propaganda/.

Luckerson, V. (2015, 9 July). Here's how Facebook's News Feed actually works. *Time*. https://time.com/collection-post/3950525/facebook-news-feed-algorithm/.

Luetge, C. (2017). The German Ethics Code for automated and connected driving. *Philosophy of Technology*, 30, 547–58.

Luria, A. R. (1968). *The mind of a mnemonist*. New York: Basic Books.

Maack, N. (2020, 22 January). Diese Stadt ist ein großer Roboter [This city is a big robot]. *Frankfurter Allgemeine*. https://www.faz.net/aktuell/feuilleton/debatten/toyotas-smart-city-diese-stadt-ist-ein-grosser-roboter-16588460.html.

Makoff, J. (2011, 16 February). Computer wins on 'Jeopardy!': Trivial, it's not. *New York Times*. https://www.nytimes.com/2011/02/17/science/17jeopardy-watson.html.

Markman, J. (2016, 8 August). Big Data and the 2016 election. *Forbes*. https://www.forbes.com/sites/jonmarkman/2016/08/08/big-data-and-the-2016-election/#29fe5d7b1450.

Martosko, D. (2013, 25 October). I'm bad at math, says Obama – but so is Congress – during visit to Brooklyn school. *Daily Mail*. https://www.dailymail.co.uk/news/article-2477130/Im-bad-math-says-Obama--Congress--visit-Brooklyn-school.

Matacic, C. (2018). Are algorithms good guides? *Science*, 359, 263.

McDaniel, B. T. (2019). Parent distraction with phones, reasons for use, and impacts on parenting and child outcomes: A review of the emerging research. *Human Behavior and Emerging Technologies*, 1, 72–80.

McDonald, A. M. and Cranor, L. F. (2008). The cost of reading privacy policies. *Journal of Law and Policy for the Information Society*, 4, 543–68.

McGrew, S., Breakstone, J., Ortega, T., Smith, M. and Wineberg, S. (2018). Can students evaluate online sources? Learning from assessments of civic online reasoning. *Theory and Research in Social Education*, 46, 165–93.

McGrew, S., Smith, M., Breakstone, J., Ortega, T. and Wineburg, S. (2019). Improving university students' web savvy: An intervention study. *British Journal of Educational Psychology*, 89, 485–500.

McNeal, G. S. (2014, 28 June). Facebook manipulated user news feeds to create emotional responses. *Forbes*. https://www.forbes.com/sites/grego rymcneal/2014/06/28/facebook-manipulated-user-news-feeds-to-create-emotional-contagion/.

Mead, M. (1928). *Coming of age in Samoa*. New York: William Morrow.

Medvin, M. (2019, 8 January). Your vehicle black box: A 'witness' against you in court. *Forbes*. https://www.forbes.com/sites/marinamedvin/2019/01/08/your-vehicle-black-box-a-witness-against-you-in-court-2/#461a44383105.

Melendez, S. (2019, 16 September). Mozilla and Creative Commons want to reimage the internet without ads, and they have $100M to do it. *Fast Company*. https://www.fastcompany.com/90403645/mozilla-and-creative-commons-want-to-reimagine-the-internet-without-ads-and-they-have-100m-to-do-it.

Mercier, H. and Sperber, D. (2011). Why do humans reason? Arguments for an argumentative theory. *Behavioral and Brain Science*, 34, 57–74.

Messerli, F. H. (2012). Chocolate consumption, cognitive function, and Nobel laureates. *New England Journal of Medicine*, 367, 1562–4.

Milner, G. (2016, 25 June). Death by GPS: Are satnavs changing our brains? *BBC*. https://www.bbc.com/news/technology-35491962.

Mønsted, B., Sapiezynski, P., Ferrara, E. and Lehmann, S. (2017). Evidence of complex contagion of information in social media: An experiment using Twitter bots. *PLoS ONE*, 12(9): e0184148.

Montaigne, M. de (2017). *Essays* (Jonathan Bennett, trans.). https://www.earlymoderntexts.com/assets/pdfs/montaigne1580book2_2.pdf. (Original work published 1580.)

Montoya, R. M., Horton, R. S. and Kirchner, J. (2008). Is actual similarity necessary for attraction? A meta-analysis of actual and perceived similarity. *Journal of Social and Personal Relationships*, 25, 889–922.

Morozov, E. (2013). *To save everything, click here: The follies of technological solutionism.* New York: Public Affairs.

Mullard, A. (2011). Reliability of 'new drug target' claims called into question. *Nature Reviews: Drug Discovery*, 10(9), 643–4.

Munro, D. (2019, 28 November). *Should tech firms pay people for their data?* Centre for International Governance Innovation. https://www.cigionline.org/articles/should-tech-firms-pay-people-their-data.

Nasiopoulos, E., Risko, E. F., Foulsham, T. and Kingstone, A. (2015). Wearable computing: Will it make people prosocial? *British Journal of Psychology*, 106, 209–16.

National Consortium for the Study of Terrorism and Responses to Terrorism. (2020). *Global Terrorism Overview: Terrorism in 2019.* https://www.start.umd.edu/pubs/START_GTD_GlobalTerrorismOverview2019_July2020.pdf.

National Geographic (2014). Greendex 2014: Consumer choice and the environment: A worldwide tracking survey. https://globescan.com/wp-content/uploads/2017/07/Greendex_2014_Full_Report_NationalGeographic_GlobeScan.pdf.

National Transportation Safety Board (2019). *Preliminary report highway HWY 18 MH 010.* https://www.ntsb.gov/investigations/AccidentReports/Reports/HWY18MH010-prelim.pdf.

Neumann, N., Tucker, C. E. and Whitfield, T. (2019). Frontiers: How effective is third-party consumer profiling? Evidence from field studies. *Marketing Science*, 38, 918–26.

Newell, A., Shaw, J. C. and Simon, H. A. (1958a). Chess-playing programs and the problem of complexity. *IBM Journal of Research and Development*, 2(4), 320–35.

Newell, A., Shaw, J. C. and Simon, H. A. (1958b). Elements of a theory of human problem solving. *Psychological Review*, 65, 151–66.

Newell, A. and Simon. H. A. (1972). *Human problem solving.* Englewood Cliffs, NJ: Prentice-Hall.

Newport, F. (2015, 9 July). Most U.S. smartphone owners check phone at least hourly. *Gallup.* https://news.gallup.com/poll/184046/smartphone-owners-check-phone-least-hourly.aspx.

Newton, C. (2018, 12 September). A partisan war over fact-checking is putting pressure on Facebook. *The Verge.* https://www.theverge.com/2018/9/12/17848478/thinkprogress-weekly-standard-facebook-fact-check-false.

Nguyen, N. (2017, 9 March). If you have a smart TV, take a closer look at your privacy settings. *CNBC.* https://www.cnbc.com/2017/03/09/if-you-have-a-smart-tv-take-a-closer-look-at-your-privacy-settings.html.

Nguyen, A., Yosinski, J. and Clune, J. (2015). Deep neural networks are easily fooled: High confidence predictions for unrecognizable images. *2015 IEEE Conference on Computer Vision and Pattern Recognition*. https://ieeexplore.ieee.org/document/7298640.

Niven, T. and Kao, H.-Y. (2019). Probing neural network comprehension of natural language arguments. *Proceedings of the 57th Annual Meeting of the Association for Computational Linguistics*, 4658–64. https://www.aclweb.org/anthology/P19-1459.pdf.

NortonLifeLock (2019). *Cyber safety insights report: Global results*. Symantec Corporation. https://now.symassets.com/content/dam/norton/campaign/NortonReport/2020/2019_NortonLifeLock_Cyber_Safety_Insights_Report_Global_Results.pdf.

Noyes, D. (2020, October). *The top 20 valuable Facebook statistics*. Zephoria Digital Marketing. https://zephoria.com/top-15-valuable-facebook-statistics/.

OECD (2017). *Key issues for digital transformation in the G20*. https://www.oecd.org/g20/key-issues-for-digital-transformation-in-the-g20.pdf.

Office of Fair Trading, United Kingdom (2007). *Research on impact of mass marketed scams: A summary of research into the impact of scams on UK consumers* (OFT Report 883). https://webarchive.nationalarchives.gov.uk/20140402214439/http:/www.oft.gov.uk/shared_oft/reports/consumer_protection/oft883.pdf.

Olson, D. R., Konty, K. J., Paladini, M., Viboud, C. and Simonsen, L. (2013). Reassessing Google Flu Trends data for detection of seasonal and pandemic influenza: A comparative epidemiological study at three geographic scales. *PLoS Computational Biology*, 9(10): e1003256.

O'Neil, C. (2016). *Weapons of math destruction*. London: Allen Lane.

Ophir, E., Nass, C. and Wagner, A. D. (2009). Cognitive control in media multitaskers. *Proceedings of the National Academy of Sciences*, 106(37), 15583–7.

Orben, A. (2020). The Sisyphean cycle of technology panics. *Perspectives on Psychological Science*, 15, 1143–57.

Orwell, G. (2008). *Nineteen eighty-four*. London: Penguin. (Original work published 1949.)

O'Toole, F. (2018). *Heroic failure: Brexit and the politics of pain*. London: Head of Zeus.

Pasquale, F. (2015). *The black box society*. Cambridge, MA: Harvard University Press.

Paul, A. (2014). Is online better than offline for meeting partners? Depends: Are you looking to marry or to date? *Cyberpsychology, Behavior, and Social Networking*, 17, 664–7.

Paulsen, D. (2006). Human versus machine: A comparison of the accuracy of geographic profiling methods. *Journal of Investigative Psychology and Offender Profiling*, 3, 77–89.

Peteranderl, S. (2020). *Under fire: The rise and fall of predictive policing*. https://www.acgusa.org/wp-content/uploads/2020/03/2020_Predpol_Peteranderl_Kellen.pdf.

Pogue, D. (2016, 1 January). How to end online ads forever. *Scientific American*. https://www.scientificamerican.com/article/how-to-end-online-ads-forever/.

Poibeau, T. (2017). *Machine translation*. Cambridge, MA: MIT Press.

Porter, T. M. (2004). *Karl Pearson: The scientific life in a statistical age*. Princeton, NJ: Princeton University Press.

Potarca, G. (2020). The demography of swiping right: An overview of couples who met through dating apps in Switzerland. *PLOS ONE*, 15(12): e0243733.

Praschl, P. (2015, 22 April). Eine Barbie mit WLAN ist das Ende der Kindheit [A Wifi-Barbie means the end of childhood]. *Die Welt*. https://www.welt.de/kultur/article139863883/.

Quinn, P. C., Eimas, P. D. and Tarr, M. J. (2001). Perceptual categorization of cat and dog silhouettes by 3- to 4-month-old infants. *Journal of Experimental Child Psychology*, 79, 78–94.

Raji, I. D. and Buolamwini, J. (2019). Actionable auditing: Investigating the impact of publicly naming biased performance results of commercial AI products. *Conference on Artificial Intelligence, Ethics, and Society*. https://www.media.mit.edu/publications/actionable-auditing-investigating-the-impact-of-publicly-naming-biased-performance-results-of-commercial-ai-products/.

Ranjan, A., Janai, J., Geiger, A. and Black, M. J. (2019). Attacking optical flow. *Proceedings of the IEEEØCVF International Conference on Computer Vision (ICCV)*, 2404–13. IEEE. https://arxiv.org/abs/1910.10053.

Rebonato, R. (2012). *Taking liberties: A critical examination of libertarian paternalism*. Basingstoke: Palgrave Macmillan.

Reed, J., Hirsh-Pasek, K. and Golinkoff, R. M. (2017). Learning on hold: Cell phones sidetrack parent–child interactions. *Developmental Psychology*, 53, 1428–36.

Reynolds, G. (2017, 12 April). An hour of running may add 7 hours to your life. *New York Times*. https://www.nytimes.com/2017/04/12/well/move/an-hour-of-running-may-add-seven-hours-to-your-life.html.

Rid, T. (2020). *Active measures*. London: Profile Books.

Rilke, R. M. (1993). *Letters to a young poet* (M. D. Herter Norton, trans.). New York: Norton. (Original work published 1929.)

Rivest, R. L. (1987). Learning decision lists. *Machine Learning*, 2, 229–46.

Roberts, S. and Pashler, H. (2000). How pervasive is a good fit? A comment on theory testing. *Psychological Review*, 107, 358–67.

Rocca, J. (2019, 7 January). Understanding generative adversarial networks (GANs). *Towards Data Science*. https://towardsdatascience.com/understanding-generative-adversarial-networks-gans-cd6e4651a29.

Rogers, S. (2012, 11 December). Census in pictures: From suffragettes to arms protesters. *Guardian*. https://www.theguardian.com/uk/datablog/gallery/2012/dec/11/census-2011-pictures-suffragettes-arms-protesters.

Ross, C. and Swetlitz, I. (2018, 14 June). IBM Watson Health hampered by internal rivalries and disorganization, former employees say. *STAT+*. https://www.statnews.com/2018/06/14/ibm-watson-health-rivalries-disorganization/.

Rötzer, F. (2019, 4 February). Jeder sechste Deutsche findet ein Social-Scoring System gut [Every sixth German finds a social scoring system good]. *Telepolis*. https://www.heise.de/tp/features/Jeder-sechste-Deutsche-findet-ein-Social-Scoring-System-nach-chinesischem-Vorbild-gut-4297208.html.

Rudin, C. (2019). Stop explaining black box machine learning models of high stakes decisions and use interpretable models instead. *Nature Machine Intelligence*, 1, 206–15.

Rudin, C. and Radin, J. (2019). Why are we using black box models in AI when we don't need to? A lesson from an Explainable AI competition. *Harvard Data Science Review*, 1(2). https://hdsr.mitpress.mit.edu/pub/f9kuryi8/release/6.

Rudin, C., Wang, C. and Coker, B. (2020). The age of secrecy and unfairness in recidivism prediction. *Harvard Data Science Review*, 2(1). https://hdsr.mitpress.mit.edu/pub/7z10o269/release/4.

Rudder, C. (2014). *Dataclysm*. London: Harper.

Ruginski, I. T., Creem-Regehr, S. H., Stefanucci, J. K. and Cashdan, E. (2019). GPS use negatively affects environmental learning through spatial transformation abilities. *Journal of Environmental Psychology*, 64, 12–20.

Russell, S. (2019). *Human compatible: Artificial intelligence and the problem of control*. New York: Viking.

Russell, S. and Norvig, R. (eds). (2010). *Artificial intelligence: A modern approach* (3rd edn). Upper Saddle River, NJ: Pearson Education.

Sales, N. J. (2016). *American girls: Social media and the secret lives of teenagers*. New York: Knopf.

Salganik, M. J. et al. (2020). Measuring the predictability of life outcomes with a scientific mass collaboration. *Proceedings of the National Academy of Sciences*, 117(15), 8398–403.

Sarle, W. S. (1994). Neural networks and statistical models. *Proceedings of the Nineteenth Annual SAS Users Group International Conference*, Cary, NC: SAS Institute, pp. 1538–50.

Schüll, N. D. (2012). *Addiction by design*. Princeton, NJ: Princeton University Press.

Schulte, F. and Fry, E. (2019, 18 March). Death by 1,000 clicks: Where electronic health records went wrong. *Fortune*. https://fortune.com/longform/medical-records/.

Schwertfeger, B. (2019). Künstliche Intelligenz trifft 'künstliche Dummheit' [Artificial intelligence meets 'artificial stupidity']. Interview with Gerd Antes. *wirtschaft + weiterbildung*, 9, 46–9.

Sengupta, S. (2011, 30 November). F.T.C. settles privacy issue at Facebook. *New York Times*.

Sergeant, D. C. and Himonides, E. (2019). Orchestrated sex: The representation of male and female musicians in world-class symphony orchestras. *Frontiers in Psychology*, 10, 1760.

Shahin, S. and Zheng, P. (2020). Big data and the illusion of choice: Comparing the evolution of India's Aadhaar and China's social credit system as technosocial discourses. *Social Science Computer Review*, 38, 25–41.

Shladover, S. E. (2016). The truth about 'self-driving' cars. *Scientific American*, 29, 80–83.

Silver, N. (2016, 24 October). Election update: Why our model is more bullish than others on Trump. *FiveThirtyEight*. https://fivethirtyeight.com/features/election-update-why-our-model-is-more-bullish-than-others-on-trump/.

Silver, N. (2018, 25 October). Election update: Where are the undecided voters? *FiveThirtyEight*. https://fivethirtyeight.com/features/election-update-where-are-the-undecided-voters/.

Simanek, D. E. (2009). *Arthur Conan Doyle, spiritualism, and fairies*. https://www.lockhaven.edu/~dsimanek/doyle.htm.

Simon, H. A. (1969). *The sciences of the artificial*. Cambridge, MA: MIT Press.

Simon, H. A. (1991). *Models of my life*. New York: Basic Books.

Simon, H. A. and Newell, A. (1958). Heuristic problem solving: The next advance in operations research. *Operations Research*, 6, 1–10.

Simonite, T. (2018, 1 November). When it comes to gorillas, Google Photos remains blind. *Wired*. https://www.wired.com/story/when-it-comes-to-gorillas-google-photos-remains-blind/.

Sinha, P., Balas, B. J., Ostrovsky, Y. and Russell, R. (in press). Face recognition by humans. To appear in *Face Recognition: Advanced Modeling and Methods*, Academic Press.

Sinha, P. and Poggio, T. (1996). I think I know that face . . . *Nature*, 384, 404.

Skinner, B. F. (1969). *Contingencies of reinforcement: A theoretical analysis.* New York: Appleton-Century-Crofts.

Skinner, B. F. (1972). *Beyond freedom and dignity.* New York: Bantam.

Smith, B. (2020, 10 January). We worked together on the internet. Last week, he stormed the Capitol. *New York Times.* https://www.nytimes.com/2021/01/10/business/media/capitol-anthime-gionet-buzzfeed-vine.html.

Smith, T., Darling, E. and Searles, B. (2011). 2010 survey on cell phone use while performing cardiopulmonary bypass. *Perfusion*, 26, 375–80.

Snook, B., Zito, M., Bennel, C. and Taylor, P. J. (2005). On the complexity and accuracy of geographic profiling strategies. *Journal of Quantitative Criminology*, 21, 1–25.

Snowden, E. (2019). *Permanent record.* New York: Metropolitan Books/Henry Holt and Company.

Society of Automotive Engineers (SAE) (2018, 11 December). *SAE issues update visual chart for its 'Levels of Driving Automation' standard for self-driving vehicles.* Press release. https://www.sae.org/news/press-room/2018/12/sae-international-releases-updated-visual-chart-for-its-%E2%80%9Clevels-of-driving-automation%E2%80%9D-standard-for-self-driving-vehicles.

Solon, O. (2017, 9 November). Ex-Facebook president Sean Parker: Site made to exploit human 'vulnerability'. *Guardian.* https://www.theguardian.com/technology/2017/nov/09/facebook-sean-parker-vulnerability-brain-psychology.

Solsman, J. E. (2018, 10 January). YouTube's AI is the puppet master of most of what you watch. *CNET.* https://www.cnet.com/news/youtube-ces-2018-neal-mohan/.

Spinelli, L. and Crovella, M. (2020). How YouTube leads privacy-seeking users away from reliable information. *Adjunct Publication of the 28th ACM Conference on User Modeling, Adaptation and Personalization*, 244–51. https://doi.org/10.1145/3386392.3399566.

Stadler, R. (2006, 9 May). Jetzt wird abgerechnet [Now's the day of reckoning]. *Süddeutsche Zeitung.* https://sz-magazin.sueddeutsche.de/gesellschaft-leben/jetzt-wird-abgerechnet-73071.

Stalder, F. (2014, 24 July). Paying users for their data. *The Mail Archive.* https://www.mail-archive.com/nettime-l@mail.kein.org/msg02721.html.

Stern, R. (2018, 21 June). Self-driving Uber crash 'avoidable', driver's phone playing video before woman struck. *Phoenix News.* https://www.phoenixnewtimes.com/news/self-driving-uber-crash-avoidable-drivers-phone-playing-video-before-woman-struck-10543284.

Stevenson, M. (2018). Assessing risk assessment in action. *Minnesota Law Review*, 103, 303–84.

Stevenson, P. W. (2016, 23 September). Trump is headed for a win, says professor who has predicted 30 years of presidential outcomes correctly. *Washington Post.* https://www.washingtonpost.com/news/the-fix/wp/2016/09/23/trump-is-headed-for-a-win-says-professor-whos-predicted-30-years-of-presidential-outcomes-correctly/?utm_term=.e3a8b731325c.

Stilgoe, J. (2019, 12 December). Who killed Elaine Herzberg? *OneZero.* https://onezero.medium.com/who-killed-elaine-herzberg-ea01fb14fc5e.

Strickland, E. (2019, 2 April). How IBM Watson overpromised and underdelivered on AI health care. *IEEE Spectrum.* https://spectrum.ieee.org/biomedical/diagnostics/how-ibm-watson-overpromised-and-underdelivered-on-ai-health-care.

Strimpel, Z. (2017). The matchmaking industry and singles culture in Britain 1970–2000. Doctoral dissertation. http://sro.sussex.ac.uk/id/eprint/71609/1/Strimpel%2C%20Zoe.pdf.

Su, J., Vargas, D. V. and Sakurai, K. (2019). One pixel attack for fooling deep neural networks. *IEEE Transactions on Evolutionary Computation*, 23, 828–41.

Suarez-Tangil, G. et al. (2019). Automatically dismantling online data fraud. *IEEE Transactions on Information Forensics and Security*, 15, 1128–37.

Szabo, L. (2019, 24 December). Artificial intelligence is rushing into patient care – and could raise risks. *Scientific American.* https://www.scientificamerican.com/article/artificial-intelligence-is-rushing-into-patient-care-and-could-raise-risks/.

Szegedy, C. et al. (2014). Intriguing properties of neural networks. *Proceedings of the International Conference on Learning Representations (ICLR).* https://arxiv.org/abs/1312.6199.

Taleb, N. N. (2001). *Fooled by randomness.* New York: Random House.

Taleb, N. N. (2010). *The black swan* (2nd edn.). New York: Random House.

Tanz, J. (2011, 20 December). The curse of Cow Clicker: How a cheeky satire became a videogame hit. *Wired.* https://www.wired.com/2011/12/ff-cowclicker/.

Taylor, A. (2018). Praise for the book *Re-engineering humanity* (by Brett Frischman and Evan Selinger. Cambridge: Cambridge University Press).

Tesla (2016, 19 October). All Tesla cars being produced now have full self-driving hardware. Press release. https://www.tesla.com/de_DE/blog/all-tesla-cars-being-produced-now-have-full-self-driving-hardware.

Theile, G. (2020, 14 February). Parship-Chef im Gespräch: 'Gut ausgebildete Frauen haben es schwerer' [Interview with head of Parship: 'It's more difficult for highly educated women']. *Frankfurter Allgemeine*. https://www.faz.net/aktuell/wirtschaft/parship-chef-ueber-das-flirten-menschen-sollten-sich-mehr-trauen-16632496.html.

Thomas, E. (2016, 28 December). Why Oakland police turned down predictive policing. *Vice*. https://www.vice.com/en/article/ezp8zp/minority-retort-why-oakland-police-turned-down-predictive-policing.

Thomas, R. J. (2020). Online exogamy reconsidered: Estimating the internet's effects on racial, educational, religious, political and age assortative mating. *Social Forces*, 98, 1257–86.

Titz, S. (2018, 3 August). Deep neural networks: Researchers outsmart algorithms in order to understand them better. *Horizons*. https://www.horizons-mag.ch/2018/03/08/gamers-can-solve-science-problems/.

Todd, P. M., Penke, L., Fasolo, B. and Lenton, A. P. (2007). Different cognitive processes underlie human mate choices and mate preferences. *Proceedings of the National Academy of Sciences*, 104, 15011–16.

Tolentino, J. (2019, 22 April). What it takes to put your phone away. *New Yorker*. https://www.newyorker.com/magazine/2019/04/29/what-it-takes-to-put-your-phone-away.

Tomasello, M. (2019). *Becoming human*. Cambridge, MA: Belknap.

Tombu, M. and Jolicoeur, P. (2004). Virtually no evidence for virtually perfect time-sharing. *Journal of Experimental Psychology: Human Perception & Performance*, 30, 795–810.

Topol, E. (2019). *Deep medicine: How artificial intelligence can make healthcare human again*. New York: Basic Books.

Topsell, E. (1967). *The history of four-footed beasts and serpents*. New York: Da Capo Press. (Original work published 1658.)

Tramer, F. et al. (2018). Ensemble adversarial training: Attacks and defenses. *ICLR 6th International Conference on Learning Representations*. https://arxiv.org/abs/1705.07204.

Tsvetkova, M., García-Gavilanes, R., Floridi, L. and Yasseri, T. (2017). Even good bots fight: The case of Wikipedia. *PLoS ONE*, 12(2): e0171774.

Turek, M. (undated). *Explainable artificial intelligence (XAI)*. Defense Advanced Research Projects Agency (DARPA). https://www.darpa.mil/program/explainable-artificial-intelligence.

Turing, A. (1950). Computing machinery and intelligence. *Mind*, 54, 433–60.

Turkle, S. (2016). *Reclaiming conversation*. New York: Penguin Books.

Twenge, J. M. (2017). *iGen*. New York: Atria Books.

Tzezana, R. (2016). Scenarios for crime and terrorist attacks using the internet of things. *European Journal of Futures Research*, 4, 18.

University of Michigan. (2016, 2 May). *Hacking into home: 'Smart home' security flaws found in popular system*. Press release. https://news.umich.edu/hacking-into-homes-smart-home-security-flaws-found-in-popular-system/.

Vigen, T. (2015). *Spurious correlations*. https://tylervigen.com/spurious-correlations.

Vodafone Institut für Gesellschaft und Kommunikation (2016, January). *Big Data: Wann Menschen bereit sind, ihre Daten zu teilen* [Big data: When are people willing to share their data]. https://www.vodafone-institut.de/wp-content/uploads/2016/01/VodafoneInstitute-Survey-BigData-Highlights-de.pdf.

van Rompay, T. J. L., Vonk, D. J. and Fransen, M. L. (2009). The eye of the camera: Effects of security cameras on prosocial behavior. *Environment and Behavior*, 41, 60–74.

von Neumann, J. (1958). *The computer and the brain*. New Haven, CT: Yale University Press.

Wachter, R. (2017). *The digital doctor*. New York: MacGraw-Hill.

Wang, W., Tang, B., Wang, R., Wang, L. and Ye, A. (2019). *Towards a robust deep neural network in texts: A survey*. ArXiv. https://arxiv.org/abs/1902.07285.

Ward, A. F., Duke, K., Gneezy, A. and Bos, M. W. (2017). Brain drain: The mere presence of one's own smartphone reduces available cognitive capacity. *Journal of the Association for Computer Research*, 2, 140–54.

Watson, J. M. and Strayer, D. L. (2010). Supertaskers: Profiles in extraordinary multitasking ability. *Psychonomic Bulletin and Review*, 17, 479–85.

Watson, L. (2015, 15 May). Humans have shorter attention span than goldfish, thanks to smartphones. *Telegraph*. https://www.telegraph.co.uk/science/2016/03/12/humans-have-shorter-attention-span-than-goldfish-thanks-to-smart/.

Webb, A. (2019). *The big nine*. New York: Public Affairs.

Wegwarth, O., Gaissmaier, W. and Gigerenzer, G. (2009). Smart strategies for doctors and doctors-in-training: Heuristics in medicine. *Medical Education*, 43, 721–28.

Weinshall-Margel, K. and Shapard, J. (2011). Overlooked factors in the analysis of parole decisions. *PNAS*, 108(42), E833.

Weiser, M. (1991, September). The computer for the twenty-first century. *Scientific American*, 94–104.

Weltecke, D. (2003). Gab es 'Vertrauen' im Mittelalter? [Did 'trust' exist in the Middle Ages?] In U. Frevert (ed.), *Vertrauen. Historische Annäherungen* (pp. 67–89). Göttingen: Vandenhoeck & Ruprecht.

Whitty, M. T. and Buchanan, T. (2015). The online dating romance scam: The psychological impact on victims – both financial and non-financial. *Criminology and Criminal Justice*, 1–9.

Wineburg, S. and McGrew, S. (2019). Lateral reading and the nature of expertise: Reading less and learning more when evaluating digital information. *Teachers College Record*, 121(11), 1–40.

Wood, J. (2005, 20 July). He made the Mini – and broke the mould. *Independent*. https://www.independent.co.uk/life-style/motoring/features/he-made-the-mini-and-broke-the-mould-301594.html.

Wu, T. (2016). *The attention merchants*. London: Atlantic Books.

Wubben, M., and Wangenheim, F. v. (2008). 'Instant customer base analysis: Managerial heuristics often "get it right"'. *Journal of Marketing*, 72, 82–93.

Young, R. A., Burge, S. K., Kumar, K. A., Wilson, J. M. and Ortiz, D. F. (2018). A time–motion study of primary care physicians' work in the electronic health record era. *Family Medicine*, 50, 91–9.

Youyou, W., Kosinski, M. and Stillwell, D. (2015). Computer-based personality judgments are more accurate than those made by humans. *Proceedings of the National Academy of Sciences*, 112, 1036–40.

Zech, J. R. et al. (2018). Variable generalization performance of a deep learning model to detect pneumonia in chest radiographs: A cross-sectional study. *PLoS Medicine*, 15(11): e1002683.

Zendle, D. and Cairns, P. (2018). Video game loot boxes are linked to problem gambling: Results of a large-scale survey. *PLoS ONE*, 13(11): e0206767.

Zhao, J. et al. (2017). Men also like shopping: Reducing gender bias amplification using corpus-level constraints. *Proceedings of the 2017 Conference on Empirical Methods in Language Processing*, 2979–89. https://www.aclweb.org/anthology/D17-1323.pdf.

Zimmerman, F. J., Christakis, D. A. and Meltzoff, A. N. (2007). Associations between media viewing and language development in children under age 2 years. *Journal of Pediatrics*, 151, 364–8.

Zuboff, S. (2019a). Surveillance capitalism and the challenge of collective action. *New Labor Forum*, 28, 10–29.

Zuboff, S. (2019b). *The age of surveillance capitalism*. London: Profile Books.

Zuboff, S. (2020, 24 January). You are now remotely controlled. *New York Times*. https://www.nytimes.com/2020/01/24/opinion/sunday/surveillance-capitalism.html.

Zuckerberg, M. (2018, 12 April). We need to rely on and build more AI tools to help flag certain content. *CNBC*. https://www.youtube.com/watch?v=riFuznlZvyY.

Zuckerman, E. (2014, 14 August). The Internet's original sin. *Atlantic*. https://www.theatlantic.com/technology/archive/2014/08/advertising-is-the-internets-original-sin/376041/.

Zweig, K. A. (2017, 7 April). Watching the watchers: Epstein and Robertson's 'search engine manipulation effect'. *Algorithm Watch*. https://algorithm-watch.org/en/watching-the-watchers-epstein-and-robertsons-search-engine-manipulation-effect/.

Notes

1 Personal conversation.
2 Lee (2018).
3 For instance, throughout her seminal analysis of surveillance capitalism, Shoshana Zuboff appears to assume this ability as generally true, such as when she speaks of 'monitoring and shaping of human behavior with unprecedented accuracy' (2019a, p. 17) or writes that 'surveillance capitalists know everything *about us*' (2019b, p. 11).
4 Breakstone, Smith, Connors et al. (2021) See also McGrew et al. (2018); Wineburg and McGrew (2019); and Chapter 11.
5 Rogers (2012).
6 National Consortium for the Study of Terrorism and Responses to Terrorism (2020).
7 Centers for Disease Control and Prevention (2020).
8 Britt (2015).
9 ERGO (2019).
10 https://www.youtube.com/watch?v=t7911kgJJZc.
11 For instance, arguing in favour of mass surveillance, the head of the German police trade union wrote that the false positive rate of 0.1 per cent is so low that it is 'acceptable, barely perceptible'. See Wendt (2020). The press release is here: https://www.bmi.bund.de/SharedDocs/pressemitteilungen/DE/2018/10/gesichtserkennung-suedkreuz.html.
12 The heated debate was fuelled by a lack of risk literacy. For instance, one commentator on Twitter correctly pointed out that the 0.1 per cent false alarm rate together with the low rate of suspects means that the vast majority of alarms are false. To see this, assume 500 suspects hanging out at train stations, of which the system correctly identifies 400 (80 per cent hit rate). Thus, there are 400 correct positives for every 12,000 false positives, which means that about 97 per cent of all positive classifications are

wrong. In response, a member of the European Parliament defended the system and tweeted: 'You should work on your maths: a 0.1 per cent error rate means 99.9 per cent hits when applied optimally. That's optimal.' She wrongly thought that a false alarm rate of 0.1 per cent means that 99.9 per cent of all classifications are correct. When the error was pointed out to her, she insisted that she knew the probability calculus but that it was irrelevant because the real issue at stake was the preventive and educative effect of face recognition systems. Politicians need risk literacy – and the humility to admit errors as well.

13 Tolentino (2019), p. 71.

14 As the saying goes, 'If you do not pay for a product, you are the product.' More precisely, the predictions made about you are the product. The coffeehouse story is inspired by an entertaining talk on corporate surveillance: see https://idlewords.com/talks/internet_with_a_human_face.htm.

15 Brin and Page (2012). The story of how the Google founders – helped by a brilliant Canadian mathematician whose loathing of advertising even exceeded that of Page – ended up creating the most powerful ad-based platform is told by Wu (2016).

16 Various companies, including Mozilla and Google Contributor, are also experimenting with micropayments (Melendez, 2019). Netflix is also interested in keeping us watching in order to keep subscription rates high, but not to satisfy a host of advertisers. Some platforms offer the option to pay not to be bombarded with advertisements, but few guarantee that those who pay are no longer tracked. For instance, business platforms such as LinkedIn and Xing offer premium memberships that allow access to data of other members (e.g., who visited one's page) but do not protect one's own data.

17 The issue of boosting users' understanding is discussed in the European Commission's report (Lewandowsky et al., 2020). Digital risk for children has been addressed by private organizations such as the DQ Institute (Chawla, 2018).

18 More precisely, the slots are auctioned and sold to the bidder for whom an algorithm calculates the highest return for the tech company, which is a function of both the bid and the expected number of users who will see or click the ad. Advertisers pay Google for clicks, so clearly Google wants you to click on the ads.

19 https://www.samsung.com/hk_en/info/privacy/smarttv/. Fowler (2019, 18 September).

20 https://www.searchenginewatch.com/2016/04/27/do-50-of-adults-really-not-recognise-ads-in-search-results/.

21 Kawohl and Becker (2017).

22 *Economist* (2018).

23 Advisory Council for Consumer Affairs at the Federal Ministry of Justice and Consumer Protection (2018). The fact that checks on scoring systems are based on reports that the credit agencies themselves have commissioned was revealed by reporters from the Bavarian public broadcaster Bayerischer Rundfunk.

24 http://2045.com/ideology/. Some writers dream of being allowed to upload our brains into this vast intelligence, once it arrives, thereby making them immortal.

25 Daniel and Palmer (2007).

26 Overstated claims about algorithms without supporting evidence can be found, for instance, in Harari (2015). I provide examples in Chapter 11.

27 See the spectrum of opinions in Brockman (2019). Also, Kahneman (2019, p. 609) poses the question whether AI can eventually do whatever people can do: 'Will there be anything that is reserved for human beings? Frankly, I don't see any reason to set limits on what AI can do.' And: 'You should replace humans by algorithms whenever possible' (p. 610).

28 Gigerenzer (2014).

29 On fear cycles, see Orben (2020).

PART 1: THE HUMAN AFFAIR WITH AI

1 Taylor, (2018).

CHAPTER 1: IS TRUE LOVE JUST A CLICK AWAY?

1 Rilke (1993).

2 Sales (2016).

3 Anderson et al. (2020).

4 Grzymek and Puntschuh (2019).

5 Parship spends about 100 million euros per year on TV, website and poster advertisements, where professional models pose as singles. Theile (2020).

6 https://www.unstatistik.de.

7 Deutsches Institut für Service-Qualität (2017).

8 https://www.elitesingles.com.

9 Cited in Finkel et al. (2012), p. 24.

10 https://www.jdate.com/en/jlife/success-stories/shlomit-ryan.

11 Finkel et al. (2012), p. 3.

12 Epstein (2013). eHarmony personnel presented a research paper claiming that married couples who met through eHarmony are happier than those who met by other means. Yet they compared newlywed eHarmony couples (average six months) with couples in the control group that were married on average for more than two years. The study neither passed the scientific review process nor was published, and one can guess why.

13 When, for instance, I contacted ElitePartner requesting an interview for this book, I was asked to send in the questions beforehand. I submitted ten questions. The response was that they were not willing to answer half of these, such as how many new paying members they have per year and how many fall in love per year. I am still waiting for their answers to the other half. There is reason to doubt that the figures released by dating agencies are trustworthy; the hyperbolic claims of the matchmaking industry have been analysed by Zoe Strimpel (2017).

14 Cacioppo et al. (2013).

15 Danielsbacka et al. (2020); Potarca (2020); Paul (2014).

16 Potarca (2020); Thomas (2020); Brown (2019).

17 Tinder also uses an algorithm, albeit one that is not based on profiles. Tinder's algorithm gives each user a secret desirability score based on how many swipes they get and from whom.

18 https://www.youtube.com/watch?v=m9PiPlRuy6E.

19 To make it simple, I use the arithmetic mean here. OKCupid's algorithm calculates the *geometric mean*, which multiplies the values and takes the square root.

20 Bruch and Newman (2018).

21 Rudder (2014).

22 Buss (2019).

23 Finkel et al. (2012), p. 30.

24 Joel et al. (2017).

25 Todd et al. (2007). See also Finkel et al. (2012).

26 Montoya et al. (2008).

27 Dyrenforth et al. (2010).

28 Finkel et al. (2012), p. 44.

29 Sales (2016).

30 Epstein (2013).

31 Hancock et al. (2007).

32 Hitsch et al. (2010).

33 Epstein (2013).

34 Epstein (2013).

35 Anderson (2016).

36 Epstein (2013).
37 Lea et al. (2009), p. 42.
38 Facebook prohibits misleading advertising, but scammers use a technique called 'cloaking' that shows Facebook's robots harmless content, unlike the message the victim reads (Kayser-Bril, 2019).
39 Office of Fair Trading, United Kingdom (2007).
40 Whitty and Buchanan (2015).
41 Suarez-Tangil et al. (2019).
42 Whitty and Buchanan (2015).
43 Tsvetkova et al. (2017).
44 Brown (2015).
45 Federal Trade Commission (2019).
46 Bostrom (2015), p. 211.
47 Youyou et al. (2015).

CHAPTER 2: WHAT AI IS BEST AT: THE STABLE-WORLD PRINCIPLE

1 Newell et al. (1958a).
2 Attributed to Richard Feynman while speaking at a Caltech graduation ceremony (source of the quote unclear).
3 Cited by Boden (2008), p. 840. A puzzling tension exists between Simon's work on decision making and bounded rationality, which focuses on uncertainty, and his work on AI, which focuses on well-defined problems such as chess. In his work on bounded rationality, Simon distinguishes between uncertainty and well-defined problems, while in his writings on AI this distinction disappears (Gigerenzer, 2021).
4 Dreyfus (1979), p. 33.
5 See Katsikopoulos et al. (2020), where it is called the 'unstable world principle', which is the same principle.
6 Kay and King (2020); Taleb (2010).
7 Makoff (2011).
8 Ferrucci et al. (2010).
9 Lee (2018).
10 Russell (2019), pp. 47–8.
11 Kumar et al. (2009). In this experiment, 50 per cent of the presented pairs showed the same person, and the other 50 per cent showed different people.
12 For this and the following example, see Katsikopoulos et al. (2020), Chapter 4.

13 Chiusi (2020), p. 195.

14 Simon and Newell (1958).

15 Krauthammer (1997).

16 See Katsikopoulos et al. (2020).

17 Aikman et al. (2021).

18 Gigerenzer et al. (2011); and Katsikopoulos et al. (2020).

19 Wachter (2017).

20 Kellermann and Jones (2013).

21 Kellermann and Jones (2013).

22 Wachter (2017).

23 Schulte and Fry (2019).

24 See Carr (2014).

25 Young et al. (2018).

26 Wachter (2017).

27 Schulte and Fry (2019).

28 A F P (2020).

29 Wachter (2017), p. 71.

30 Gigerenzer and Muir Gray (2011).

31 Gottman and Gottman (2017), p. 10; https://www.gottman.com/about/research/; Gottman et al. (1998).

32 See Heyman and Slep (2001).

33 https://www.gottman.com. See also Barrowman (2014).

34 Roberts and Pashler (2000).

35 Heyman and Slep (2001).

36 Heyman and Slep (2001).

37 Heyman and Slep (2001). The difference between 65 per cent and 21 per cent is called 'overfitting'.

38 For the field of behavioural economics, see, for example, Berg and Gigerenzer (2010).

39 Fitting was also the rule in statistics, such as in the *Journal of the American Statistical Association*; see Breiman (2001).

40 Until the 1990s, one would have had to search hard to find any predictions in cognitive modelling in general. See Roberts and Pashler (2000); and Brandstätter et al. (2008).

41 Bailey et al. (2014).

42 https://quoteinvestigator.com/tag/niels-bohr/.

43 Russell and Norvig (2010).

44 Strickland (2019).

45 Ross and Swetlitz (2018).

46 Topol (2019).

47 Best (2013).
48 Schwertfeger (2019).
49 Brown (2017).

CHAPTER 3: MACHINES INFLUENCE HOW WE THINK OF INTELLIGENCE

1 Weiser (1991).
2 Turing (1950).
3 Gigerenzer and Goldstein (1996); and Gigerenzer and Murray (2015).
4 Daston (1994); and Gigerenzer and Goldstein (1996).
5 Babbage was similarly influenced by the division of labour introduced in the English textile industry that used punch cards to programme weaving machines. This so impressed Babbage and many of his contemporaries that 'factory tourism' came into vogue. See Daston (1994); and Gigerenzer (2001).
6 There are many versions of this story. This condensed version is based on one of the first accounts that mentions the numbers 1 to 100 by Franz Mathé in 1906. See Hayes (2006).
7 Cited in Wood (2005). This quote has also been attributed to another Sir Alec, namely Alec Guinness. See also the former US president Barack Obama (Martosko, 2013) and the former German chancellor Gerhard Schröder (Stadler, 2006).
8 Gleick (1992).
9 Daston (2018).
10 https://www.computerscience.org/resources/women-in-computer-science/.
11 Von Neumann (1958); Turing (1950). On the differences between von Neumann's, Turing's and Simon's views of the relation between the computer and the brain or mind, see Gigerenzer and Goldstein (1996).
12 Newell et al. (1958b); Newell and Simon (1972).
13 Simon uses clear words: 'the hypothesis is that a physical symbol system of the sort I have just described has the necessary and sufficient means for general intelligence' (1969, p. 28).
14 Simon (1991).
15 Cohen (1998).
16 Gigerenzer and Goldstein (1996).
17 Gigerenzer (1991); and Gigerenzer and Murray (2015).

CHAPTER 4: ARE SELF-DRIVING CARS JUST DOWN THE ROAD?

1 Elon Musk in a video message to the World Artificial Intelligence Conference in Shanghai, July 2020. https://bdtechtalks.com/2020/07/29/self-driving-tesla-car-deep-learning/.

2 https://twitter.com/senblumenthal/status/981257797269688321.

3 Uber sold its autonomous car division (Uber ATG) in December 2020.

4 National Transportation Safety Board (2019); Stern (2018).

5 Stilgoe (2019).

6 Efrati (2018).

7 Stilgoe (2019).

8 In 2016, for instance, Nissan CEO Carlos Ghosn proclaimed regarding his cooperation with Microsoft, 'In 2020, you're going to have what we call a totally autonomous-driven car,' before adding: 'This is different from the driverless car ... 2020 for the autonomous car in urban conditions, probably 2025 for the driverless car' (Dillet, 2016). See also Elias (2019).

9 Dickmanns and Zapp (1987).

10 Shladover (2016).

11 Shladover (2016).

12 Daston (2022).

13 See Geirhos et al. (2020) on shortcut learning.

14 Simonite (2018).

15 Szegedy et al. (2014).

16 Here are some statisticians' complaints about the new jargon in AI. What is now called the *input layer* is known as *independent variables* in statistics, and the *output layer* is a new term for *dependent variables*. What is called a *neural network* is in essence the same as a nonlinear regression or a discriminant analysis, for numerical estimation and classification, respectively. Moreover, algorithms that can learn have been developed long ago. One of these is *regression*, which learns weights from data, as in supervised learning. In statistics, unsupervised learning also has a long tradition, with a toolbox of methods such as cluster analysis and factor analysis. Despite this similarity between classical statistics and AI, one key difference is that statistical applications typically fit their models to a given sample of data, whereas neural networks get the data *sequentially* and update their algorithm after each feedback. See Sarle (1994).

17 Kosko (2015).

18 Szegedy et al. (2014).

19 These tiny systematic perturbations that fool deep neural networks can be found with the help of evolutionary algorithms. The technique is also called 'hard-negative mining', that is, identifying 'adversarial examples' to which the network falsely attaches low probabilities of being the correct number or object. The same perturbation can cause misclassifications not only for the examples shown here, but also for other training sets and with other networks. To shield networks, one strategy has tried to include adversarial examples in the training set, but even that method remains vulnerable to simple attacks (Tramer et al., 2018).

20 Wang et al. (2019).

21 The images that fool deep neural networks were generated with evolutionary algorithms or gradient ascent methods (Nguyen et al., 2015).

22 Su et al. (2019). On the logic of adversarial networks see Rocca (2019).

23 Brooks (2015).

24 Titz (2018).

25 Ranjan et al. (2019).

26 Dingus et al. (2016).

27 Webb (2019), p. 183. To deal with these problems, engineers are working on multisensory systems, which use a combination of vision, laser (lidar) and location measures. For instance, the location is linked to a map with information about speed limits, so that a 65-mph speed limit sign 'detected' by the vision system could be disregarded.

28 Gleave (2020).

29 Luetge (2017).

30 Awad et al. (2018).

31 Fleischhut et al. (2017).

32 Steven E. Shladover. Personal communication, December 2020.

33 https://www.sparkassen-direkt.de/auto-mobilitaet/telematik/. The example is taken from the first German telematics insurer, Sparkassen.direkt. Rapid acceleration is defined as exceeding $0.235 \text{ g} = 2.3\text{m/sec}^2$, and harsh braking as exceeding $0.286 \text{ g} = 2.8\text{m/sec}^2$. The company eventually discontinued offering telematics insurance because the cost of the black box was too high. Nevertheless, it became a financial success but for other reasons: its publicity attracted new customers. Due to new regulations in the European Union, all new cars must have an e-call system, that is, a black box that notifies the police in the case of a severe car accident. This regulation makes telematics insurance more profitable.

34 ERGO (2019). The study used a representative sample of 3,200 people living in Germany.

35 Medvin (2019).
36 Doll (2016).
37 Fowler (2019, 27 December).
38 Maack (2020).
39 Bliss (2019).
40 National Geographic (2014).
41 Branwen (2011).
42 See Geirhos et al. (2020).
43 Szabo (2019).
44 Zech et al. (2018).
45 See, for instance, Youyou et al. (2015).
46 Koh (2021); Geirhos et al. (2020).

CHAPTER 5: COMMON SENSE AND AI

1 Calaprice (2011). The quote is attributed to Einstein.
2 Coleridge (1838).
3 Church (2019). The 85 billion nerve cells in the brain consume about 20 per cent of the body's energy; thus, the average power consumption of an adult is 100 watts.
4 Tomasello, *Becoming Human*.
5 Gigerenzer, *Gut Feelings*.
6 Kruglanski and Gigerenzer, 'Intuitive and Deliberate Judgments.'
7 Poibeau (2017).
8 For illustrations of translations from Chinese, French and German into English, see Hofstadter (2018).
9 https://www.deepl.com/en/translator#de/en/Papstschuss. The information is fluid on DeepL, meaning that these translations may change with time.
10 Poibeau (2017).
11 Poibeau, (2017), p. 71.
12 Kayser-Bril (2020).
13 Niven and Kao (2019). Similarly, Gururangan et al. (2018) conclude that because of neural networks' ability to discover spurious but efficient cues in the data, the success of natural language models to date has been overestimated.
14 Kurzweil (2012), p. 7.
15 Quinn et al. (2001).
16 Sinha et al. (2006).
17 Brunswik (1956).
18 Sinha and Poggio (1996).

19 Asch (1951).
20 Szegedy et al. (2014).
21 Burell (2016).
22 Lake et al. (2017).
23 Nguyen et al. (2015).
24 Lake et al. (2017).
25 Hsu (2015).
26 Luria (1968).

CHAPTER 6: ONE DATA POINT
CAN BEAT BIG DATA

1 Anderson (2008).
2 Harford (2014).
3 Daston (2017).
4 Daston (2017), pp. 161–2.
5 Google engineers trained the algorithms on data from years 2003–7 and tested them on data from 2007–8. Ginsberg et al. (2009).
6 Olson et al. (2013).
7 Lazer et al. (2014).
8 Copeland et al. (undated).
9 Nevertheless, bestselling authors continue to suggest to the general public that Google Flu Trends, like IBM's Watson for Oncology, is a huge success story for big data. I recall a talk held in Munich in May 2014 by Viktor Meyer-Schönberger, first author of the 2013 bestseller *Big Data*, in which he still presented Google Flu Trends as the showcase of big data even though by that time Google Flu Trends had long lost its nose for where the flu was going. The hundreds of business executives in the audience were visibly impressed. Two years later, Harari (2015, pp. 390–91; 2016) still talks about Google's 'magic' and presents the story in a similar way to impress the general reader.
10 Anderson (2008).
11 Brown (1838).
12 Katsikopoulos et al. (2020, 2021).
13 Katsikopoulos et al. (2020, 2021) Our analysis was inspired by the appendix in Lazer et al. (2014), who reported various more or less complex rules that predict better than Google Flu Trends. For those interested in the statistical details, note that these rules included a simple regression with a two-week lag as the only predictor that had the same error as the recency heuristic. The regression model differs from the recency heuristic

in that one still needs to compute and update the regression coefficients every time one makes a prediction. This is no improvement over the recency heuristic. Lazer reported that a hybrid model that combines Google Flu Trends with lag data performs best. Yet this hybrid model needs all the elaborate calculations performed by Google Flu Trends in the first place.

14 See Artinger et al. (2018); Green and Armstrong (2015); and Katsiko-poulos et al. (2020).

15 Dosi et al. (2020).

16 Porter (2004).

17 Anderson (2008).

18 Ginsberg et al. (2009).

19 Vigen (2015).

20 Aschwanden (2016).

21 Advisory Council for Consumer Affairs at the Federal Ministry of Justice and Consumer Protection (2018), p. 62. In the financial world, being fooled by randomness is a frequent event; see Taleb (2001).

22 Mullard (2011); and Begley (2012).

23 Chalmers and Glasziou (2009).

24 Leetaru (2018).

25 Bergin (2018).

26 Anderson (2013).

27 Neumann et al. (2019).

28 Salganik et al. (2020).

29 Clayton et al. (2020).

30 Chiusi (2020). For instance, Danish municipalities had been experimenting with an algorithm for identifying children in vulnerable families until the data protection authorities intervened.

31 Istituto Superiore di Sanità (2020). The report is based on available data from 18 November 2020.

32 Gigerenzer (2014).

PART 2: HIGH STAKES

1 Feynman et al. (1985), p. 345.

CHAPTER 7: TRANSPARENCY

1 European Union (2016), Article 5 (1a).

2 Calaprice (2011). The quote is attributed to Einstein.

3 Loomis v. Wisconsin, 881 N.W.2d 749 (Wis. 2016), cert. denied, 137 S.Ct. 2290 (2017).

4 Liptak (2017).

5 See Gigerenzer (2003), Chapter 11, p. 186.

6 Grisso and Tomkins (1996), p. 928.

7 The study analysed more than 1,000 rulings of eight Israeli judges (Danziger et al., 2011). For a critique of its conclusions, see Weinshall-Margel and Shapard (2011); and Glöckner (2016).

8 DeMichele et al. (2020).

9 Epstein (1995).

10 Dressel and Farid (2018).

11 Dressel and Farid (2018).

12 Matacic (2018).

13 This is the average of the value for individuals (63 per cent) and the value of the majority vote in groups of twenty (67 per cent).

14 Geraghty and Woodhams (2015). The Dressel and Farid study was replicated by Lin et al. (2020) with similar results, except when the base rates of recidivism were low (only 11 per cent) *and* the human participants did not get feedback and thus could not learn about the low base rates. With low base rates of recidivism, COMPAS fared no better than the most simple algorithm of always predicting no recidivism.

15 See DeMichele et al. (2020); and Rudin et al. (2020).

16 Angelino et al. (2018).

17 Rudin and Radin (2019). If you are interested in reading more on how machine learning tools extract the most important features, see Katsikopoulos et al. (2020). The definition of transparency in this section is also taken from this work.

18 https://advancingpretrial.org/psa/factors/#fta.

19 My colleagues and I have worked on making decision lists more transparent by curtailing their size, which, in machine learning, is typically unrestricted (Katsikopoulos et al., 2020).

20 https://advancingpretrial.org/psa/research/.

21 See Stevenson (2018) for the problems and traps of measuring the performance of algorithmic risk assessment tools.

22 Grossman et al. (2011).

23 Peteranderl (2020).

24 Gorner and Sweeney (2020).

25 Peteranderl (2020).

26 Thomas (2016).

27 Hauber et al. (2019).

28 Snook et al. (2005).

29 See Bennell et al. (2007); and Paulsen (2006).

30 Gigerenzer et al. (2011).

31 Sergeant and Himonides (2019).

32 Dastin (2018). See O'Neil (2016) for how big data increases inequality.

33 Buolamwini and Gebru (2018).

34 Raji and Buolamwini (2019).

35 Zhao et al. (2017). This article also developed measures that succeeded in reducing the increase in gender bias by almost half but couldn't fully eliminate it.

36 Among the two-thirds of pictures classified as 'woman', two-thirds are expected to be correct (because two-thirds of all the pictures are women). Similarly, among the one-third of the pictures classified as 'man', one-third is expected to be correct (because only one-third of all the pictures are men), which results in $2/3 \times 2/3 + 1/3 \times 1/3 = 5/9$ correct answers, about 56 per cent.

37 Chin (2018). Google says that over 20 per cent of technical roles are filled by women, but that is not the figure for machine learning.

38 Hao (2020).

39 https://googlewalkout.medium.com/standing-with-dr-timnit-gebru-isupporttimnit-believeblackwomen-6dadc300d382.

40 Gigerenzer et al. (2007).

41 https://www.hardingcenter.de/en.

42 Benoliel and Becher (2019).

43 McDonald and Cranor (2008).

44 Zuboff (2019b), pp. 166–8.

45 Advisory Council for Consumer Affairs at the Federal Ministry of Justice and Consumer Protection (2017).

46 Rudin and Radin (2019).

47 https://www.fico.com/en/newsroom/fico-announces-winners-inaugural-xml-challenge.

48 Rudin (2019). For the medical domain, see Holzinger et al. (2017).

49 Katsikopoulos et al. (2020).

50 Turek (undated), pp. 7–10. See also Gunning and Aha (2019).

51 See, for instance, Gigerenzer et al. (2011); Green and Armstrong (2015); Jung et al. (2017); and Katsikopoulos et al. (2020, 2021).

52 Artinger et al. (2018); Wubben and Wangenheim (2008).

53 In machine learning, these rules are known as 1-rules, learned by the 1R program; see Holte (1993).

54 Rivest (1987).

55 The fact that tallying can be as or even more accurate than black box algorithms in situations of uncertainty has been known in psychology since Dawes and Corrigan (1974); Einhorn and Hogarth (1975); and Czerlinski et al. (1999). A comparison between tallying and machine learning algorithms can be found in Katsikopoulos et al. (2020).

56 Markman (2016).

57 Silver (2016).

58 Lichtman (2016). The following presentation is adapted from Katsikopoulos et al. (2020).

59 Stevenson (2016).

60 In the US presidential election of 2020, the Keys predicted correctly that Biden would win. The polls again underestimated Trump, but most got the final result right.

61 Spinelli and Crovella (2020).

62 Pasquale (2015).

63 See Gigerenzer (2003), p. 91.

64 Advisory Council for Consumer Affairs at the Federal Ministry of Justice and Consumer Protection (2018). The members of the Council were divided about whether scoring services should report all features or only the most relevant to the public.

65 See Articles 13 and 22 of the GDPR (European Union, 2016).

66 https://docs.google.com/forms/d/e/1FAIpQLSfdmQGrgdCBCexTrpne7 KXUzpbiI9LeEtdoAm-qRFimpwuv1A/viewform.

CHAPTER 8: SLEEPWALKING INTO SURVEILLANCE

1 Zuckerman (2014).

2 Snowden (2019).

3 Nasiopoulos et al. (2015) report that wearing smart glasses increases socially accepted behaviour, but only as long as people do not forget about the eye trackers. On the positive effect of security cameras on prosocial behaviour, see van Rompay et al. (2009).

4 Cho (2020). On Venezuela, see Berwick (2018).

5 Kostka and Antoine (2019).

6 Kostka (2019).

7 Advisory Council for Consumer Affairs at the Federal Ministry of Justice and Consumer Protection (2018).

8 ERGO (2019).

9 Rötzer (2019).

10 Christl (2017).

11 Leetaru (2018).

12 Barnes (2006).

13 Vodafone Institut für Gesellschaft und Kommunikation (2016).

14 NortonLifeLock (2019).

15 ERGO (2019).

16 Freed et al. (2018).

17 In Dave Eggers's satire of Silicon Valley *The Circle*, a cult-like internet company – a mixture of Google and Facebook – reigns the world. At company rallies, employees chant 'sharing is caring' and 'privacy is theft'.

18 Farnham (2014).

19 Johnson (2010); Sengupta (2011).

20 *Economist* (2018).

21 Zuboff (2020).

22 Brin and Page (2012), p. 3832.

23 Zuboff (2019b), pp. 71–5.

24 Zuckerman (2014).

25 Zuboff (2019b).

26 Zuboff (2019b), p. 87.

27 Zuboff (2019b), pp. 118–20.

28 https://www.techtransparencyproject.org/articles/googles-revolving-door-us.

29 Baltrusaitis (2019).

30 Elliott and Meyer (2013).

31 Cahall et al. (2014).

32 For more details, see Zuboff (2019b).

33 Watson (2015).

34 Smith et al. (2011).

35 Twenge (2017). I should note that the questions of whether these associations are causal and how large the effect is are a matter of intense discussion in psychology. See also Turkle (2016).

36 Lanier and Weyl (2018); Lanier (2019).

37 Here I have updated a calculation made by Felix Stalder (2014).

38 Noyes (2020).

39 Facebook (2020).

40 For other estimates, see Munro (2019). Some higher estimates are based on dividing Facebook's revenue by the number of users, which ignores the fact that revenue is not income, and also that Facebook needs to retain some of the income for profit.

41 Melendez (2019); Pogue (2016).

42 Eames (1990). Mattel has sold more than a billion Barbies.

43 K. Bondy, cited in Gigerenzer (2003), pp. 23, 260.

44 Praschl (2015).

45 Digital Courage (2016). Other companies followed and produced their own smart dolls, such as My Friend Cayla, a toy that was classified as an illegal transmitter and forbidden in Germany. Illegal transmitters are well-known from cold war movies where spies record private conversations using pens and cigarette lighters with hidden microphones built in.

46 Hu (2018).

47 Tzezana (2016).

48 University of Michigan (2016). See also Davis et al. (2020).

49 Elsberg (2017).

50 https://www.samsung.com/hk_en/info/privacy/smarttv/. In 2015, Samsung TVs were found to be listening to everything they could hear. Since then, the company maintains it has changed the system to record only what you say when spoken to directly. The pattern is familiar: companies continually test how far they can go, that is, to what extent the privacy expectations of the public have deteriorated, and only react after protest. In 2017, the Federal Trade Commission rebuked the TV industry for being deceptive and unfair and told the industry to be up front and give the customers a chance to opt in. The industry countered with even more small print that few will take the time to read; the majority will simply click 'agree'. Fowler (2019, 18 September); Nguyen (2017). The survey mentioned was conducted with the insurer ERGO in Germany, 2019.

51 https://www.washingtonpost.com/news/the-switch/wp/2017/03/08/ex-cia-chief-to-stephen-colbert-no-the-government-is-not-spying-on-you-through-your-microwave/.

52 Weiser (1991).

53 The best account of nudging and its underlying philosophy can be found in Rebonato (2012).

54 Epstein and Robertson (2015).

55 Epstein and Robertson (2015); and Zweig (2017).

56 Ten per cent undecided voters is the average of the 2016 and 2012 US presidential elections. Silver (2018).

57 Bond et al. (2012).

58 See, for instance, Zuboff (2019a, 2019b).

59 Coppock et al. (2020). See also Howard (2020).

60 Kramer et al. (2014). As an aside, the editor of the journal in which the Facebook article was published explicitly expressed ethical concerns.

61 Booth (2014); and McNeal (2014).

62 Snowden (2019).

63 Zuckerberg (2018). See also Morozov (2013).

64 Shahin and Zheng (2020).

65 Kostka (2019).

66 Zuckerman (2014).

67 Greenwald (2014).

68 Snowden (2019).

69 Snowden (2019).

70 Lotan (2014).

71 https://www.youtube.com/watch?v=A6e7wfDHzew.

72 Kostka and Zhang (2018). Shenzhen, a city near Hong Kong with over 12 million inhabitants, was the first large city in the world to have its taxis and buses run entirely on electricity.

73 For instance, surveillance cameras hang from rooftops and poles across Ecuador, from the Amazonian jungle to the Galapagos Islands. Ecuador has implemented a Chinese system called ECU-911, and other countries in Asia, Europe and Africa appear to be following suit.

74 The term 'Great Firewall' was coined by *Wire Magazine* in 1997. See Griffiths (2019).

75 Griffiths (2019), p. 64.

76 Griffiths (2019), p. 118. The censored search engine Google.cn went online in January 2006.

77 Isaac (2016).

CHAPTER 9: THE PSYCHOLOGY OF GETTING USERS HOOKED

1 Skinner (1972).

2 Eyal (2014), p. 164. In a more recent book, *Indistractable: How to Control Your Attention and Choose Your Life* (2019), Eyal swerved in the opposite direction, becoming a champion of how to get unhooked.

3 Skinner distinguished two kinds of intermittent (variable) reinforcement and two kinds of fixed reinforcement, resulting in four schedules of reinforcement. (1) In a *fixed ratio schedule*, a behaviour is reinforced after it happened exactly x times. (2) In a *variable ratio schedule*, a behaviour is reinforced after it happened a variable number of times. (3) In a *fixed interval schedule*, a behaviour is reinforced if it occurred after a fixed time. (4) In a *variable interval schedule*, a behaviour is reinforced if it

occurred after a variable interval of time. The two variable reinforcement schedules create a steady rate of behaviour and the variable rate schedule the highest response rate. The fixed interval schedule leads to the lowest response rate, and, after a reinforcement, the behaviour stops and is only gradually taken up again.

4 Halpern (2014).
5 Lindström et al. (2021).
6 See Lindström et al. (2021).
7 Solon (2017).
8 https://www.facebook.com/notes/facebook/facebook-gets-a-facelift/2207967130.
9 Zuboff (2019b), p. 458.
10 Luckerson (2015).
11 Haynes (2018).
12 Solsman (2018).
13 Spinelli and Crovella (2020). These authors also show that YouTube's recommender system more likely directs privacy-seeking users (e.g., those who disable cookie placements or use Tor) towards unreliable sources than those logged into a Google account. YouTube's policy change in 2019 has somewhat reduced this 'leading away' effect, but it remains in force.
14 https://suntrics.com/tech-blogs/longest-snapchat-streak-a-brief-guide/.
15 https://99firms.com/blog/snapchat-statistics/.
16 Tanz (2011).
17 Fletcher (2010).
18 Eyal (2014), p. 175.
19 Zendle and Cairns (2018).
20 https://www.england.nhs.uk/2020/01/countrys-top-mental-health-nurse-warns-video-games-pushing-young-people-into-under-the-radar-gambling/.
21 Gibbs (2018).
22 Ward et al. (2017).
23 Newport (2015).
24 Schüll (2012), p. 215.
25 Schüll (2012), p. 109.
26 Addiction Resource.net (2020).
27 Schüll (2012), p. 58. Besides video poker, *multiline video slots* also exemplify the escape-gambling, time-on-device type of play.
28 Schüll (2012), p. 33.
29 Schüll (2012), p. 2.

CHAPTER 10: SAFETY AND SELF-CONTROL

1 Montaigne (2017), Book 2, Chapter 17.
2 Smith (2020).
3 Centers for Disease Control and Prevention (2020).
4 Kleinhubbert (2013).
5 Gendron (2016).
6 http://www.txtresponsibly.org/share-your-stories/.
7 Kleinhubbert (2013).
8 Tombu and Jolicoeur (2004).
9 Ophir et al. (2009).
10 Watson and Strayer (2010). The citation is from the abstract.
11 Gliklich et al. (2019).
12 https://www.flightsafetyaustralia.com/2018/07/flying-to-distraction/.
13 Kim (2015).
14 Connolly (2018).
15 Allen (2017).
16 For an overview of studies reported here, see McDaniel (2019).
17 Reed et al. (2017).
18 Zimmerman et al. (2007).
19 Clifford et al. (2020). Kozyreva et al. (2020) review research on digital self-control.
20 BEA, Final Report AF 447, p. 185, as cited in Hartmann (2017).
21 Hartmann (2017).
22 Federal Aviation Administration (2013). See also Carr (2014), pp. 1–2.
23 Brumfiel (2016).
24 Brainbridge (1983).
25 Ruginski et al. (2019).
26 Baraniuk (2016).
27 Milner (2016); and CNS/ATM (2017).

CHAPTER 11: FACT OR FAKE?

1 Mead (1928).
2 Lee (2018).
3 Locke (1975), pp. 656–7.
4 Topsell (1967).
5 Simanek (2009).
6 Newton (2018).
7 Götz et al. (2019).

8 Lavin (2020).

9 Islam et al. (2020).

10 O'Toole (2018).

11 O'Toole (2018).

12 Carroll (2020). On repetition and persuasion in general, see Armstrong (2010).

13 Gigerenzer (1984).

14 Mønsted et al. (2017).

15 See https://www.unstatistik.de (April 2017); the media headline is from https://www.ispo.com; https://www.woman.at. The original study is Lee et al. (2017).

16 Reynolds (2017).

17 Tesla (2016).

18 Hawkins (2019).

19 Ewing (2020).

20 Topol (2019).

21 This kind of argument to surrender to AI authority can, for instance, be found in Harari (2016).

22 See Gigerenzer (2014), Chapter 5.

23 Lewis (2003).

24 Lewis (2003), p. 247.

25 See Hirsch and Hirsch (2011).

26 Gigerenzer et al. (1989).

27 Hirsch and Hirsch (2011), p. 32.

28 Barra (2011).

29 See, for instance, Harari (2015), p. 374.

30 Frederik and Martijn (2019).

31 Frederik and Martijn (2019).

32 Blake et al. (2015).

33 Coviello et al. (2017).

34 An analysis of fifteen advertising experiments on Facebook, each with between 2 million and 140 million users, independently showed that correlational methods overestimate the effect of advertising. See Gordon et al. (2019).

35 Blake et al. (2015). A related argument is that even if ads have no measurable direct effect, they may have a long-term effect on brand recognition. But companies with highly recognized brand names such as eBay spent most of their ad budget on customers already familiar with the brand who specifically searched for it, which makes brand keyword advertising redundant.

36 Lewis and Rao (2014).

37 Lewis and Reiley (2014).

38 See Huang et al. (2020).

39 See Huang et al. (2020).

40 Frederik and Martijn (2019).

41 McGrew et al. (2018).

42 McGrew et al. (2018), p. 178.

43 https://www.minimumwage.com/2014/10/denmarks-dollar-forty-one-menu/.

44 Wineburg and McGrew (2019).

45 Wineburg and McGrew (2019).

46 McGrew et al. (2019); Breakstone, Smith, Wineburg, (2021).

47 https://ccconline.libguides.com/c.php?g=242130&p=1609638. See Kapoun (1998).

48 https://www.faktabaari.fi/assets/FactBaR_EDU_Fact-checking_for_edu cators_and_future_voters_13112018.pdf. For the role of behavioural science in promoting techno savvy, see Lorenz-Spreen et al. (2020); and Kozyreva et al. (2020).

49 Weltecke (2003).

50 Mercier and Sperber (2011).

51 Howard (2020).

52 Rid (2020).

53 Advisory Council for Consumer Affairs at the Federal Ministry of Justice and Consumer Protection (2017).

54 Helbing et al. (2017).

Image Credits

p.33 'You caught his eye' dating service message. Source: FTC 2019.

p.45 Fast-and-frugal trees. Source: Katsikopoulos et al. (2020).

p.63 'Women computers'. Source: © NASA.

p.70 Levels of automation in cars. Source: © SAE
International from SAE J3016™ Taxonomy and Definitions for Terms Related to Driving Automation Systems for On-Road Motor Vehicles (2018-06-05), https://www.sae.org/standards/content/j3016_201806/.

p.76 Neural networks. Source: Szegedy et al. (2014).

p.77 Deep neural networks Based on Szegedy et al. (2014) and Nguyen et al. (2015, © IEEE).

p.79 Colour patches that confuse neural networks. Source: © The Max Planck Institute for Intelligent Systems 2019.

p.102 Bill Clinton and Al Gore. Reprinted by permission from Springer Nature: Sinha & Poggio (1996).

p.103 Identifying faces from a distance. Source: Sinha et al. (2006).

p.105 Deep neural network errors. Source: Szegedy et al. (2014).

p.107 Neural network classification. Based on Szegedy et al. (2014) and Nguyen et al. (2015, © IEEE). Reprinted with permission from Nugyen et al. (2015).

p.108 Image captions generated by a deep neural network. Image credits, from left to right: Gabriel Villena Fernández/Wikicommons (https://commons.wikimedia.org/wiki/File:Cowboy_show_-_cowboys_on_horses.jpg), picture alliance/AP Images, and picture alliance/APPhoto/Dave Martin. Similar images can be found at twitter.com/interesting_jpg. Source: Lake et al. (2017).

p.114. Flu predictions. Source: Katsikopoulos et al. (2022).

p.118. Source: Messerli (2012) © (2012) Massachusetts Medical Society.

p.121. Data points. https://tylervigen.com/old-version.html.

p.165. The privacy paradox. Numbers based on Norton LifeLock, Cyber Safety Insights Report: Global Results.

p.185 Homo sapiens to homo digitalis. Source: © iStock by Getty Images.

p.215 Smartphone bed. Shown is the original German version, distributed by the Auerbach Foundation, http://www.diy-4u.de/wp-content/uploads/2017/06/19046716_43188701384048l_100988876_n.png.

p.220 woodcut rhinoceros. Source: unicorn: https://commons.wikimedia.org/wiki/File:Oftheunicorn.jpg; rhinoceros: https://commons.wikimedia.org/wiki/File:D%C3%BCrer_rhino_full.png.

p.238 Civic online reasoning test. The original image can be found at: https://imgur.com/gallery/BZWWx. Source: Perduejn/Wikicommons.

p.239. Civic online reasoning test. Source: https://www.minimumwage.com/2014/10/denmarks-dollar-forty-one-menu/.

p.241 average time check. Source: Wineburg and McGrew (2019).

Index